# UNRAVELLING THE THREADS:
# A GUIDE TO THE WILSONS
# OF STENSON
# 1664 to 1880

Malcolm J. Harrison

# UNRAVELLING THE THREADS: A GUIDE TO THE WILSONS OF STENSON IN THE COUNTY OF DERBYSHIRE 1664 to 1880

Malcolm J. Harrison

© Malcolm J. Harrison 2008

ISBN 978-0-9557382-0-3
EAN 9780955738203
Printed by Healeys Printers Ltd, Unit 10-11, The Sterling Complex,
Farthing Road, Ipswich, Suffolk IP1 5AP
and published by
M. J. Harrison, "Colum Publishing"
78 Dulwich Road, Holland on Sea, Essex CO15 5LZ.

2008

# Contents

Page

Illustrations.

Foreword by Richard Garratt Wilson.                                    vii

Introduction.                                                            1

1.    From small beginnings: The Wilsons of Stenson, Derbyshire.        7

2.    Weaving a Yarn: the Entry of the Wilsons into the Silk Trade.     17

3.    Elizabeth Collett and her Descendants.                           33

4.    Daniel West: Whitefield's Forgotten Trustee.                     43

5.    Thomas Wilson of Highbury, Islington.                            58

6.    John Wilson of Upper Street, Islington and the Lea-Wilsons.      71

7.    Stephen and Ann Collett Wilson of Church Street.                 78

8.    William Wilson of Milk Street and The Wortons, Oxfordshire.      89

9.    Joseph Wilson of Highbury and the Maitland Wilsons of
      Stowlangtoft.                                                   109

10.   From Spitfields to Calcutta:
      Daniel Wilson 5th Bishop of Calcutta.                           119

APPENDIX

      A.    Table of Wilsons: 1664-1880                               144

      B.    Elizabeth Collett and her Descendants                     145

SELECT BIBLIOGRAPHY                                                   170

# List of Illustrations

1. Family tree: by E. F. Wilson. *viii*

2. Stenson Farm: *c.*1835 by Harriet Ann Moore. 6

3. Silk Dress *c.*1853. 16

4. Memorial Plaque to the Colletts and Pellys. 42

5. Daniel West's residence and the birthplace of Daniel Wilson, Spitfields. 44

6. The Lord Mayor's Banquet: Mansion House: 1839. 70

7. Nether Worton, Oxfordshire. 90

8. Over Worton, Oxfordshire. 94

9. Holy Trinity Church, Over Worton. 95

10. Stowlangtoft Hall, Suffolk. 108

11. Little Massingham Rectory, Norfolk. 115

12. Holy Trinity Church, Over Worton, *c.*1804. 120

13. Islington Parish Church. 130

# Foreword

As a little boy in Epsom, where my grandfather was the Town Clerk and lawyer to Lord Rosebery, I was often taken to his house. A revered figure called Bishop Daniel Wilson was often mentioned there, as the most distinguished of the (collateral) ancestors.

Years later, on my first visit to India, I went to the Cathedral which Bishop Wilson had built in Calcutta and there saw his urbane bust still seemingly conducting the ecclesiastical business of the 19th century. His efforts did not always endure. At Shimla, where the British dignitaries used to retire for the hot summer, the vicar of the local church well knew of Daniel Wilson, claiming that there was a foundation stone laid by him. But, a century on he was unable to find it.

Daniel Wilson, fifth Bishop of Calcutta and Metropolitan of all India, was a man of his time. He took Evangelism to his heart, and expressed it with an independent spirit. But he was his own man, possessed of a drive and energy which culminated in Calcutta's gothic Cathedral, which Wilson planned, arranged to finance, and of which he oversaw the architecture.

The Cathedral alone was the extraordinary achievement of only a few years. His business-like attitude to affairs must be linked, as Malcolm Harrison explains in his book, with the prominence of both sides of his family in the trade and industry of London. His father was a silk manufacturer and one member of the Wilson family became Lord Mayor of London. The family's links with the East India Company went back to the late seventeenth century, and there were even family relations with the "white rajah" Brookes of Sarawak. Another part of the Wilson family tree showed Thomas Brooke's three children by his "Indian companion" from Bihar, and these children were sent to England for their education, of whom the two daughters went to Mile End Green along with Daniel Wilson's three younger sisters.

The Construction of the Cathedral was not the only substantial innovation made by Wilson. He took the step of completely excluding the caste system from the native Churches of South India. That was in 1835.

All in all, he was a Church leader in India who was distinguished for his resolution and independence, preaching vigorous sermons as a channel for the fruitful traffic that was to proceed from Britain to India, and also the vivifying cultural exchanges between India and the West. Bishop Daniel Wilson was an underrated figure whose story along with other members of the Wilson family is here narrated by Malcolm Harrison with much new material and correction of earlier accounts.

Richard Garratt Wilson.
(Former editor Far Eastern Economic Review)

*Family tree: by E. F. Wilson.*

# Introduction

## Tying up loose ends: The Wilsons of Stenson, Derbyshire*(i)*

"Our beginnings was small the latter has greatly increased." So said Thomas Wilson [II] at a Banquet given by Lord Mayor Samuel Wilson at the Mansion House in 1839 to which 117 members of the family were invited.[1] From the few strands that we have at our disposal regarding the early history of the Wilson family the most that we are offered from the biographies of Daniel Wilson and Thomas Wilson [II] is a thumb nail sketch concerning their origins.[2] This is in stark contrast to the lengthy apologia that the authors of the two memoirs offer: sanitized biographies totally lacking in any imagination. Only later when we turn to the anonymous legend of the Wolfsons are we provided with any sense of romantic colouring and yet even here the author never delves into the origins of the Wilsons.[3] Likewise the family sketch by Harriet Ann Wilson (née Moore) adds nothing new to our knowledge, the writer being dependent on Bateman's life of Daniel Wilson.[4] Nor do more recent biographical sketches on Daniel Wilson add to our knowledge: the authors relying on Bateman.[5]

From the barest of evidence provided by Bateman the only information that we are offered is that it is possible to trace the Wilsons of Stenson back to the year 1657 where there is a reference to a William and Elizabeth in the Parish Registers. However there is no evidence to show that it is from them that the Wilsons of Stenson who are the subject of this study are descended.[6]

Likewise, there is no evidence to show that there is any connection between John Wilson (1755-1835) of Stenson and John Wilson (1763-1838) from whom Ronald Binge the Jazz musician was descended. They are two quite distinct and unrelated families. John Wilson of Stenson died unmarried in 1835 leaving the farm at Stenson to his niece, Mary Wayte (née Moore). The John Wilson from whom Ronald Binge was descended was the son of James and Mary Wilson of Ashover. He married in 1789 Mary Bucknall.[7] Any suggestion therefore that they are the same person is based on a fundamental mistake.

But, to return to the Wilsons of Stenson. According to an inventory of Mary Wilson who died on the 30th February 1686 it was her son, John Wilson (1664-1714) who inherited the estate at Stenson.[8] Consequently, it is her son John Wilson [I] who forms the starting point in this study on the Wilsons of Stenson.

As a family they were probably indistinguishable from any other family that lived in that part of the Trent Valley, a point not lost on Thomas Wilson [II] who states that "it was a family originally possessing no note of eminence distinguishing it from the mass of English yeoman."[9] And yet, by the time that

Lord Mayor Samuel Wilson entertained the Wilson clan to the banquet on the 5th of April 1839 in the Egyptian Hall many of its members had indeed distinguished themselves in a variety of ways. Amongst these mention should be made of Stephen Wilson [I], who in 1754 established the first family branch of the silk trade in London. Then there is Thomas Wilson, [I] who along with Daniel West was one of the founding fathers of the Hoxton Academy (later Highbury Academy). At least four members of the Wilson family including Daniel West were members of the Lay Committee of the London Missionary Society that had been formed in 1795, whilst William Wilson [I] of Milk Street and the Wortons, Oxfordshire, served as a Lay member of the Church Missionary Society and First Chairperson of the Oxfordshire Auxiliary Bible Society. Others, such as Samuel Wilson pursued a career in the Corporation of the City of London, rising in 1838 to the rank of Lord Mayor of London, the only silk weaver to hold this office, whilst his brother, Stephen Wilson (1777-1860), made his mark in the silk industry by introducing into England in 1820 the Jacquard machine. And there is Daniel Wilson who had originally been intended for a career in the silk trade but chose instead to enter the ministry eventually going on in 1832 to become the 5th Bishop of Calcutta.

For the unsuspecting faced with a long list of people many of whom shared the same surname and in some cases the same forename it must be admitted that some degree of confusion often resulting in mistakes is understandable if not inevitable as we have already observed.

In order, therefore to make the task of those readers not familiar with many of the people referred to in this study easier I have provided a Genealogical table of the extended family from 1664 to 1880.

Consisting of Ten chapters the first two chapters of the Guide to the Wilsons focus firstly on the Wilsons of Stenson from 1664 to 1835 and then secondly on the entry of the Wilsons into the silk trade.

Chapters Three to Ten consist of a series of biographical studies of various members of the family, commencing with Elizabeth Collett and concluding with Daniel Wilson, her great grandson. At first sight, the inclusion of a chapter on Elizabeth Collett might come as a surprise to those members of the Wilson family who are not familiar with her name. Apart from a brief reference to her by Gertrude Jacob and Steven Runciman in their studies on the White Rajah, she might otherwise be relegated to a footnote in the pages of history. That however would be a mistake for what has not been realized is that Elizabeth Collett was the collateral ancestress of Daniel Wilson, 5th Bishop of Calcutta, the White Rajahs of Sarawak, and the seven beautiful Pattle sisters and thus almost the whole of the Bloomsbury set.[10]

That said it is necessary to make clear at the outset that this study or Guide to the Wilsons of Stenson is not intended to be an exhaustive biographical study or a detailed history of the Wilsons or indeed of individual members of the family. Their history proper deserves greater treatment, which is beyond the scope of this modest study. Rather it is intended to be a Guide to the Wilsons of Stenson, Derbyshire enabling those not familiar with this territory to avoid the same pitfalls and errors that have befallen past and present writers.

It remains for me to add some words of acknowledgement to the late Mr and Mrs J. Brereton of Little Massingham, Helen Brown, Rosemary and Tony Jewers, Francis and Margaret Rushbrooke-Williams, and their two daughters, Debbie Mackinlay (née Rushbrooke-Williams) and Sarah Di-Lenardo (née Rushbrooke-Williams), Richard Garratt Wilson for his hospitality and help over many years, John Wilson Smith, John Worden Wilson and his wife for their support, encouragement and hospitality over many years, Dr Julian Wilson, Mr and Mrs Bird (née Lee-Wilson) and their daughter, Alison Horne (née Bird) for their hospitality, Mrs Ann Taylor, Elizabeth Cooper (née Fitzroy Wilson), Mrs Joan Davies of Twyford Derbyshire, Mr Robin Compton, Mr Richard Compton of Newby Hall Ripon, Mr J Foreman one time owner of Stenson Farm Derbyshire, Dr Roger Dalton, Dr. J. Latham, Mr and Mrs Macdonald of Stowlangtoft Hall (now a Nursing Home), Professor Andrew Porter Rhodes Professor of Imperial History, King's College London, Dr C. Binfield Professor Associate of the University of Sheffield, Peter Redman for his hospitality, Revd J.S. Reynolds, Revd J. Walsh, Laurie Short, Revd Dr Graham Kings, Vicar of St Mary Islington, David Bateman (a descendent of the Batemans of Bunhill Row), Zena Godfrey and Jenny Thompson (née Godfrey), whose great grandfather, the Revd Edward Godfrey, M.A. was a Chaplain in the East India Company. I would also like to express my gratitude to the late Ray Turner, one time Church Warden of St Mary Islington, the Churchwardens of Over Worton, Mr and Mrs Charles Thatcher and Mr and Mrs Malcolm Axtell for making available to me the Parish records and for their kind hospitality and support over many years.

I wish also to thank the various organizations and individuals who have over the years patiently dealt with my requests: Christine Kelly of the Banbury Museum, Ingrid A. Roderick of the Bible Society, Ken Thomas Company Archivist of Courage Ltd, Miriam Wood Archivist Derby Record Office, Lisa Bates Librarian Local Studies Library Matlock, Hackney Archives Department, Gloucester Record Office, Hereford and Worcester Record Office, W.W. Breem Librarian and Keeper, The Honourable Society of the Inner Temple, Mrs J. Pennington, Assistant Archivist Lancing College Sussex, J,M. Ayton Archivist The Central Library Manchester, Miss Rachel Watson County Archivist Northamptonshire Record Office, S.J. Barnes County Archivist Oxford County Council, Andrew Byrne of The Spitalfields Trust, R.J. Evans Archivist Vestry House Museum London Borough of Waltham Forest, Tower

Hamlets Local History Library, Elizabeth Williams Librarian Partnership House Mission Studies Library, Catherine Wakeling USPG Archivist, Dorian Leveque of the India Office British Library, Steven Tomlinson Bodleian Library, University of Oxford, Lucy McCann, Librarian Rhodes House, Oxford, the Librarian University College London, Ruth Kenny Archivist National Portrait Gallery London, the Librarian The Local history Library, London Borough of Islington, Linda Rhodes Librarian Local History Library London Borough of Barking and Dagenham (Valence House), CSL. Davies Fellow and Tutor of History and Keeper of Archives Wadham College Oxford, Revd F.T. Holt Rector of St Clement Worcester, Miss Diana Chardin Librarian Trinity College Cambridge, Jean Grice, Archivist of the Braintree Museum, David Humphreys Managing Director of Humphreys Silk Manufacturing Company Castle Hedingham, Mrs. J Smith, Hon. Librarian United Reformed Church History Society, also Mrs Margaret Thompson Administrator of the URCH Society, Cambridge, Revd Dr S. Orchard Principal of Westminster College, Cambridge, the Librarian of the Royal College of Surgeons, Susan Hinley, The Essex Record Office, Suffolk Record Office, Michael Hinnels of the Coventry Record Office, Mr John Creasey Emeritus Librarian Dr Williams's Library, The Librarian The Worshipful Company of Goldsmiths, The Librarian The Guild hall Library, London.

Lastly and most importantly, I wish to express my gratitude to my wife, Pam and my children, Richard and Dianne who have not only learned to live with the Wilson family over a long period of time but have also been of assistance to me in my investigations and encouraging me to continue with the task of completing the guide. I trust that this study on the Wilson family will reward their patience and steadfastness over many years.

## Notes and References:

(i) The Wilsons of Stenson are not to be confused with the Family of John and Mary Wilson (née Bucknall) of Derby. See: Harrison, M.J. The Wilsons of Derbyshire: a Note. JURCHS. January 2008.

1. Wilson, J. (1846) Memoir of the Life and Character of Thomas Wilson, Esq. By his Son. London. Hereafter referred to as Memoir of Thomas Wilson. See also: Plummer, A. (1972) The London Weavers Company: 1600-1970. London: Routledge and Kegan Paul.

2. See: Bateman, J. (1860) Life of the Right Revd Daniel Wilson, D.D. London: John Murray. 2 vols. Wilson, J. (1846) Memoir of Thomas Wilson. London. See also: Edwards, J. (1860-1861) Notes on the Parish Registers of Barrow and Twyford: The Reliquary: vol. 1. p.231-235.

3. J.W.W. (n.d.) The Legends of the Wolfson Family. London: J.A. Squire: Crown Steam Printing Works.

4. Wilson, Harriet Ann. (1901) A Family Sketch. Touching the Wilson, Moore,

Douglas and Fox Families written for my Children and Grand children. (Unpublished Diary privately owned.)

5. See: Loane, Marcus. (1951) Oxford and the Evangelical Succession. London: Lutterworth Press. ch.5. Daniel Wilson: 1778-1858. See however; Reynolds, J.S. (1952) The Evangelicals at Oxford: 1735-1871. Oxford: Clarendon Press who makes use of a wider range of original sources than does Marcus Loane in his study.

6. Bateman, J. (1860) Life of Daniel Wilson. London: John Murray. vol. 1. Bateman is incorrect when he states that the Wilsons of Stenson can be traced back to a William and Elizabeth Wilson. The latter are a different family.

7. See: Harrison, M.J. The Wilsons of Derbyshire: A Note. Journal of the Reformed Church History Society. Jan. 2008. This is a response to the article by S. Orchard: The Wilson Family and Derbyshire. JURCHS. vol. 6 no. 8. May 2001. p.570-589.

8. Litchfield Joint Record Office: Inventory of Mary Wilson: 1686.

9. Wilson, Joshua. (1846) Memoir of Thomas Wilson. London.

10. See: Harrison, M.J. Daniel West: Whitefield's Forgotten Trustee. Journal of the United Reformed Church History Society. June 2006. See also: Harrison, M.J. From Spitalfields to Calcutta: Daniel Wilsons Love of India. Indian Church History Review. June 2006. See also: Olsen Victoria. (2003) From Life: Julia Margaret Cameron and Victorian Photography. London: Aurum Press. Runciman, S. (1960) The White Rajahs a History of Sarawak from 1841-1946. Cambridge: Cambridge University Press.

*Stenson Farm: c.1835 by Harriet Ann Moore.*

# 1. From Small Beginnings
## The Wilsons of Stenson, Derbyshire: 1664-1835[i]

The story of the Wilsons of Stenson who are the subject of this Guide begins on a small farm in Stenson, a hamlet in the combined parish of Twyford and Barrow upon Trent, South Derbyshire, whose windswept lands are broken up by a series of intersecting channels that descended from a small flat gravelled terrace to the flood plains of the River Trent.[1]

The original farmhouse long since demolished consisted of a parlour and kitchen with rooms or chambers upstairs. Rebuilt in the late 18th century the farmhouse underwent further extension in 1832 with the addition of a new parlour and bedroom.[2]

Between the farmhouse and the road that ran from Stenson farm to Twyford was a magnificent row of elm trees giving the farmhouse its distinguished appearance. These trees no longer exist having been destroyed by the ravages of Dutch elm disease that swept England in the 1970s. The farm itself was probably in the region of 200-250 acres consisting in part of water meadows providing rich grazing land for the livestock. In addition to the water meadows were the arable fields devoted to the growing of wheat, oats, rye, peas and barley of which barley was the main cash crop.[3]

From the inventory of Mary Wilson, dated 1686, we learn that in addition to keeping cattle and sheep, she also kept bees, pigs, hens and ducks. It is more than probable that there was an orchard and kitchen garden.[4]

By today's standards the farm might appear to be small but by the standards of the time not only was it large enough to provide them with a good standard of living but also it was large enough to ensure that all members of the family including servants and labourers had a role to play. Whilst the men folk including the young sons were busy carrying out the seasonal tasks of hedging, ditching, ploughing, sowing, haymaking, harvesting and sheep shearing the women, including the daughters, were busy milking the cows, collecting the eggs, feeding the livestock and assisting in the dairy with the making of cheeses, butter and cream. Although some of the dairy products were kept for consumption in the home, the majority of the dairy products were sold in the local markets or at the annual cheese fairs held in Ashbourne, Burton, Derby and Nottingham.[5]

To what extent the Wilsons of Stenson were enterprising and progressive farmers is not known, but given that not only did they rent land from the Harpurs of Calke Abbey but were also able to settle their younger sons in a commercial enterprise in London is a clear indication that they were in fact the sort of farmers who kept one eye on the management of their land and one eye on their cash crops. Of these, malt barley for which they received a premium was the main cash crop.

According to Defoe the Trent Valley was an area renowned for its prodigious yield of barley most of which was destined for the breweries notably those in Burton on Trent.[6]

This town owed its origins to the brewing of ale as early as the 11th century when Wulfric founded a Benedictine Abbey in 1004. With the dissolution of the Monasteries during the reign of Henry the VIIIth, the brewing industry managed to survive the crisis. By 1620, Burton ale was available in London, being transported by road then by river to Hull before being taken by sea to London. During the 18th century, Burton ale was also being exported to the Baltic States and to Russia. This however came to a halt during the Napoleonic wars. In addition, the Burton brewers were to export their fine pale ale to India from which the name IPA has its origins.

From the farmhouse, it was possible to see the barges sailing up and down the River Trent laden with their precious cargo of malt barley. Although there was a landing stage at Barrow upon Trent, it is more than likely that the Wilsons took their farm produce overland, or before the cutting of the Trent-Mersey canal, to Willington Docks, which was situated near the River Trent.[7]

As well as benefiting from having a ready market so close at hand to which they were able to send their barley, farmers such as the Wilsons also benefited from the breweries by having a regular supply of food stuffs with which to feed their livestock during the winter months. Instead, therefore of having to send their cattle to market every winter to be slaughtered they were able to keep their cattle over the winter thereby improving the quality and size of their herd and in so doing of meeting the needs of an ever-increasing population with quality meat.[8] At the same time they were able to increase their milk yield resulting in a higher production of dairy products, most of which was destined for the local markets.

Situated at the centre of an export market that was dependent on quality barley destined for the local brewing industry in Burton upon Trent, succeeding generations of Wilsons must have recognized the importance of commerce as a means of ensuring that their younger sons were able to make their way in the world. However, it was not to the silk mills of Derby or the breweries of Burton upon Trent to which they sent their younger sons but in the first instance to the silk trade in Coventry and then at a later stage to London. Nevertheless, in order for their sons to succeed in the wider world of commerce this meant providing them with an education that equipped them for such a life.

Exactly where the Wilsons sent their sons to school is not known. There were a number of private schools in and around Derby and it may well be that it was to one of these rather than Derby Grammar School or the Dissenting Academy in Findern that they were sent there being no evidence at this stage that they were Dissenters. Only later do we learn that John Wilson [IV] entertained Dissenters and attended the Dissenting chapel in Barrow upon Trent. We also learn from the memoir of Thomas Wilson junior that John Wilson [IV] was the first trustee of the Chapel in Brookside, Derby.[9]

As to the nature of the education which their daughters received it is more than probable given their status that they received an education with girls of a similar background to their own either at a local private school or an academy in Barrow or Derby. Such education as they received was of a general nature including reading, writing, arithmetic, painting and drawing and possibly music, thereby equipping them for a life of service in the home.[10] Descended from the classic breed of yeomen farmers, the Wilsons were not gentry, but they were relatively prosperous and ambitious for their children, especially for their younger sons.[11]

Whereas however it was not unusual for young ladies of their status to remain at home until they married, the same cannot be said for the younger sons. On completing their education at the age of fourteen or thereabouts they were then expected to leave home and make their way in the wider world of business or commerce whilst the eldest son remained at home until he inherited the farm from his parents.

At this stage in time, John Wilson [I] with whom this study on the Wilsons takes its starting point was in the fortunate position of owning two farms, one at Twyford, that he left to his eldest son Thomas, whilst John [II] inherited the farm at Stenson.[12] (See: Table 1). From the few details that we know about John Wilson [I] we learn from the inventory of his mother, Mary Wilson that as her only lawful and natural son he inherited at the age of twenty four the farm at Stenson in 1686. Two years after his mother's death, he married Mariae Holden by whom he had five children, of whom only three survived to adulthood. These were, Thomas (b.1693), John (1696-1747) and Sarah (1697-c.1717). (See: Table 1) Although John Wilson [I] had left the farm at Stenson to his younger son John [II], it was not until after the death of his mother, Mary Wilson (née Holden) in 1718 that John [II] eventually came into possession of Stenson Farm. By this time, he had married Ann Henshaw, the eldest daughter of John and Lucy Henshaw (née Cooper) of Weston upon Trent, near Barrow. Over a period of twenty-three years, they had twelve children of whom only seven survived to adulthood. (See: Fig. 2). Given the high infancy mortality at this time, this was in fact a very good survival rate.[13]

According to one of his sons, John Wilson [II] was a conscientious father who showed great concern for his children and in particular for his younger sons for whom there was very little if any future on the farm at Stenson.

Unfortunately, he was not in a position to purchase any farms for them and as a result, they had no choice but to leave home and find an opening in some commercial enterprise. Whether John Wilson [II] had any links with commerce or business is not known, but far from leaving his sons to secure a living for themselves it is recorded that he used to accompany them so as to ensure that they were placed in a suitable enterprise. The first of his sons to be placed in a commercial enterprise was his second son Stephen [I] (1723-1755), who entered into a small silk firm in Coventry. A shrewd and successful business-man Stephen [I] established in 1754 a branch of the business in the City of London, which at this stage was the leading centre for finished silk goods and the main source of raw material for the silk industry. In September 1755, Stephen [I] contracted a fever from which he died leaving the business to his widow Mary, who renegotiated the terms of the partnership with her brother in law Thomas Wilson [I]. This time it was agreed that Mary should remain in Coventry whilst Thomas [I] who by this time had married Mary Remington went to London. It was to this branch of the business situated in Wood Street, Cheapside that succeeding members of the Wilson family were sent. Amongst these were Thomas Wilson [II], the elder son of Thomas and Mary Wilson (née Remington), their younger son, Joseph Wilson, from whom Field Marshall Maitland Wilson was descended and Mary Wilson's (née Fullalove) two sons, John and Stephen Wilson [II]. They were later joined by their Derbyshire cousin William [I], the second son of John and Ann Wilson (née Cocks) of Stenson.[14]

But, to return to John Wilson [II]. On his death in 1747 from a fever he contracted whilst in London the farm at Stenson passed to his eldest son, also called John [III]. Entries in the Parish Records state that he had married Ann Cocks, the eldest daughter of Widow Cocks of Duffield. Six children were born to John and Ann, all of whom survived to adulthood. (See: Table 3) How-ever, Ann died soon after the birth of her youngest daughter Mary, leaving John Wilson [III] to care for the needs of six children, the youngest barely six months and the eldest just nine years of age. Whether he was able to call on other members of the family, including his sister in law to assist is not known, but there is no indication that he farmed the children out to nurses in the village or sent them to other members of the family for adoption. Given his apparent prosperity and status it is more than probable that he was able to employ servants to care for his children as well as carry out the necessary domestic tasks within the home, leaving him free to concentrate on the management of the farm.

In keeping with the family tradition, John saw to it that his children received an education that reflected their status. Whereas however his two daughters, Ann and Mary received an education that prepared them for marriage either to a wealthy farmer or merchant his three younger sons received an education that equipped them for a life in commerce.[15]

While his two daughters, Ann (1758-1803) and Mary (1763-1796) were expected to remain at home until such times as they married, his three younger sons, William (1756-1821), Thomas (1760-1829) and Stephen (1762-1814) were sent to London where they were entered into an apprentice in the silk industry. During the time that his three sons served their apprenticeship, which was normally a period of seven years, John Wilson [III] paid for all their apparel, board and lodgings including their laundry whilst his eldest daughter Ann, made their shirts.[16]

The only son remaining at home was John Wilson's eldest son, John Wilson [IV] who inherited the farm on the death of his father in 1789. John Wilson [IV] never married. Any suggestion that it was from him that Ronald Binge was descended is a clear case of mistaken identity.[17] By the time of John's death in 1835, apart from his niece, Mary Wayte (née Moore) to whom he left Stenson Farm, there were no other members of the family of Wilsons of Stenson remaining in Derbyshire. Many of his relatives, including his brothers and sisters had died whilst other members of the wider Wilson family had long since moved to London and the surrounding areas where many were to make their name in society.[18]

As the eldest son, John [IV] devoted his life to the management of the farm and the rearing of a fine herd of longhorn and shorthorn cattle. By this stage, advances had been made in farming and in particular in animal husbandry. Up until the late 18th century the longhorn was the dominant cattle in Britain, but at the turn of the 18th century Bakewell's longhorn cattle were being replaced by the more successful cattle bred by the Collings brothers of Durham. These shorthorn dual-purpose cattle gave a high milk yield and produced a good beef calf that met the needs of the market. Recent studies have also indicated that many farmers were also supplementing their cattle feed with spent grain obtained from the breweries in and around Burton on Trent. Because the spent grain was so rich in proteins and phosphorus, this enabled the more enter-prising farmers such as John Wilson [IV] to not only feed their cattle over the winter but also increase the size of their herds. This allowed him to set aside more land for grazing resulting in a higher milk yield per cow, leading ultimately to a higher production of cheese and butter.[19]

Evidence from a Farm sales advertisement in the Derby Mercury for January 1835 indicates that in addition to the rearing of longhorned cattle for which John Wilson [IV] had a well earned reputation he also kept a herd of dairy shorthorn cows which gave a good milk yield and prime meat suitable for the meat market.[20]

The other major developments in agriculture was the invention of the seed drill, the Ransome plough and the use of other laboursaving devices such as the reaper that had been invented by the Revd Patrick Bell in 1828. For small but progressive and innovative farmers such as John Wilson [IV], the use of laboursaving devices and the introduction of new crops and improved breeds of cattle meant that they were able to maximize their profits and keep down their labour costs resulting in more efficient farming and greater financial prudence.

During his lifetime the old farmhouse, which had been rebuilt sometime in the late 18th century, was further extended in 1832 with the addition of a parlour and bedroom. It was here that his great niece Harriet Ann Wilson (née Moore) frequently stayed as a young child, a fact that she recorded in her Family Sketch.[21]

In addition to all this John Wilson (IV) took an active role in the local Congregational chapel in Barrow upon Trent. This was a chapel funded partly by his uncle Thomas Wilson [I] of Highbury, who had been responsible for the funding and building of the chapel in Brookside Derby, where John Wilson [IV] was the first Trustee, a post that he held from 1783 until his death in 1835.[22]

With the death of John Wilson [IV] in 1835 the farm passed to his niece, Mary Wayte to enjoy for life. She was the daughter of Ambrose and Ann Moore, (née Wilson) and had married first, John Hickson of the Wortons, Oxfordshire, then second George Wayte of Repton.[23] On her death, the farm passed to her brother Ambrose Moore, a silk weaver of Milk Street, London and the Depot Derby, which he then passed on to his descendants in whose hands the farm remained until 1881.[24]

Although the sale of the farm in 1881 marks the end of one part of the story of the Wilsons of Stenson it is however not the end of their story. Many of them were to make a name for themselves in society. Amongst these mention should be made of Lord Mayor Samuel Wilson, (1791-1881) the only member of the Weavers Company to achieve this status and Stephen Wilson of Old Jewry (1777-1860) (elder brother of Samuel) who introduced the Jacquard machine into England. Then there is Daniel Wilson, (1778-1858) the 5th Bishop of Calcutta, John Dover Wilson, (1885-1969) a leading authority on Shakespeare, Field Marshall Henry Maitland Wilson, later Baron Maitland Wilson of Stowlangtoft and Libya, (1881-1964) Edward Francis Wilson (1845-1915) a missionary to the Indians at Algoma, Canada, and Charlotte Wilson (née Martin) 1854-1944) a member of the Fabian Society, anarchist and feminist and recipient of the OBE. These are just a few members of this family who in the words of one of its members was a family originally possessing no great note of eminence to distinguish it from the mass of English yeomen.[25]

*Notes and References:*

(i)  The Wilsons of Stenson are not to be confused with John and Mary Wilson (née
     Bucknall) of Derby from whom Ronald Binge the composer and jazz musician was
     descended. They are two distinct and unrelated families. See: Harrison, M.J The
     Wilsons of Derbyshire: a note. JURCHS, Jan. 2008.

1.   Stenson is a small hamlet in the combined parish of Twyford and Barrow upon
     Trent an area of continuous settlements from the Neolithic period to present times.
     See: Wilson, J. (1846) Memoir of Thomas Wilson. London. Also: Bateman, J.
     (1860) Life of Daniel Wilson. London: John Murray.

2.   Wilson, Harriet Ann. (1901) A Family Sketch (privately owned) The diary contains
     a sketch c.1832 showing the extensions that had been carried out at this stage. It is
     probable that the house depicted in the sketch was demolished and rebuilt in the
     1850s when the farm came into the possession of Ambrose Moore. (1788-1873).
     According to the inventory of Mary Wilson 1686, the original farmhouse consisted
     of a parlour, kitchen and three bedrooms.

3.   According to John Foreman whose family had farmed at Stenson from the turn of
     the 19th century having purchased it from the Wilsons, half the land would have
     been devoted to grazing whilst the lower land towards the Trent was dedicated to
     growing crops and in particular barley which was suited to the light well drained
     soil of the Trent Valley.

4.   Litchfield Joint Record Office (LJRO). 5th Feb 1686. Inventory of Mary Wilson.

5.   See: Henstock, A. (1969) Cheese Manufacture and Marketing in Derbyshire and
     North Staffordshire 1670-1870. Derbyshire Archaeological Journal. vol. 89. See
     also: Dalton, R. (1998) Reportage of the Michaelmas Cheese Fair at Derby in the
     Derby Mercury 1780-1880. Derby Miscellany. vol. 15, part 2. Autumn.

6.   Defoe, D. (1962) A Tour Through the Whole Island of Great Britain. ed., G.D.H.
     Cole. London J. M Dent.

7.   From Stenson to Burton the main forms of transport would either be overland
     or by river. Before the cutting of the Trent Mersey canal c.1776-7 the main
     landing stage would have been at Willington, which is not more that 5 miles from
     Stenson Farm. See: Chambers, J.D. (1957) The Vale of Trent 1670-1800 Economic
     History Supplement. Also: Owen, C.C. (1968) The Early History of the Upper
     Trent Navigation. Transport History vol. 1 no. 3.

8.   Charles, D. (2002) Farming and the Countryside: Past Present and Future. Notting-
     ham: Nottingham University Press, in which he notes that when Bakewell bred his
     cattle and sheep he did so in response to a market that wanted fat meat.

9.   Wilson, Joshua. (1846) Memoir of Thomas Wilson. London in which he points
     out that there was no indication at this stage that the Wilsons attended either the
     Presbyterian meeting house in Derby or the meeting house in Findern which was
     close to Stenson. Likewise there is no evidence that the Wilsons were educated
     either at the Dissenting Academy at Findern or the Grammar School in Derby.
     See Tacchelta, B. ed. (1901) Derby School Register: 1570-1901. London. On
     the Dissenting Academy at Findern see: Transactions of the Congregational

Historical Society. vol. vii, Early Nonconformist Academies: Derby and Findern.

10. Hughes, K. (1998) George Eliot: the Last Victorian. London: Fourth Estate, who makes the point that life on the farm especially for young daughters was extremely harsh and far removed from the idyllic scene portrayed in paintings. As such it is not surprising that the Wilson girls turned their backs on the farm and married merchants.

11. Hughes, K. (1998) ibid. p.11 who points out that yeomen farmers were freeholders and were much harder to place in society than tenant farmers.

12. LJRO. 2nd April 1717: John Wilson who left land at Findern to his eldest son, Thomas and the Stenson Farm to his second son, John.

13. See Chambers, J. D. (1957) The Vale of Trent 1670-1800 Economic History Supplement. The high mortality rates in the Wilson families of John Wilson [I] 1689-1699 and John Wilson [II] 1718-1746 correspond with the bad years of 1692-1729 and 1741-1742 referred to by Chambers in his study on infant mortality rates for the period 1670-1800.

14. Wilson, J. (1846) Memoir of Thomas Wilson. London. See also: Bateman, J. (1860) The Life of Daniel Wilson. London: John Murray. 2 vols.

15. Ann Wilson, eldest daughter of John and Ann Wilson (née Cocks), married Ambrose Moore a merchant of the City of London whilst Mary, the youngest daughter, married William Green, also a merchant of the City of London.

16. Letter to Ann Wilson from William Wilson: 11th May 1773 in which he complained about the shirts that she made as either being too large or too small.

17. See: Orchard, S. The Wilson Family of Derbyshire. JURCHS. vol. 6. no. 8. May 2001 where he mistakenly confuses John Wilson (1755-1835) with John Wilson (1763-1838) who married Mary Bucknall and from whom Ronald Binge the jazz musician was descended. They are two distinct and unrelated families. See also: Harrison, MJ. The Wilsons of Derbyshire: a Note. JURCHS, Jan. 2008.

18. Amongst those Wilsons who made their mark in society were Thomas Wilson senior and junior, Daniel Wilson, Bishop of Calcutta, Lord Mayor Samuel Wilson, Stephen Wilson of Old Jewry, Joshua Wilson, and Joseph Wilson of Highbury and Stowlangtoft from whom the Maitland Wilsons of Stowlangtoft are descended.

19. See: Dalton, R. 91997) Agricultural Changes in Southern Derbyshire: 1800-1870. East Midland Geographer. Vol. 20 also Dalton, R. (1999) The Relationship of the Brewing Industry of Burton upon Trent to Local Dairy Farming in the 18th and 19th centuries. East Midland Historian. vol. 9.

20. Derby Mercury. 1835 Farm Sales Advertisement: Jan 7th 1835 in which the salesman, Mr Brearey commented on the excellence of John Wilson's stock of longhorn cattle.

21. Wilson, Harriet, Ann. (1901) A Family Sketch. (Privately owned.)

22. Wilson, Joshua. (1846) Memoir of Thomas Wilson. London. See also: Harrison, M.J. Patrons and Church Builders: The Wilsons of Highbury and Islington: a paper

given at a seminar organised by the Friends of Union Chapel and the Victorian Society. London. September 24th 2005. Forthcoming publication 2008.

23. Wilson, Harriet, Ann. (1901) A Family Sketch. (Privately owned) Mary Wayte was the only surviving daughter of Ambrose and Ann More (née Wilson). Her second husband, George Wayte, was a member of a family that came from Milton, near Repton.

24  On the death of Mary and George Wayte the farm passed to Mary's brother, Ambrose Moore (1788-1873) and was sold by his son, Cunningham Wilson Moore in 1881 to the Foremans. Today the only evidence that remains of the Wilsons of Stenson are the tombstones that flank the footpath at Twyford Parish Church.

25  Amongst those to achieve DNB status in the Wilson family are: Thomas Wilson junior, Daniel Wilson, Bishop of Calcutta, John Dover Wilson, Henry Maitland Wilson (Field Marshall and 1st Baron) and Charlotte Wilson (née Martin)

*Silk Wedding Dress c.1853.*
*Photo courtesy: Mr & Mrs Axtell, Over Worton. Original owned by the Wilsons of Nether/Over Worton (n.d.).*

# 2. Weaving a yarn: the entry of the Wilsons into the Silk Trade

Sent to Coventry by his father, Stephen Wilson [I] was the first member of the Wilson family of Stenson, Derbyshire to enter the silk trade.[1]

Born in 1723 Stephen was the second son of John [II] and Ann Wilson (née Henshaw) who owned a small farm in Stenson, a small hamlet in the combined parish of Barrow and Twyford, South Derbyshire.[2]

From the few details that we have about Stephen Wilson [I] we learn that he married Mary Fullalove, the eldest daughter of Elizabeth Fullalove, a widow of Coventry, a member of a family that was connected by marriage to the Remingtons, thus putting them amongst the ruling families in Coventry. In addition to the Remingtons, these included the Freemans, the Oldhams and the Whitewells all of whom served on the Corporation of the City of Coventry.[3]

By marrying Mary Fullalove, it is clear that Stephen [I] married well, leading ultimately to useful family and business connections within what appears to have been a close knit community amongst the leading families of Coventry. Thus, we find that in 1754 his brother Thomas [I] married Mary Remington, only daughter of John Remington a member of the Corporation of Coventry. At a later stage, Stephen's daughter, Ann Wilson, married Thomas Oldham whilst his second daughter Elizabeth Wilson married William Freeman. Later Catherine West, the youngest daughter of Daniel and Ann West (née Brooke), married William Whitewell, son of John Whitewell, Alderman of Coventry.[4]

All this was in the future. In the meantime, Stephen [I] who had established a very successful business in the Foleshill area of Coventry opened up in 1754 a branch of the family business in Wood Street, Cheapside, London, which at this stage was the leading centre for finished goods, and the main source of raw material for the silk industry.[5]

In the same year, he entered into a partnership with his younger brother, Thomas [I] who had recently married Mary Remington, only daughter of John Remington, a wealthy merchant and member of the ruling elite in Coventry. The terms of the partnership were that Thomas [I] was to manage the manufacturing business in Coventry leaving Stephen [I] to supervise the London branch. Within one year of entering into partnership with his brother, Stephen [I] died from a fever he contracted whilst in London leaving his wife to manage the business and look after four children, all of whom were under the age of six. He was thirty-two years of age.[6]

Although the position that Mary Wilson (née Fullalove) found herself in was not unique, she was nonetheless fortunate in being able to call on the support of her immediate family. She was also in the advantageous position of having two sons who in time would hopefully enter the family business. Failing that she could pass the business on to one of her two daughters: after all such arrangements were not that unusual. However, until her children, and in particular her sons were of age the most obvious course of action open to her was to re-negotiate the terms of partnership with her brother in law, Thomas Wilson [I]. This she duly did for we learn that two months after her husband's death, Mary Wilson entered into a new partnership with her brother in law, Thomas Wilson. It was agreed that Thomas [I] would move to London leaving her to manage the family branch in Coventry.[7]

THOMAS WILSON [I] (1731-1795)

Thomas Wilson [I] was the second member of the Wilson family to enter the silk trade. Like his brothers, he too would have received an education at a neighbouring school before being placed in a suitable commercial enterprise. However, it was not to Coventry or Derby that he was taken by his father John [II], but to London with the intention of being settled into an appropriate business. During the time that they were in London his father, John Wilson [II] fell ill and as a result, the visit was cut short. On the return journey to Stenson, his father's condition rapidly deteriorated and he died at Leicester on June the 11th 1747. He was buried at Twyford.

Two years later Thomas [I] made a trip to St Kitts, but after staying there for about three years and escaping many dangers, he returned to England in 1752. Given Thomas Wilson's attitude to the Slave trade it may well be that during his time in St Kitts he witnessed the full horrors of what John Wesley called 'the vilest trade that ever saw the sun.' Following his return to England in 1752, Thomas settled in Coventry where he entered for a short time in business with his brother, William. In spite of the fact that this proved to be an ill-fated partnership notwithstanding, in 1754 his elder brother Stephen [I], invited him to become a partner in his silk business. Following the death of Stephen [I] in 1755 his widow re-negotiated new terms with her brother in law in which it was agreed that Thomas [I] should take responsibility of the London branch of the business in Wood Street, Cheapside, leaving her to supervise the Foleshill (Coventry) business. By this stage, Thomas [I] had married Mary Remington, the only daughter of John Remington of Coventry.

On arriving in London Thomas and his wife, Mary lived firstly in St Peter's Precinct, for which they paid a rent of £2.10s.10d for property in St Peter's Street, off Wood Street, Cheapside.[8] Later, in 1759 they are listed, as living at 124 Wood Street, Cheapside where they rented a large and extensive premise that was to be the family home for the next eighteen years. It was here in this branch of the family business that succeeding members of the Wilson family were apprenticed before setting up their own business in the silk trade.

## JOHN WILSON (1751-1826)

With John Wilson, the eldest son of the late Stephen Wilson [I] we come to the first member of the 2nd generation of Wilsons to follow in his late father's footsteps when he was placed into the silk trade. In 1765, John entered into the family business with his mother, Mary Wilson, (née Fullalove) and her brother in law, Thomas Wilson [I]. During the period in which he was apprenticed to his mother and uncle, Thomas Wilson [I] John spent a great deal of his time in Coventry which at this stage was the main centre for the manufacture of ribbons. Following the completion of his apprenticeship in 1772 John was made a partner in the family business first with his mother and uncle Thomas Wilson [I], then from 1786 until 1794 with his uncle, and his cousin also called Thomas. From 1794 until 1798, the firm was a co-partnership between John and Thomas Wilson [II]. In 1798, Thomas Wilson [II] retired early from the business leaving John the sole manager of the family business. that had been established by his father, Stephen Wilson [I] in 1754.⁹

## STEPHEN WILSON [II] (1753-1813)

The next member of the late Stephen Wilson's family to be placed in the silk industry was Stephen Wilson [II], the younger son of Stephen and Mary Wilson (née Fullalove). This Stephen, hereafter referred to as Stephen of Church Street Spitalfields, is however not to be confused with his more illustrious cousin, Stephen Wilson of Old Jewry, (member of the firm of Lea and Wilson) who was responsible for introducing the Jacquard machine into England in 1820.¹⁰

Although there is no reference to Stephen Wilson [II] (of Church Street, Spitalfields) in the records of the Weavers Company as having served his apprenticeship in the firm of Thomas, Mary and John Wilson of 121 Wood Street, Cheapside, it is more than probable that he served the seven years required before entering into partnership in 1774 with Daniel West of Church Street, Spitalfields.¹¹ In the same year he married Anne Collett West, eldest daughter of Daniel and Anne West (née Brooke).¹² Later, in 1793 he is listed as being a partner for a short period of time with Harvey, Ham and Perigal of Spital Square.¹³ By this time his father in law, Daniel West was cited as being resident in Southampton Row where he remained until his death in 1796. In addition to taking an active part in the life of the Weavers Company Stephen Wilson also took an active role in the affairs of the Fishmongers Company where he served on the livery and as auditor to the Company.¹⁴

From 1799 until 1813, the year of his death he is listed as being a silk manufacturer at 6 Church Street, Spitalfields and 12 Goldsmith Street, Cheapside, then in 1811 he is listed as being in partnership with two of his sons, Robert Brooke Wilson and Stephen Wilson at 12 Goldsmith Street, Cheapside. After his death in 1813, the business passed into the hands of his sons, Robert Brooke Wilson, Stephen Wilson and Thomas Wilson where it remained until 1829.[15]

## WILLIAM WILSON (1756-1821) of Milk Street

With William Wilson [I] the second son of John and Ann Wilson (née Cocks), we come to the third member of the second generation of Wilsons to enter the family business in Wood Street Cheapside London. Following the completion of his education in 1770 William [I] was sent to London by his father John Wilson [III], where he resided with Thomas Wilson [I] and his family at 124 Wood Street, Cheapside. Although there is no entry in the Court Minute Books of the Weavers Company regarding his apprenticeship, William Wilson [I] is listed as having been made free by redemption on the 3rd of February 1778.[16] On the 28th of September, 1778 he was elected to the Court of Weavers.[17] The following year he married Elizabeth West, second daughter of Daniel and Ann West (née Brooke), of Church Street, Spitalfields.

Between 1785 and 1790, he is cited as being a silk weaver resident at 10 Goldsmith Street, but later in 1791, he is listed as residing at 31 Milk Street, Cheapside that he rented first from a Thomas Flight and then from John Remington for the yearly rent of £76.[18] It was here in the Milk Street business that Stephen Wilson [I] sent his eldest son, Daniel Wilson in 1792 with the aim of him following in the family business.[19] As events turned out this was not to be. In 1797, Stephen Wilson [II] agreed to his son withdrawing from the silk trade in order to enter the ministry of the Church of England.[20]

Other members of the Wilson family to be apprenticed to William Wilson were his own two sons, Joseph (1786-1855) and William [II] (1791-1867) and their cousin, Ambrose Moore, the only surviving son of William's sister, Ann Moore (née Wilson).

## AMBROSE MOORE (1788-1873)

In 1802 Ambrose Moore, was sent by his mother Ann Moore (née Wilson) to London to be apprenticed along with William's eldest son, Joseph, to his uncle, William Wilson in what was considered one of the most lucrative silk companies in the City.[21] Though he was born in London Ambrose spent most of his early childhood in the city of Derby where his mother resided in Friar Gate, Derby. Such education that he had was of a limited nature, a fact that he regretted. During the time that he was apprenticed to his uncle, he sought to make good his lack of education by reading and studying, especially legal matters that related to the silk trade. Following the completion of his apprenticeship Ambrose was made free in 1809 by servitude and in the following year he was made a partner in the family business with his cousin, Joseph Wilson, the eldest son of William Wilson [I]. In a letter written to his sister, Eleanor he describes the business as being one of the most profitable in silk manu-facture.[22] By this stage his uncle, William Wilson [I], had begun to withdraw from the business and retired to his estates in Oxfordshire. Although technically William's eldest son, Joseph was the senior partner in the business, effectively he was a sleeping partner, having retired early from the business in order to devote his time to a variety of philanthropic causes dear to his heart.[23] This left the operational running of the business to William's nephew Ambrose, who like his uncle was equally rigorous in his attention to the business and to the activities of the Weavers Company. Thus, we find that in 1822 he was elected Renter Warden and then in 1825 to the post of Renter Bailiff. In the following year, he was elected to the post of Upper Bailiff, the highest post in the company.[24]

In 1823, he purchased the Ordnance Depot in Normanton Road, Derby that had been designed by James Wyatt, which Ambrose Moore then had converted into a silk factory. At each corner of the yard stood four small houses or cottages originally intended for the soldiers. It was here in one of these cottages with its garden Ambrose Moore and his family lived when they were in Derby.[25]

Apart from his uncle, William Wilson [I] of 31 Milk Street, Cheapside, and his distant cousin, Stephen Wilson of Lea and Wilson Old Jewry, he was the only other member of the family to give evidence before the Select Committee of the House of Commons on the silk industry. Like Stephen Wilson of Old Jewry, he supported the abolition of the Spitalfields Acts on the grounds that it was unjust to those who were industrious. He also considered that the Acts prevented improvements in the trade. In his evidence in 1840 before the Committee on the working conditions of the mills in Derby, he demonstrates a total lack of concern for the welfare of those in his employment. When asked about the length of hours that children between the ages of 9 to 13 should work his reply was that he did not consider it unhealthy for them to work 10 or more hours per day with only 10 minutes break for dinner and an additional break of 10 minutes between dinner and supper. To what extent his indifference to the working conditions of these mill children was markedly dissimilar to that of other mill owners in the country is a moot point but what is so disquieting is the manner in which he puts profit before the conditions of his workers. His purpose was to make money – not lose money irrespective of how injurious the system might be to those in his employment. Equally disconcerting is the fact that his brother in law, Dr Douglas Fox, Medical Superintendent supported Ambrose Moore in his evidence before the committee.[26]

Whereas the ringing of the bell at 6 a.m. may have been a novelty with Ambrose Moore's own children, for those children in his employment, most of them under the age of ten, the tolling of the bell told the same old story.

Likewise, his own children may have been fascinated by the steady rhythm of the beam engine but to those tiny factory children the ceaseless and monotonous beat served only to reinforce for the workers that their sole purpose was to make a profit for the owner.

In 1842, Ambrose Moore sold the mill to Samuel Morley giving him more time to concentrate on his business in London and the activities of the Weavers Company. By 1849, he had virtually retired from the business, thus bringing to an end a family enterprise that had survived for nearly seventy years.

## JOSEPH WILSON (1756-1851)

In 1780 Joseph Wilson, the youngest son of Thomas Wilson [I] was apprenticed to the firm of Mary Wilson (née Fullalove), Thomas Wilson [I] and John Wilson.

Although there is no reference in the Records of the Weavers Company to this fact it is probable that he fulfilled the necessary requirements laid down by the Company enabling him to take up the Freedom of the Weavers Company. However it was not until 1791, a gap of ten years, before he obtained his freedom by redemption, a decision that coincided with his being made a partner with his uncle, John Remington, a member of a wealthy family of merchants of Coventry.[27] In 1792 he was joined by his brother in law Samuel Mills, who is described as being registered as a Land Tax Agent for John Remington.

Unlike his father, Thomas Wilson senior, or his cousin, John Wilson of Upper Street, neither of whom seemed to have become involved in the affairs of the Weavers Company we find that after taking up his freedom Joseph chose to take an active role in the affairs of the Company. From the records of the Weavers Company, we learn that in 1795 along with his brother in law Samuel Mills, he was elected auditor of the Weavers Company. In the same year he was elected Renter Bailiff, a post that he held for two years. Thereafter he rose steadily through the ranks of the Weavers Company rising eventually in 1820 to the rank of Upper Bailiff, the highest position in the Weavers Company.[28] However his involvement in the business affairs of the Company seemed not to have distracted him from his occupation in the manufacture of silk crepe or mourning crepe. Thus, we find that in 1809 he engaged George Courtauld to manage a branch of his business that he had established in Braintree. In the event, it proved to be an ill-fated partnership concluding in 1817 with a court decision that went against Joseph Wilson.[29] Despite losing the case it was not until 1843 that Joseph Wilson eventually sold the business at Braintree to Samuel Courtauld. But for that initial encounter with George Courtauld that spring morning in 1806 it might have been the firm of Wilson and Remington Mills that the people of Braintree might have remembered today. That however is another episode in the history of the Wilson silk industry.

STEPHEN WILSON (1777-1860) of Old Jewry

The next phase or stage in the history of the Wilson involvement in the silk trade moves on to Stephen Wilson of Lea and Wilson of 26 Old Jewry who as we have already noted is not to be confused with his cousin, Stephen Wilson [II] of Church Street, Spitalfields and the father of Daniel Wilson, later Bishop of Calcutta. Stephen Wilson who was born in 1777 was the second son of John and Elizabeth Wilson (née Wight). In 1791, he was apprenticed to Richard Lea of Old Jewry and Beckenham and obtained his freedom of the Weavers Company by redemption in 1799.[30] In the time honoured manner not only did he marry Sarah Lea, the second eldest daughter of his master but also went on to become a partner in his father in law's business. It was to this business that his younger brother, Samuel was apprenticed.

From the few details known about him, it is recorded that he spent the period 1803 to 1807 incarcerated in a French prison with his cousin, Robert Brooke Wilson, younger brother of Daniel Wilson.[31] Exactly why they had been detained in a French prison in Paris is unknown but it may well be that they had been apprehended while they were endeavouring to obtain details on the jacquard machine.

Although in the history of the Weavers Company Stephen is overshadowed by his more illustrious brother, Samuel Wilson, the only member of the Weavers Company to rise to the rank of Lord Mayor, this should not detract from his achievement of having introduced into England in 1820 the Jacquard loom. By so doing he revolutionized the English silk industry. According to a letter written in 1820 we learn that Stephen Wilson of Old Jewry sent one of his servants, Thomas Smith to France to obtain drawings and if possible obtain a hook, a pasteboard and some patterns and ribbons. Having obtained the necessary details, Stephen Wilson then set up a factory in Streatham in which he installed the Jacquard looms.[32] It was however not until much later that the Jacquard loom was adopted on a large scale by other manufacturers.

Like his cousin Ambrose Moore, partner in the firm of Wilson and Moore of Milk Street, Stephen Wilson of Old Jewry was an ardent advocate for the repeal of the Spitalfield Act giving evidence to the Select Committee of the House of Commons on the silk industry.

Accused by Peter Moore, MP of being an exporter and capitalist who in consequence was only interested in obtaining goods at a cheap rate for exportation and had no concern with the manner in which the workmen were paid Wilson retorted that his workmen received 17 shillings for plain work and 35 shillings per week for figured work: a far higher amount than most manufacturers paid their workers for the same amount of work.[33]

As a leading figure in the Weavers Company, he is recorded as serving on a committee in 1821 to collect funds for the relief of the poor in Spitalfield, raising over £40,000. During his career in the silk industry he served on a number of committees for the Weavers Company and held the office of Upper Bailiff on two further occasions.

## SAMUEL WILSON (1791-1881)

In 1806 Stephen Wilson's younger brother, Samuel Wilson (1791-1881), was apprenticed to the firm of Lea & Wilson of 26 Old Jewry. In 1813, he obtained his freedom and was made a partner with his elder brother Stephen, in the firm of Lea and Wilson of Old Jewry. By 1821, the firm had moved to Streatham where Stephen installed the jacquard machines. After holding a number of offices in the Weavers Company, including that of Upper Bailiff Samuel went on to hold office as Alderman, then Sheriff and finally Lord Mayor of the City of London, from 1838-1839.[34]

## *Conclusion*

By the 1840s the numerous firms set up by various members of the Wilson family had either closed or been taken over by larger companies. These included the smaller firms such as Stephen and Thomas Wilson of Bread Street,[35] Stephen and Thomas Wilson of 12 Goldsmith Street,[36] and Melville Wilson of Wilson, Stephenson and Co of 124 Wood Street, Cheapside.[37] In addition to these smaller family businesses there were the major firms. Thus, we find that in 1843 Joseph Wilson of Wilson and Remington Mills sold his firm in Braintree to the Courtaulds,[38] whilst Ambrose Moore sold his business in Derby to Samuel Morley, c.1840.[39]

Although the Wilsons were not the only silk manufacturers in the City of London or indeed in Spitalfields, what is remarkable is the way that so many of the firms established by the Wilsons survived for such a long period of time. Equally significant is the length of time that members of the Wilson family dominated the upper echelons of the Weavers Company. Thus, we find that from 1774 until 1884 if we take into account co-sanguinal relatives over 27 members of the Wilson family are listed as having held the office of Renter Bailiff and Upper Bailiff. These included such prominent members as Daniel West, William Wilson, Joseph Wilson of Highbury, Ambrose Moore, John Remington Mills, Stephen Wilson of Old Jewry, Alderman Samuel Wilson and his son Cornelius Lea Wilson. Of these, the one of whom the Company is most justly proud is Lord Samuel Wilson. He was the only member of the Company and for that matter the Wilson family to hold the office of Lord Mayor: an event that he celebrated by inviting 117 members of the Wilson clan to a banquet held in the Egyptian room of Mansion House.[40]

*Notes and References:*

1. Wilson J. (1846) Memoir of Thomas Wilson. London. See also Rothstein, N.K.A (1961) The Silk Trade in London: 1702-1766. London University M.A.

2. Wilson, J. (1846) Memoir of Thomas Wilson. London. Stenson was a small hamlet in the combined parishes of Barrow upon Trent and Twyford.

3. See: Hinman, M.J. (1980) Men who Ruled Coventry 1725-1780. Coventry: Coventry & Warwickshire Historical Association. Of the families who were amongst the ruling elite in Coventry were the Oldhams, Remingtons, Whitewells and Freemans all of whom intermarry into the Wilson family that originally came from Stenson, Derbyshire. According to Hinman the Fullaloves were 3rd ranking amongst the ruling families of Coventry.

4. In the private calendar of Stephen Wilson, 1795-1802. there are references to the Oldhams, Freemans and Whitewells. As Michael Hinman has shown in his study on the men who ruled Coventry, they were all amongst the ruling elite in the City.

5. Rothstein, N.K.A. (1961) The Silk Industry in London: 1702-1766. London University. M.A. In her dissertation she lists a Stephen Wilson and Co of Aldermanbury 1755-1793. This is probably a reference to the firm established by Stephen Wilson (I) (1723-1755 in Wood Street, Cheapside that is in the Aldermanbury and Cripplegate Ward. See also: Wilson, J. (1846) Memoir of Thomas Wilson. London. On Wood Street, Cheapside, see: Gordon, Caroline & W. Dewhirst. (1985) The Ward of Cripplegate in the City of London. London: Ward Cripplegate Club. Wood Street was well sited being on the main staging and carrying routes to Coventry, Derby, Leicester, Manchester and Nottingham. Apart from the Castle, the most important Coaching Inn in Wood Street, Cheapside was The Swan with two necks, whilst at the north end of Wood Street was the Mitre Inn.

6. See: Wilson, J. (1846) Memoir of Thomas Wilson. London.

7. Wilson, J. (1846) Memoir of Thomas Wilson. London.

8. London Register Rates: (1758-1759) in which Thomas Wilson is listed as being resident in St Peter's Precinct. See also: Wilson, J. (1846) Memoir of Thomas Wilson. London.

9. Wilson, J. (1846) Memoirs of Thomas Wilson. London.

10. See: Rothstein, N.K.A. (1990) Silk Designs of the 18th century. London: Thames and Hudson.

11. London Directory, 1775 in which Stephen Wilson [II] is listed as being in partnership with Daniel West of 7 Church Street, Spitalfields. See also: Bateman, J. (1860) Life of Daniel Wilson. London: John Murray. 2 vols.

12. Bateman, J. (1860) Life of Daniel Wilson. London. 2 vols.

13. See: Rothstein, N.K.A. (1990) Silk Designs of the 18th century. London: Thames and Hudson in which she cites that Stephen Wilson was a partner for a short time with a Mr Perigal of Spital Square, Spitalfields.

14. According to an entry in his Private Calendar: 1795-1802 Stephen Wilson records that he was elected a member of the Fishmongers Company along with John

Remington and that he was elected to the Livery where he served as auditor to the Company.

15. Universal British Directory, 1799 in which Stephen Wilson is listed as being at 12 Goldsmith Street, Cheapside In 1811 he is listed with his sons as a silk manufacturer. By 1829 his three sons, Robert, Stephen and Thomas had died.

16. GUILDHALL LIBRARY: Gld Mss. Court Minute Books: Weavers Company: 4655/17/1765-1785.

17. GUILDHALL LIBRARY: Gld Mss. Court Minute Books: Weavers Company. 4655/17/1765-1785.

18. GUILDHALL LIBRARY: Gld Mss. Court Minute Books: Weavers Company: 4655/18/1785-1798. See also: Suffolk Record Office: Bury St Edmund's Branch. HA/530/4/1-9/1: Abstract of Title deeds relating to Milk Street, Cheapside. Given the size of the premises with its own millrace it is more than probable that William Wilson was engaged in the manufacture of Broad loom silk. See Bateman, J. (1860) Life of Daniel Wilson. London: John Murray in which he gives a brief description of the premises and the size of the work force employed by William Wilson.

19. Wilson, J. (1846) Memoir of Thomas Wilson. London. See also: Harrison, M. J: Patrons & Church Builders: The Wilsons of Highbury and Islington. A paper given at a Seminar organized by the Friends of Union Chapel and the Victorian Society. September. 2005 Forthcoming: 2008.

20. Bateman, J. (1860) Life of Daniel Wilson. London: 2 vols.

21. GUILDHALL LIBRARY: Gld Mss: Court Minute Books: Weavers Company 4655/19/1798-1825. The only other reference to Ambrose being apprenticed to his uncle, William Wilson of Milk Street is to be found in the Family sketch written by his daughter, Harriet Ann Wilson, (née Moore) in 1901. (Privately owned.)

22. In her Family Sketch Harriet Wilson (née Moore) records that her father, Ambrose Moore was made a partner in his uncle's business, which he describes as being one of the most lucrative companies in the city. This Joseph Wilson, the eldest son of William and Elizabeth Wilson, (née West) is not to be confused with Joseph Wilson of Highbury Place, the second son of Thomas and Mary Wilson of Highbury, Islington.

23. Bateman, J. (1860) Life of Daniel Wilson. London: 2 vols., in which Joseph is described as being the founder of the LDOS. See also: Brown, F.K. (1960) Father of the Victorians: the Age of Wilberforce. Cambridge: Cambridge University Press.

24. GUILDHALL LIBRARY: Gld Mss. Court Minute Books: Weavers Company: 4655/20/1825-1850.

25. Wilson, H.A. (1901) Family Sketch written by the daughter of Ambrose Moore. (Privately owned.)
See also: Simpson, R. (1826) History and Antiquities of Derby. 2 vols.

26. See: Report to the General Board of Health: Preliminary Enquiry into the sewerage, drainage and supply of water and the sanitary conditions of the

inhabitants of the borough of Derby: E. B. Cressy. Superintendent inspector. London: HMSO. 1849. See also: HCSC: BPP Report from the Select Committee on the Act for the regulation of Mills & Factories: 1840. vol. 1.

27. GUILDHALL LIBRARY: Gld Mss. Court Minute Books: Weavers Company. 4655/18/1786-1798.

28. GUILDHALL LIBRARY: Gld Mss. Court Minute Books: Weavers Company: 4655/18/1786-1798.

29. Essex Record Office: Chelmsford Branch. D/F/3/2/94: Letters: Papers & Deeds relating to George Courtauld and Joseph Wilson: c.1809-1817. See also: Coleman, D.C. (1969) Courtaulds: an Economic and Social History. Oxford: Clarendon Press. 2 vols.

30. GUILHALL LIBRARY: Gld Mss: Court Minute Books: Weavers Company: 4655/19/1798-1825.

31. In her Family Sketch, Harriet Wilson refers to Stephen having been imprisoned in the Bastille along with Robert Brooke Wilson, younger brother of Daniel Wilson. See also HCSC (PP) Select Committee on the Silk Trade, 1818.

32. See: Rothstein, N.K.A. (1977) The Introduction of the Jacquard Loom to Great Britain: in Studies in Textile History in memory of Harold B Burnham. ed. Veronika Gervers. Ontario: Ontario Museum.

33. HCSC. (P P) Select Committee on the silk Trade: 1818.

34. Plummer, A. (1972) The London Weavers Company: 1600-1970. London: Routledge Kegan and Paul. See also: Wilson, J. (1846) Memoirs of Thomas Wilson, London.

35. Stephen and Thomas Wilson were the younger sons of John and Ann Wilson (née Cocks) of Stenson, silk manufacturers of Bread Street, Cheapside.

36. Stephen and Thomas Wilson of 12 Goldsmith Street were the younger sons of Stephen Wilson [II] formerly of Church Street, Spitalfields and then from 1799 of 12 Goldsmith Street.

37. Melville Wilson who married Louisa Stephenson was the son of Thomas Wilson of Bread Street, Cheapside.

38. See: Coleman, D. C. (1969) Courtaulds: an Economic and Social History. Oxford: Clarendon Press.

39. Derby Museum & Art Gallery: Although Samuel Morley owned no less than 4 silk mills along the Normanton Road no mention is made in Glover (1843) or Bagshaw of Morley being listed at The Depot, Normanton Road. I am grateful to Roger Shelley, Keeper of Industrial and Social History for this information.

40. Plummer, A. (1972) The London Weavers Company: 1600-1970. London: Routledge Kegan & Paul.

## SILK MANUFACTURERS IN THE WILSON FAMILY:

1. Stephen Wilson [I] (1723-1755) Coventry and 121 Wood Street, Cheapside.

2. Thomas Wilson [I] (1731-1794) Partner with his brother, Stephen Wilson [I] 1754: then made partner with his widow, Mary Wilson of Coventry and 121 Wood Street, Cheapside.

3.  John Wilson (1751-1826) son of Stephen Wilson [I] of Coventry: and 121 Wood Street Cheapside, partner with his mother & uncle, then uncle and cousin: then with his sons, Stephen and Thomas Wilson until his death in 1826. By 1841, the firm had ceased trading.

4.  Stephen Wilson [II] (1753-1813) second son of Stephen Wilson [I] of Coventry. Partner with his father in law, Daniel West of Church Street, Spitalfields. Later he is listed in 1799 as trading at 12 Goldsmith Street, Cheapside on his own and in 1812 with his sons, Stephen, Robert and Thomas Wilson. By 1829, the firm had ceased trading.

5.  William Wilson (1756-1821) Milk Street, Cheapside and The Wortons, Oxfordshire: under the partnership of Wilson, Robinson and Moore, later Wilson and Moore.

6.  Thomas Wilson (1760-1829) brother of Stephen Wilson with whom he was a partner in Bread Street, Cheapside.

7.  Stephen Wilson (1761-1814) in partnership with his brother Thomas Wilson Bread Street, Cheapside and Grace Church, City of London.(8)

8.  Thomas Wilson [II] (1764-1843) son of Thomas Wilson retired from business in 1794.

9.  Joseph Wilson (1766-1851) 30 Milk Street, Cheapside and Highbury, Islington. In partnership with John Remington, then in 1810 the firm is listed as Joseph Wilson and G Courtauld (Braintree) From 1821 until c.1840 the firm is listed as being Wilson and Remington Mills. (See: entry no. 13.)

10. Stephen Wilson (1777-1860) Son of John Wilson of Upper Street: partner in the firm of Lea and Wilson of Old Jewry.

11. Joseph Wilson (1786-1855) Sleeping partner: Wilson, Moore and Robinson of 31 Milk Street, Cheapside, London and The Old Depot, Normanton Road, Derby.

12. Ambrose Moore (1788-1873) nephew of William Wilson of Milk Street, Cheapside: made a partner in the firm along with his cousin, Joseph Wilson of Clapham and Nether Worton, Oxon. By 1823 is listed as Wilson, Moore and Robinson, The Old Depot, Normanton Road Derby and 31 Milk Street Cheapside. In 1835, the firm is listed as being Wilson and Moore, 2, Devonshire Street, London and The Depot Mills, Derby.

13. John Remington Mills (1798-1879) Partner in the firm of his uncle, Joseph Wilson of Milk Street, Cheapside and Highbury, Islington. Retired from the business in 1840.

14. Wilson, (Melville) Stephenson & Co. He was the son of Thomas Wilson of Bread Street. They traded at 124 Wood Street, Cheapside. In 1841 the firm is listed as Wilson, Keith and Co.

## SILK FIRMS: 1754-1846

| | |
|---|---|
| Remington Mills and Wilson. | 30 Milk Street, Cheapside. 14 Lamb's Passage, Bunnhill Row, City of London. |
| Wilson, Moore and Co. | 31 Milk Street, Cheapside. 21 Spital Square, Spitalfields. |

| | |
|---|---|
| Wilson, Stephenson & Co. | 124 Wood Street, Cheapside. |
| Thomas Wilson: (1760-1829) | 30 Grace Church Street, City of London. |
| | Bread Street, Cheapside. |
| Thomas Wilson, John Wilson. | 121 Wood Street, Cheapside. |
| Stephen Wilson. | 12 Goldsmith Street, Cheapside, and |
| | 6 Church Street, Spitalfields. |
| Lea & Wilson. | 26 Old Jewry. Cripplegate. |

Significant Dates of Silk Manufacturers:
(Wilson & related members of the family)

| | |
|---|---|
| 1754/5: Stephen Wilson<br>& Thomas Wilson | Ribbon Weavers: Coventry & Wood Street, Cheapside.[1] |
| 1755: Mary Wilson<br>& Thomas Wilson | Ribbon Weavers:<br>Coventry & Wood Street. |
| 1758: Daniel West | Satin Weaver, Wood Street, Spitalfields. |
| 1760: Daniel West | Satin Weaver, Wood Street, Spitalfields. |
| 1763: Thomas Wilson<br>and Co | Ribbon Weavers, Wood Street, Cheapside. |
| 1763: Daniel West & Wren | Satin Weavers, Church Street, Spitalfields. |
| 1768: Daniel West | Satin Weaver, Church Street, Spitalfields. |
| 1770: Thomas Wilson | Ribbon Weaver, 124, Goldsmith Street, Cheapside. |
| 1771: John Remington | Silk Weaver, 30, Milk Street, Cheapside. |
| 1771: Lowndes, Remington &<br>Briggs | Silk Weavers, 30, Milk Street, Cheapside. |
| 1773: Daniel West | Satin Weaver: 7, Church Street, Spitalfields. |
| 1774: Daniel West | Satin Weaver: 7 Church Street, Spitalfields. |
| 1775: West, D & Stephen Wilson | Satin Manufacturers: 7 Church Street, Spitalfields.[2] |
| 1775: Wilson, Thomas,<br>Mary & John | 121 Wood Street, Cheapside.[3] |
| 1780: Remington & Layton | 30 Milk Street, Cheapside. |
| 1785: Wilson, T & Co | 121 Wood Street, Cheapside. |

| | |
|---|---|
| 1790: William Wilson | 10 Goldsmith Street, Cheapside. |
| 1790: Wilson, T & John | 121, Wood Street, Cheapside. |
| 1790: Wilson, T & S | 4 Bread Street, Cheapside. |
| 1790: Remington & Wilson | 30 Milk Street, Cheapside. |
| 1793: Harvey, Perigal, Ham & Wilson, S | Spital Square. |
| 1794: John Wilson | Coventry & 121 Wood Street, Cheapside. |
| 1797: S.Wilson & West | 7 Church Street, Spitalfields. |
| 1799: Stephen Wilson | 6 Church Street, Spitalfields, & 12 Goldsmith Street, Cheapside. |
| 1799: William Wilson | 31 Milk Street, Cheapside. |
| 1810: Joseph Wilson & G. Courtauld | Braintree.[4] |
| 1810: W.Wilson & A. Moore | 31 Milk Street, Cheapside. |
| 1812: Stephen Wilson & Sons | 12 Goldsmith Street, Cheapside. |
| 1816: S&T Wilson | 11 Goldsmith Street, Cheapside & 121 Wood Street, Cheapside. |
| 1818: Stephen & Robert Brooke Wilson | 12 Goldsmith Street, Cheapside. |
| 1821: Wilson, J&A Moore | 31 Milk Street, Cheapside. |
| 1821: Wilson & Remington Mills | 30 Milk Street, Cheapside & Braintree. |
| 1823: Lea Wilson. Bourefield & Wilson | 26 Old Jewry, Cripplegate.[5] |
| 1823: Wilson, Moore and Robinson | The Old Depot, Normanton Road Derby, & 31 Milk Street,Cheapside, London. |
| 1835: Wilson & Moore A. Depot Mills, Derby | 2 Devonshire Street, London & Moore, |
| 1841-1846: Wilson, Keith & Co | 124 Wood Street, Cheapside.[6] |

## Notes

1.  See: Rothstein, N.K.A. (1961) The Silk Industry in London. (M.A: London University) who lists a Stephen Wilson and Co of Aldermansbury: 1755-1799. (p.36) This is probably a reference to the firm that Stephen Wilson (1723-1755) established at 121/124 Wood Street, Cheapside that is in the Ward of Aldermans-

bury. Following his death it became a co-partnership between his widow, Mary Wilson and Thomas Wilson (1731-1794) then Thomas, Mary and John Wilson (1751-1826) and then John, Stephen and Thomas Wilson. (See note 5.)

2. In 1773/4, numbers were inserted in the houses.

3. The premises of Stephen Wilson and Co were on the corner of Wood Street/ Goldsmith Street: Directories cite the firm as being either in Goldsmith Street or Wood Street, Cheapside.

4. Coleman, D.C. (1969) The Courtaulds: An Economic and Social History. Oxford: Clarendon Press. 2 vols.

5. See: Rothstein, N.K.A. (1990) Silk designs of the 18th century in the Collection of the V&A, London. London: Thames and Hudson, in which she observes that in 1823 they are listed as Lea, Wilson, Bourefield and Wilson of 26 Old Jewry, Cripplegate.

6. See: Rothstein, N.K.A (1990) op cit: in 1841 the firm at 121-124 Wood Street is listed as Wilson, Keith & Co: by 1846 they had become Keith & Shoobridge and Daniel Keith & Co, of 124 Wood Street, Cheapside.

## Entries of Wilsons and members of the Family in the Records of the Weavers Company

Office Holders in the Weavers Company:

1774:   Daniel West: Renter Bailiff.[a]
1776:   Daniel West: Upper Bailiff.[a]
1780:   Benjamin Mills: Upper Bailiff.[1]
1791:   Richard Lea: Upper Bailiff.[2]
1801:   William Wilson: Renter Bailiff.
1802:   William Wilson: Upper Bailiff.
1804:   Samuel Mills: Upper Bailiff.[3]
1811:   Stephen Wilson.[4]
1818:   William Wilson/Stephen Wilson.[4]
1819:   Samuel Mills: Upper Bailiff: (post declined by W.Wilson: 14th July 1819).
1820:   Joseph Wilson: Upper Bailiff.[5]
1826:   Ambrose Moore: Upper Bailiff.[6]
1828:   Joseph Wilson.[5]
1829:   Stephen Wilson.[4]
1831:   John Remington Mills.[7]
1832:   Samuel Wilson: (Alderman).[8]
1837:   Lea Wilson.[9]
1840:   Ambrose Moore.[6]
1845:   John Remington Mills.[9]
1847/8: Ambrose Moore.[6]
1853:   Edward Wilson.[10]
1857:   Cornelius Lea Wilson.[11]
1862/3: Colonel Samuel Wilson.[8]
1872:   Cornelius Lea Wilson: (elected to replace Edward Fox: who died in office).

1884:    Cornelius Lea Wilson.

*Notes:*
(a) Daniel West: partner with his son in law Stephen Wilson [II] of Church Street.
1. Benjamin Mills, father of Samuel Mills, son in law to Thomas Wilson, senior of Highbury: (1731-1794).
2. Richard Lea: father in law to Stephen Wilson and Alderman Samuel Wilson: of Old Jewry.
3. Samuel Mills was land agent and land tax collector for Remington Mills & Wilson of Milk Street.
4. Stephen Wilson of Lea & Wilson, of Old Jewry and Streatham: according to the Minutes of the Weavers Company August 1818 was Bailiff with William Wilson who declined the post of Upper Bailiff 14th July 1819.
5. Joseph Wilson: (son of Thomas Wilson of Highbury) of Remington Mills and Wilson, 30 Milk Street, Cheapside. (see Burkes' Landed Gentry: J.Wilson of Stow-langtoft, Suffolk).
6. Ambrose Moore, nephew to William Wilson of Milk Street, Cheapside: made partner in his Uncle's firm in 1810. In 1823 he established a silk manufactory in the Old Depot, Derby. The firm was sold in the 1840s to Samuel Morley.
7. John Remington Mills: son of Samuel Mills: retired from the firm of Remington Mills and Wilsons in 1840: (see Burkes' Landed Gentry).
8. Alderman Samuel Wilson: brother to Stephen Wilson of Old Jewry: only member of the Weavers Company to become Lord Mayor.
9. Lea Wilson: son of Stephen and Sarah Wilson (née Lea) of Old Jewry.
10. Edward Wilson: son of Stephen and Sarah Wilson (née Lea) of Old Jewry.
11. Cornelius Lea Wilson: son of Alderman Samuel Wilson and Jemima Wilson (née Lea of Old Jewry and Beckenham).

*References:*
Burkes' Landed Gentry.
Gld Mss. 4655 Court Minute Books.
Plummer, Alfred. The London Weavers Company. London: Routledge Kegan & Paul, 1972.
London Trade Directories:
Gld Mss Weavers Company.
Parliamentary Papers: Silk Industry.
Rothstein, N. (1990) Silk Designs of the 18th century in the Collection of the V&A London: Thames and Hudson.

# 3. Elizabeth Collett and her descendants[i]

Tradition has it that Elizabeth Collett, the second daughter of Thomas and Isabella Collett (née Castle), was descended from one of the daughters of Sir Thomas Vyner of Eastbury Manor, Barking.[1]

Sir Thomas Vyner was the only surviving son of Thomas Vyner of North Cerney in Gloucestershire by his second marriage to Anne Ellis. In 1600, Thomas was sent to London where he resided with his stepsister and her husband, Samuel Moore, a goldsmith and member of the Worshipful Company of Goldsmiths. Following the completion of his apprenticeship Thomas Vyner was made a member of the Goldsmiths Company and a Freeman of the City of London, rising eventually to the rank of Prime Warden, the highest office in the company, and Lord Mayor of the city of London. In 1653/4 he was knighted by Oliver Cromwell and after the interregnum was created a Baronet by King Charles 2nd.[2]

In 1649, Thomas Vyner purchased Westbury, in Barking, followed in 1650 by the purchase of Eastbury Manor. On his death, these two estates descended to his sister, Edith and her heirs in whose hands the estates remained until the end of the 17th century.[3]

At first sight this account of Elizabeth Collett's pedigree might sound plausible: howbeit there is another version of the same account which claims that Elizabeth Collett was descended from Edith the eldest sister of Sir Robert Vyner's father, William Vyner, step brother to Sir Thomas Vyner.[4]

Fascinating though these claims might be there is in fact no genealogical evidence in the history of the Vyners in support of the claim that Elizabeth Collett was descended from the Vyners.[5] Likewise there is no evidence that her husband, Robert Brooke, was descended from the Brookes of Warwick.[6]

Whilst it is not too difficult to see why such a link between Elizabeth Collett and the Vyners was created, this is a legend that was probably conjured up by the phrase the White Rajahs of Sarawak to give credibility and substance to James Brooke's prestige as Rajah and Governor of Sarawak. All that was needed was for him to obtain a knighthood after which he obviously hankered. That said, what should not be overlooked is the fact that but for a pedigree that he claimed went back to Sir Thomas Vyner it is doubtful if he would have received the Freedom of the Worshipful Company of Goldsmiths let alone the Freedom of the City of London.[7]

However to return to Elizabeth Collett and her true pedigree. As we have already noted Elizabeth Collett was the second daughter of Thomas and Isabella Collett (née Castle) formerly of Goodmanfields Whitechapel, and then of Barking. Her father, Thomas Collett was a maritime Captain in the services of the East India Company and Captain of the East Indiaman, *The Grantham*.[8] In the Church of St Margaret's Barking is a memorial plaque bearing amongst many others the name of Captain Thomas Collett and two of his daughters, Grissel Pelly, (née Collett) and Susanna Court, (née Collett).[9]

Thomas Collett's name also appears on two Benefactors Boards in the Church, one in what is now the Refectory where he is listed as being a benefactor to the poor of the parish. The other Board is in the South aisle of the Church where he is listed along with his brother, Captain Jonathan Collett as having purchased six acres of land the rents of which were to be laid in penny loaves and distributed to the poor in the parish.[10]

We also learn from other sources that Thomas had two more children. These were Thomas (1704-1718), who died in India and was buried in the grounds of Fort William, Calcutta and Elizabeth (c.1700-1751), the wife of Captain Robert Brooke, the subject of this study.[11]

Although there is no reference to Elizabeth Collett on the Memorial Plaque bearing the name of her father, Thomas Collett, we learn from his will that she had married Robert Brooke, whom Thomas Collett described as being a "mariner of Goodmanfields, Whitechapel."[12] This was a highly desirable residential area amongst maritime captains and merchants in the services of the East India Company and where her uncle, Captain Jonathan Collett of the EIC and her brother in law, Captain John Pelly, also resided.[13] From this evidence, we may deduce that Robert Brooke was a person of substance or potential substance.[14]

Five children were born to Elizabeth and Robert Brooke, two daughters and three sons of whom only their two daughters and one son survived to adulthood. These were Ann (1722), Elizabeth (1725) and Robert (1727). The other two sons, Thomas and Jonathan died early in life.[15]

According to the will of Robert Brooke, it was their eldest daughter, Ann who married Daniel West, one of the executors to Robert Brooke's will.[16] Later, Daniel West was to become financial advisor and confidante to the Countess of Huntingdon and one of George Whitefield's trustees.[17]

Ann and Daniel West were the grandparents of Daniel Wilson, (1778-1858) who went on to become Bishop of Calcutta, a position that he held from 1832-until his death in 1858. By the standards of the day, this was a remarkable achievement given that India had been the graveyard of the preceding four Bishops in a space of only eighteen years.[18]

The second daughter of Elizabeth and Robert Brooke, also called Elizabeth, is cited as having married Thomas Pattle, a maritime Captain in the EIC and part owner with her brother, Robert, of the East Indiaman, *The Speke*.[19] Elizabeth and Thomas Pattle had four children, three daughters and one son. The three daughters were, Mary (1740), Ruth (1741-1829) and Elizabeth (1752). Of these Mary and Elizabeth probably died in early childhood whilst Ruth, their only surviving daughter, married her uncle, Robert Brooke, the only surviving son of Elizabeth and Robert Brooke.[20]

As to Elizabeth and Thomas's only son, also called Thomas (1742-1818) he married first Sarah Hasleby whilst in India and then shortly after Sarah's death in 1812 or thereabouts he married Susannah Wilson.[21] There is no evidence however that she was related to the family of Wilsons from whom Daniel Wilson was descended.

Thomas had ten children by Sarah, his first wife, five sons and five daughters of whom only three sons survived to adulthood: Thomas Charles (1773-1815), James (1775-1845) and William. Of these the most significant was James Pattle.

Leaving aside the myths surrounding James Pattle as recorded by Virginia Woolf, according to the records of the East India Company; we learn that he was born in India where he stayed for the first seven years of his life before being sent to England. After completing his education at the age of sixteen, he returned to India following in the footsteps of his father by serving in the East India Company eventually rising to the position of Senior Judge of the Court of Appeal in the Murshidabad district.[22]

James Pattle and his wife, Adeline Maria, whom he married in 1811, remained in India where they brought up their family of nine daughters and one son. Only seven of their ten children survived to adulthood: Adeline (1812-1836), Julia Margaret (1815-1879), Sarah (1816-1867), Maria (1818-1892), Louisa (1821-1873), Virginia (1827-1910) and Sophia (1829-1911).[23] By the time of James and Adeline's death in 1845, only four of their six surviving daughters remained for some time in India with their respective husbands. These were Julia Margaret, Sarah, Maria and Louisa, the two younger daughters, Virginia and Sophia, having returned to England where they were to make their mark on English culture and society.[24] James and Adeline's eldest daughter, Adeline (1812-1836) who had married Colin Mackenzie died at sea. She was twenty-four years of age.[25]

Returning to Elizabeth and Robert Brooke, their third surviving child was a son, also called Robert who married Ruth Casson Pattle, the only surviving daughter of Elizabeth and Thomas Pattle. Such a marriage was technically illegal as Ruth was the niece of Robert Brooke.

Ruth and Robert Brooke had one son, Thomas (1760-1835) who also followed the example of his uncle, Thomas Pattle, by going out to India in 1779 as a Bengal Writer in the services of the East India Company.[26] In the Private Calendar of Stephen Wilson (1795-1802) he is referred to as Cousin Thomas Brooke of Calcutta.[27]

Although Thomas Brooke is said to have been a childless widower he had it seems adopted the practice common amongst Writers in Calcutta of taking a Bibi or Companion by whom he had at least three children.[28] The three children were Charles William (1784-1836), Sophia (c.1785) and Julia (n.d.).

It is not known when they were sent to England for their education but according to an entry in the Private Calendar of Stephen Wilson, the three children lived with their grandmother, Ruth Brooke.[29] By this time, she is recorded as living in Mortlake and then in 1814 had moved to Reigate where she lived with her grandson, James Brooke, son of Thomas and Anna Maria Brooke (née Stuart). According to one of James Brooke's biographers, she was said to have given generously to the poor in Reigate and to missionaries. How much of this rubbed off on her grandson is not known but it is interesting to note that when James went to Sarawak he set about establishing a Christian mission under the auspices of the Church of England. All this was in the future but in so doing, he was in fact following in a family tradition.[30]

But to return to Ruth Brooke's son, Thomas Brooke of Calcutta. In addition to having three children by his Bibi, the Moher Bibi of Arah in Bihar, Thomas Brooke is recorded as having a further eight children by his second wife, Anna Maria Stuart, whom he married on February 1st 1793. Of these only five survived to adulthood: Harriet Grace (1794), Henry Stuart (1798-1820), Emma (1802-1870), James (1803-1868) and Margaret (1805-1864).[31]

In 1816, Thomas Brooke retired from his position as a Senior Judge in the Court of Appeal in Murshidabad and settled in Bath. In his will dated 1835 he left to each of his three surviving children by his wife, Anna Maria, £30,000.[32] To his two surviving children by his Mohar Bibi, Charles William and Sophia, he left £1,000. In addition, he left £1,000 to Charles with the proviso that he should provide the Mohar Bibi of Arah with a pension.[33]

As to James, the only surviving son of Thomas and Anna Maria Brooke, (née Stuart) following the death of his father in 1835, he purchased a schooner and after a series of misadventures sailed to the Indian Archipelago where in 1841, he was appointed the 1st White Rajah of Sarawak.[34]

After serving as the 1st Rajah of Sarawak for twenty-two years he returned to England in 1863 where he retired to his cottage at Burrator in North Devon. By this time, his health was rapidly declining and on June the 11th 1868, he died. Before his death in 1868, he appointed his nephew, Charles Johnson, the second son of his sister, Emma, to succeed him as the 2nd Rajah of Sarawak.[35] He in turn was succeeded by his son, Charles Vyner, thereby perpetuating and reinforcing the Vyner tradition.

To what extent James Brooke or his biographers were responsible for the story linking his great great grandmother, Elizabeth Brooke (née Collett) with Sir Thomas Vyner is open to question but given James Brooke's ability in legend making such a possibility is not beyond the bounds of reason. After all here was a legend in the making and what better person than James Brooke to create such a story.[36] Notwithstanding, in so doing he has in fact given Elizabeth Brooke (née Collett) a place in history that she justly deserves.

*Notes & References:*

(i) *On the Colletts of Barking and their descendents see: Harrison, M.J. From Barking to Calcutta and Sarawak. The Link, St Margaret's Barking: Dec. 2005, also Borneo Chronicle: Spring/Summer, 2006. Elizabeth Collett was the second daughter of Thomas Collett, a Captain in the maritime services of the East India Company. It is from her that Daniel Wilson, 5th Bishop of Calcutta, James Brooke, 1st White Rajah of Sarawak and the 7 beautiful daughters of James Pattle are descended. From this we can see the pivotal role that she played in a family that produced Civil servants, academics, writers and intellectuals: not to say the whole of the Bloomsbury Group that centred around Virginia Woolf (née Stephen) and her sister Vanessa Bell (née Stephen) No study apart from my own research makes this link between all these distinguished families.*

1. See for example: Jacob, G.L. (1876) The Raja of Sarawak. London. 2 vols.: who claims that James Brooke was seventh in descent from Sir Thomas Vyner. See also: Runciman, S. (1960) The White Rajahs: a History of Sarawak from 1841-1946. Cambridge: Cambridge University Press.

2. See for example: Keppel, H. (1846) The Expedition to Borneo of *HMS Dido* for the Suppression of Piracy. London: 2 vols. See also: Notes and Queries. 2nd series: no. 53. Jan 3. 1857. Oxford University Press.

3. See: Vyner, C. (1887) The Vyners: A Family History. Leamington: See also: The Victoria County History of Essex: vol. v. ed. J.E. Oxley. London: Oxford University Press.

4. See: Keppel, H. (1846). The Expedition to Borneo of *HMS Dido* for the Suppression of Piracy. London. 2 vols.

5. See: Vyner, C. (1887) The Vyners: a Family History. Leamington. In his study, Charles J Vyners does not refer to the Colletts or to Elizabeth Collett. Nor is there any evidence in the pedigrees of the Vyners and their descendants in either the Gloucester Record office or the Essex Record Office.

6. See: Brooke G.E. (1918) The Brookes of Horton in the Cotswolds. Singapore: Methodist Publishing House. Gilbert Brooke is however incorrect when he states that Charles William Brooke and his son, John Cheap Brooke were descended from the Brookes of Cavan. Charles William Brooke was the son of Thomas Brooke by his Bibi, the Moher Bibi of Arah in Bihar. See: PCC/Prob/11/1835 Will of Thomas Brooke in which he leaves £1,000 to his son Charles William Brookes on condition that he provides the Moher Bibi with a pension.

7. See Saunders, G.E. (1992) Bishops and Brookes: the Anglican Church Mission and the Brooke Raj in Sarawak: 1841-1941. London: OUP. See also: Barley, N. (2003) White Rajah: a Biography of Sir James Brooke. London: Abacus.

8. See OIOC: British Library. L MAR/B617B Thomas Collett: 11 Sept, 1717 Journal of an intended voyage in the ship *"Grantham"*. See: Farrington, A. (1999) Biographical Index of EIC Maritime Service Officers: 1600-1834. London: B.L. also; Farrington, A. (1999) Biographical Index of EIC Ships: 1600-1834. London: B.L. The *Grantham* which was owned by his brother, Jonathan Collett, was built in 1711 at Johnson's, later the Blackwall Yard owned by Jonathan Collett.

9. Of the four children of Thomas and Isabella Collett only the names of Grissell and Susanna, wife of Mr Court appear on the memorial plaque in the Church of St Margaret's Barking.

10. See The Victoria County History of Essex. vol. v. ed. J.E. Oxley. London: Oxford University Press, 1965.

11. According to the records of the EIC Thomas Collett junior (1704-1718) was buried at Fort William, Calcutta. See: British Library: India Office. OIOC: Biographical Files: N/1/1/f28.

12. See: PCC/Prob/11/726/1743 Thomas Collett.

13. Jonathan Collett is listed as being resident in Goodmanfields. He is also listed in 1747 as having been the proprietor of the Blackwall yards at present being used by the EIC. See: Hobhouse, H, ed. Survey of London: Poplar, Blackwall & Isle of Dogs: The Parish of All Hallows. London: The Athlone Press, 1994. vol. xliv. See also: Green, H.B. & Wigram, R. (1881) Chronicles of Blackwall Yard. London. 2. vols. John Pelly married 1st Elizabeth Langthorne, then Grissel Collett, eldest daughter of Thomas Collett. See List of Tombstones & Inscriptions at St Margaret's churchyard: (1930) Barking District Council where Ruth Hinde, (née Casson) is cited as being the wife of Henry Hinde of Upton. Their daughter, Elizabeth (1717-1761) married John Pelly junior. The Pellys were related also to the Hindes and the Cassons of Upton Park, Barking thus linking the Pellys to the Pattles of St Katherine's by the Tower back to the Brookes by the marriage of Thomas Pattle to Elizabeth Brooke, second daughter of Robert and Elizabeth Brooke, née Collett.

In 1732, John Pelly was appointed a Captain in the maritime services of the EIC on the recommendation of Jonathan Collett. In 1744, he was sworn in as an Elder Brother of the Corporation of Trinity House. On John Pelley see: Fry, Katharine. (1888) History of the Parishes of East & West Ham. London. See also: Pelley, D. (2001) Upton Connections: 1732-1816. A Story of Families. Durham: Pentland Books.

14. I owe this point to Anthony Farrington, Keeper of the India and Oriental Office, British Library.

15. See will of Thomas Collett: PCC/Prob/11/726/1743: in which he leaves a bequest to his grandchildren, Ann, Elizabeth, Robert and Jonathan. He then adds a codicil to the will in which he leaves three hundred pounds to his fifth grandchild, Thomas. Brooke, the youngest child of Elizabeth and Robert Brooke.

16. PCC/PROB/11/878/1762: Robert Brooke. See Boyles: Marriage Index: 1738-1837: a Daniel West is listed as marrying Ann Brooke in St Paul's Cathedral, 1750.

17. See: Bateman, J. (1860) Life of Daniel Wilson. London: John Murray, 2 vols. See also: Harrison, M.J. Daniel West: Whitefields Forgotten Trustee. JURCHS. vol. 7. no. 8. June 2006. See also: The Cheshunt Foundation @ Westminster College, Cambridge: A1/9/8-A1/12/13 & A.4/7/8 Correspondence to George Whitefield and the Countess of Huntingdon from Daniel West. As a wealthy silk manufacturer, he also acted as Trustee and confidential advisor to both George Whitefield and the Countess of Huntingdon.

18. On Daniel Wilson see: Bateman, J. (1860) Life of Daniel Wilson. London: John

Murray. 2 vols. See also: Harrison, M.J. Daniel Wilson and his Love of India. June 2006. Indian Church History Review. The first four Bishops were: Thomas Fanshawe Middleton (1814), Reginald Heber (1823), John Thomas James (1827), and John Matthias Turner (1829-1831).

19. Thomas Pattle was the eldest son of Edward Pattle (*d.*1728) and his first wife, Ruth Casson (m. 1709). It is probable that she was related to William Casson (*d.*1705) whose name appears on a memorial to the Cassons, Hindes and Pellys in the Churchyard of St Margaret's Barking. If this is correct, this links the Pattles with the Cassons and the Hindes and the Pellys of Aveley and Upton House, Barking, Essex. On *The Speke* see: Farrington, A. (1999) (1999) Biographical Index of EIC Maritime Service Officers: 1600-1834. London: B.L. also; Farrington, A. (1999) Biographical Index of EIC Ships: 1600-1834. London: B.L.

20. Although Hardwickes Marriage Act of 1753 had by this stage passed into law it seems that no attempt was made to prevent such a marriage taking place. It would seem that so long as she had her parents consent such a marriage was not illegal. Robert Brooke was the part owner of the EIC ship, *"The Speke"* and a maritime Captain in the services of the East India Company.

21. See: OIOC B.L. N/1/2/f.175 Biographical Index which records that on 10th June 1770 Thomas Pattle married Sarah Hasleby at Cossimbazar, India. In 1795 Thomas Pattle, son of Thomas & Elizabeth Pattle, (née Brooke) returned to Calcutta where he served as a Senior Judge in the Supreme Court in Murshidabad, then at Cawnpore until his retirement in 1810. In the Private Calendar of Stephen Wilson: 1795-1802, there is a reference to Thomas Pattle returning to India in the December of 1795, leaving his wife, Sarah in England with her son, Henry. See also: Boyd, E. French. (1976) Bloomsbury Heritage: their Mothers and their Aunts. London: Hamish Hamilton. Appendix A. See also: British Library: OIOC. Bengal: Past and Present, 1909: Bengal Kalendar, 1800. After the death of his wife, Sarah he married Suzanne Wilson. She is not however related to the Wilsons of Stenson.

22. It is probable that Virginia was responsible for the creation of the myth associated with James Pattle, her great grandfather that was included in the book of photographs by her great aunt, Julia Margaret Cameron entitled: Victorian Photographs of Famous Men and Fair Women. ed. Tristram Powell with an introduction by Virginia Woolf and Roger Fry. rev. edn. Boston: A&W Visual Library. 1973. See also: Boyd, Elizabeth French. (1976) Bloomsbury Heritage: their Mothers and their Aunts. London: Hamish Hamilton. App. C. See also: Olsen, Victoria. (2003) From Life: Julia Margaret Cameron & Victorian Photography. London: Aurum. Press. See also: Pemble, John, ed. (1985) Miss Fane in India. Gloucester: Alan Sutton.

23. On the Pattle sisters See: Olsen, Victoria. (2003) From Life: Julia Margaret Cameron & Victorian Photography. London: Aurum Press.

24. See: Boyd, Elizabeth French. (1976) Bloomsbury Heritage: their Mothers and their Aunts. London: Hamish Hamilton.

25. See James, Lawrence. (1997) The Making & Unmaking of British India. London:

Little Brown & Co. in which Colin Mackenzie is cited as having married as his second wife, Helen, an ardent Evangelical who kept a Diary: Life in Mission *et al.* See also: Olsen, Victoria. (2003) ibid

26. On Thomas Brooke see: OIOC. B.L. OIR/O/6/1-20: (1794-1841) Bengal Civil Service: Personal Series. See also: OIOC/O/6/21-36: 1740-1850; Prinsep. C.C. Bengal, Madras & Bombay Civilians: Thomas Brooke.

27. Wilson, Stephen. (1795-1802) Private Calendar. Stephen Wilson married Ann Collett West, eldest daughter of Daniel and Ann West, (née Brooke) and grand daughter of Elizabeth Brooke (née Collett) from whom she obtained her middle name of Collett.

28. See: Runciman, S. (1960) The White Rajahs. Cambridge: CUP. On the practice of keeping a Bibi See: Dalrymple, W. (2001) The White Mogul. London: Harper Collins where he refers to the Calcutta Writers and the practices that they followed. The word Bibi is equivalent to the English Mother or Mrs. The taking of a Bibi was a practice that Wellesley and later Cornwallis sought to eradicate amongst the Writers in the service of the EIC. See also: Jasanoff, Maya. (2006) Edge of Empire. London: Harper Perennial.

29. According to Stephen Wilson, the two granddaughters of Ruth Brooke were educated at Miss Jones' School in Stepney Green with his own younger daughters. He does not record where Charles William Brooke received his education, before going to Bengal where he enlisted as a Cadet in the Bengal Native Army. See: B.L. OIOC: L/MIL/9/111/f.49: Cadet 1800: In 1801 both Charles and his sister, Sophia returned to India. Reece in his entry on James Brooke in the New Oxford Dictionary of National Biography is incorrect when he states that Charles William had been brought up with the second family. By the time of the birth of James Brooke in 1803, Charles William was 19 and had returned to India where he served as an officer in the Bengal native Army. Likewise, Gilbert Brooke is incorrect when he states that Charles William Brooke was descended from the Brookes of Cavan.

30. See: Jacob, G.L. (1876) The Raja of Sarawak. London: 2 vols. It is significant to note that it was Gertrude Jacob who recounts that on his return to England where he received his education that James Brooke divided his time with his parents in Bath and his grandmother, Mrs Ruth Brooke at Reigate. She also recounts the story told by Keppell that Elizabeth Brooke (née Collett) was descended from Sir Thomas Vyner, one time Lord Mayor and Prime Warden of the Worshipful Company of Goldsmiths. On this, she is incorrect.

31. Barley is incorrect when he describes Anna Maria Stuart as being illegitimate. She was the natural daughter of Colonel William Stuart, 9th Lord Blantyre of a Scottish Regiment. Technically, it was from Emma Johnson (née Brooke) wife of the Revd F. C. Johnson that the Rajahs of Sarawak were descended. The second Rajah was Charles Anthoni Johnson (1829-1917) who succeeded James Brooke in 1868. Charles Anthoni Johnson changed his name to Brooke in response to his Uncle's request. Barley is incorrect when he states that Margaret Savage, (née Brooke) the wife of the Revd Anthony E. Savage, died without issue. She had one daughter, Ann Maria Frances Savage.

32. See: PCC/Prob/11/1835. Will of Thomas Brooke of Bath.
33. See: PCC/Prob/11/1835. Will of Thomas Brooke of Bath.
34. See: Runciman, S. (1960) The White Rajahs. Cambridge: Cambridge University Press. See also: Borneo Chronicle. Spring/Summer 2005. vol. 50. no. 11.
35. In 1863, James Brooke disinherited his nephew, John Brooke Johnson, later Brooke Brooke, Rajah Muda of Sarawak in favour of Charles Anthoni Johnson. Before his death in 1868 James Brooke appointed his nephew Charles Johnson, the second son of Emma and the Revd F.C. Johnson as his successor. It is from Charles and his wife Margaret Brooke (née de Windt) that the 3rd and final Rajah of Sarawak was descended. Margaret De Windt was the 1st cousin of Charles Brooke, being the niece of the Revd Francis Charles Johnson. See Bodleian Library: Rhodes House: Basil Brooke Papers; (BBP) MSS Pac.s.90: Box 3/11: pedigree of the Brookes, Johnsons and Grants.
36. See: Saunders, G.E. (1992) Bishops and Brookes: the Anglican Church Mission and the Brooke Raj in Sarawak: 1841-1941. London: OUP. See also: Barley, N. (2001) White Rajah: a Biography of Sir James Brooke. London: Abacus.

MEMORIAL PLAQUE: ST MARGARET'S BARKING. To the Colletts and Pellys

"In a vault near this place is deposited the body of Mrs Susanna Pytts daughter of Captain Jonathan Collett and wife of Edmund Pytts, who died April 2nd 1742 aged 34 years, Also the body of Captain Thomas Collett, late of this Parish who died April 12th 1743 aged 67 years, also the body of Mrs Susanna Collett, wife of the above said Jonathan Collett who died January 23rd 1745 aged 71 years, also the body of the above said Jonathan Collett who died May 14th 1746 aged 65 years , also the body of Mrs Susanna Court, daughter of the above said Thomas Collett who died January 5th 1757 aged fifty years: also the body of Mrs Grissel Pelly, wife of Captain John Pelly and daughter of the above said Thomas Collett who died November 26th 1759 aged 60 years. Captain John Pelly, one of the Elder Brothers of Trinity House died February 14th 1762, aged 79."

*St Margaret's, Barking, Essex.*

# 4. Daniel West: George Whitefield's forgotten Trustee[i]

Within a stone's throw of Hawksmoor's Christ Church is 6 Church Street, Spitalfields considered to be one of the finest residences in Spitalfields and from 1763 to 1794 the home of Daniel West, one of Whitefield's worthy, trusty and tried friends and grandfather of Daniel Wilson.[1]

This is an impressive 4-bayed, three storeyed building constructed in fine red brick surmounted by a superb door case with Ionic columns and a unique carved console hood that gives the house a distinguished appearance without making it ostentatious.[2]

Equally splendid is the magnificent oak stair case, an exquisite work of art, excelled only by the stair case in the Ministers house at no 2 Fournier Street.[3] The stair case at no 6 Church Street with it's delightfully turned and twisted balustrades and fluted ionic columns with matchless carved tread ends and hand rails, down which his grandson Daniel Wilson would slide rises to the first floor which is dominated by the large front room that occupies the full width of the house.[4]

What gives this house such an impressive frontage is the emphasis that the builder, William Taylor gave to the first floor with its four full height windows and high ceiling giving the room a light airy atmosphere.[5]

Here in this grand room with its raised and fielded panelling Daniel West would have received his guests: Thomas Wilson, [I & II] John Eyre, John Newton, Thomas Haweis, Benjamin Mills, Samuel Brewer, George Whitefield and Selina, Countess of Huntingdon, just to name a few of whom it is probably true to say that Whitefield and the Countess must rank as the most distinguished.[6]

This was emphatically a merchant or master weavers house, one of those grand roomy and comfortable houses, says Daniel Wilson that abounded in the old fashioned parts of London.[7]

At first sight it might appear strange that someone of whom so little is known – a person of very little significance should live in a residence as grand as any to be found even in Mayfair.[8] But, in fact it is impossible to overlook the significance of this quite remarkable person: one of the last links of a past age that went back to Whitefield.

Born in 1726 Daniel West was the son of a silk weaver also called Daniel of Vine Court, Wood Street, Spitalfields. Little is known about his father except that he was married to an Elizabeth and that they had three children of whom only two survived to adulthood. These were Daniel and Elizabeth. From the records of the Worshipful Company of Weavers we learn that Daniel West

*Daniel West's residence and the birthplace of Daniel Wilson, Spitalfields.*

senior had been apprenticed to a John Partridge by whom he had been made free in 1721.[9] Apart from having been admitted to the Weavers Company there is no evidence to show that he took an active part in the affairs of the Company and yet, the very fact that he could afford to live in Wood Street, considered to be a desirable area, would indicate that the Wests were very far from poor.[10]

In 1740 Daniel West junior as he is referred to in the records of the Weavers Company was apprenticed to his father.[11] However it was not until 1752 that Daniel West junior obtained his freedom, the same year that his first child Elizabeth Brooke was born.[12]

His wife, Anne Brooke, whom he married in 1750 was the eldest daughter of Captain Robert and Elizabeth Brooke (née Collet) of Goodman Fields Whitechapel, a highly desirable residential area for maritime captains.[13] Although Robert Brooke is cited in Burke's Landed Gentry as being descended from the Brookes of Horton there is in fact no evidence to support this claim.[14] His more notable claim to fame however is the fact that he and his wife, Elizabeth Collet, daughter of Captain Thomas Collett were the great grand-parents not only of Daniel Wilson, 5th Bishop of Calcutta (1832-1858), but also of James Brooke, the first White Rajah of Sarawak (1848-1863) and James Pattle, father of the seven surviving Pattle sisters.[15]

In 1758 Daniel West is listed as being a resident in Wood Street, Spitalfields, considered to be a highly desirable area of Spitalfields: the same year that he is cited as being elected to the Livery of the Weavers Company, thus marking the beginnings of a distinguished career with the Worshipful Company of the Weavers.[16] By 1763 they had moved to a joint residence in Church Street an even more prestigious street, where he is cited as being in partnership with a Mr Wren.[17]

Later, in 1774 he is cited in the London Directory as being in partnership with a Stephen Wilson: his future son in law.[18] By this time Daniel Wilson had started to make his way through the ranks of the Weavers Company being elected Auditor, then Renter Bailiff, finally rising to the rank of Upper Bailiff the highest post in the Weavers Company and one normally restricted to the socially and economically elite within the Company.[19] That Daniel West was able to rise to the highest office in the Company is a clear indication that not only was he in fact wealthy but above all he was a person of integrity, just the right sort of person to hold a position of responsibility in any walk of life.

In addition to being involved in the affairs of the Weavers Company we also find that Daniel West took an active role in the life of Whitefield's two Tabernacles, Moorefields and Tottenham Court Road where for twenty five years he served as a Trustee: a post that he held until his death in 1796.[20]

Of Daniel West's religious background we are completely in the dark apart from the fact that in 1757 he appears as a signatory to the Rules and Orders of a Christian Society that met weekly in Bethnal Green to study the Bible, sing hymns, pray and meet the pecuniary and physical needs of its members and their families.[21] This would indicate that he had undergone a conversion experience, but whether it was as a result of the preaching of the Revd Samuel Brewer, a close friend of the family or through George Whitefield we are not told: though by the time that he had completed his apprenticeship in 1747 the Evangelical revival was already underway.[22] Whether he ever listened to Whitefield preaching nearby in Moorefields is not known but, given Whitefield's popularity and power to draw the crowds such a possibility cannot be ruled out. The park was a fashionable meeting place for the crowds who would often gather together to watch such activities as bear-baiting, cock-fighting, wrestling or dog fighting. It was also a regular place where Wesley, Whitefield and many other ministers would preach to the crowds. Not far away was Wesley's chapel, built on the site of the old foundery, whilst nearby was the Tabernacle that Whitefield's followers had built in 1741. This was clearly a source of embarrassment to Whitefield as it was close to the Foundery where Wesley and his followers met, and so as to avoid any further criticism and distress to the cause of the Gospel, Whitefield had another Chapel erected on a plot of land in Tottenham Court Road. Together these two chapels formed what was knows as the Whitefield Trust of which Daniel West was one the Trustees.[23]

Even though Whitefield and his followers found themselves outside the established Church, the two Chapels continued to observe the full rites of the Church of England and as such the members and their Ministers would have regarded themselves as being "Members of Christ's Catholic and Apostolic Church."[24]

Those who attended the two Chapels occupied what might be called the middle ground of English Religion whereby they mixed with Churchmen and Dissenters. Thus we find that even though Daniel West was a Trustee of the Tabernacle he would often attend the local Parish churches to hear the preaching of Ministers like William Romaine, Henry Foster, John Newton, Richard Cecil or Basil Woodd.[25]

This ability to move freely between Church and Chapel as exemplified by Daniel West and for that matter Thomas Wilson is an indication that any attempt to define Evangelicalism too narrowly is fraught with danger.[26]

As a young man Daniel West would have been open to the influence of many fine preachers both within the traditional Dissent movement and also within the Anglican church, but perhaps the greatest influence in his life was the preaching of George Whitefield which was far greater than any history book might suggest, because of the lives that he touched both directly and indirectly. Amongst these were the apprentices, journeymen, merchants and masters of the City of London and in particular the life of Daniel West and Thomas Wilson.[27] And in this connection it is with Daniel West and the generation of Thomas Wilson [I] that the influence and impact of George Whitefield and the Countess of Huntingdon can be seen at it's best.[28] Although it has often been suggested that George Whitefield lacked in Wesley's organizational skills, nonetheless he was alive to the importance of providing members with the opportunity to share in the wider ministry of the Two Chapels or Society[29] Thus there was the opportunity for all, regardless of wealth or status to become Class or Band Teachers, Band leaders, Door-Keepers, or as in the case of Daniel West to be appointed one of two Trustees to the Trust. That Daniel West should be entrusted to such a position by George Whitefield is a good indication not only of the confidence in which he was held by Whitefield but, also by the members of the Society. Likewise we also find that he acted as a personal financial advisor to the Countess of Huntingdon, a further indication of the trust in which he was held. Above all it is a clear reflection of his own personal piety. From a purely administrative perspective it is clear that he was eligible to hold such a position. During his long and distinguished career in the Worshipful Company of Weavers he would have developed those skills and qualities that would have fitted him for this position. These qualities would have included a minute attention to detail, careful and precise book-keeping or auditing of the Trust's accounts as well as the habits of neatness and personal skills, all of which when taken together were the result of his own up-bringing and training in early life. But to these everyday qualities or talents should be added those qualities which though not quantifiable in the same manner as these ordinary human qualities, are none-the-less equally if not more important as they go to make up the total personality of this remarkable person. These qualities are what might best be called spiritual or religious qualities: the quality of his faith and his earnest desire to live and honour God, a point not lost on the writer of his obituary.[30]

Whereas membership of the Tabernacle was in the hands of the Conference the responsibility for the management and upkeep of the two Tabernacles lay with the Trustees who were accountable to the whole Conference for their actions and decisions. Along with the other Trustee Robert Keene, he would have been responsible for the upkeep and maintenance of the Ministers houses, the alms houses and the two schools. They would also have been responsible for the payment of the stipends of the Ministers as well as raising funds, paying the bills, distributing the payment of relief to the poor and sick of the two chapels: a task that they would probably have delegated to the Band leaders and Visitors appointed by the Society. As such there would always have been tasks for members to perform irrespective of gender, age or status. In addition to all this it would have been their responsibility to ensure that the pulpits of the Two

Tabernacles were regularly filled with preachers who, in the words of Thomas Wilson [I] were of a "warm lively affectionate manner and who were able to address the conscience."[31] There is no doubt that the duties of the Trustee was time consuming and physically demanding and yet, despite suffering from a painful disorder of the bladder for the last thirteen years of his life, it was said of Daniel West that he was always regular in his duties in the Tabernacle and with never a murmur on his lips. As if his responsibilities both within the Tabernacle and for that matter in the Weavers Company were not enough, we find Daniel West along with Robert Keene, Benjamin Mills, Thomas Wilson, Revd Samuel Brewer, Joseph Barber, Revd John Clayton and the Revd John Kello taking an active role in the formation of the Hoxton Academy. Founded in 1778 for the training of Dissenting Ministers it owed its creation two years previously to the formation of the Evangelical society. Amongst those who might rightly be considered to the founding fathers of these two organizations were: Thomas Wilson [I] Benjamin Mills and the Revd Rowland Hill.[32]

Later, in 1795, one year before his death, Daniel West was appointed one of twelve lay Directors to the Board of the London Missionary Society. It is interesting to note that of the 12 lay directors appointed, three were members of the Wilson family: Thomas Wilson [II], his brother, Joseph Wilson of Highbury and their cousin, John Wilson of Upper Street Islington who served as a Lay examiner for Candidates. Other members of the board included the Revd Thomas Haweis, the Revd Daniel Bogue and the Revd John Eyre of Ram's Chapel.[33] Formed in 1795, the London Missionary Society was originally interdenominational or ecumenical in spirit and drew support from the different branches of the Church. In its early stages it operated mainly in the South Seas, though later it cooperated with the Church Missionary Society by sending missionaries to Africa of whom David Livingstone is probably the most famous.[34]

In addition to all these activities we also find that along with Benjamin Mills, he was appointed by the Weavers Company a Trustee of the Linborough Trust set up by the terms of the will of James Linborough, July 1774. By the terms of his will he had set aside a capital sum of £3,000 in 3% Consolidated Bank Annuities to be used to establish a series of lectures to be known as the Linborough lecture. These lectures were to be held on a Sunday evening commencing with the first Sunday in September and concluding on the last Sunday in April. Amongst those who attended these lectures were the Wests and Wilsons, including Daniel Wilson who as a young person showed a marked irreverence during the service: ... "sitting in a careless, lounging manner and often laughing and talking ..."[35] The first Minister to be elected by the Weavers Company to deliver the Linborough lectures was the Revd Henry Foster of Long Acre Chapel, London who held the post for three years and was paid a salary of £50 per annum. At the end of the series there was a grand meal held in the hall of the Weavers Company. Other Ministers invited to deliver the lectures were the Revd Richard Cecil of St John, Bedford Row, Revd Thomas Scott of Lock's Chapel, the Revd Josiah Pratt, Curate to Richard Cecil, and the Revd Charles Simeon of Cambridge. What is interesting about this list is the fact that all these speakers were members of the Eclectic Society formed in 1783, the same year that the Linborough lectures were first held. The Eclectic society would meet fortnightly at St John's Bedford Row where Richard Cecil was the Vicar and Josiah Pratt was his curate. With the exception of Simeon all were 'Oxford men' and all exerted a significant influence in the development and spread of Evangelical religion in London.[36]

From this we begin to see the part that Daniel West also played in the spread of Evangelicalism in and around London providing a clear example of the influence of this remarkable lay person over a long period of time. Above all, we begin to obtain a picture of a person who along with his family enjoyed a rich and various religious life whereby they mingled freely with Anglicans and Dissenters on equal terms, even though there were those who clearly disapproved of such cooperation and collaboration.

At the same time we are able to appreciate the rich atmosphere into which his grandson, Daniel Wilson, later Bishop of Calcutta, was born and though as a young person he was to react against the piety of his family, what cannot be overlooked is the debt that he owed to his mother, considered to be the power-house in the family, and his grand-father, the last in a line that went back to George Whitefield.

What little that we know about Daniel West it would appear that he was a somewhat shy and retiring person who sought to avoid the public limelight, preferring instead to carry out his duties both in the Weavers Company and at the Tabernacle in a quiet and dignified manner. Yet, if he chose to remain in the background this should not detract from the fact that both within the Weavers Company and within the Calvinistic wing of Dissent he is an important figure.

Apart from a few brief and terse references in Bateman's life of Daniel Wilson and the memoir of Thomas Wilson [II], the only other reference to him that is of any significance is in the Evangelical Magazine. Yet, even here the details about his life are sparse, the author preferring to concentrate on his death bed scene, which, whilst serving as a model for other Christians was in fact far removed from the events as depicted by his son in law, Stephen Wilson in his Private calendar.[37] That said, the obituary in the Evangelical Magazine, probably written by John Eyre a close friend of the family, is a remarkable tribute to a very remarkable person.[38]

Yet, despite the lack of information about this very private person what cannot be ignored or overlooked is the fact that he was a person who fulfilled the traditional success story of the 18th century. As we have observed his was a very distinguished career in the Weavers Company in which he rose to the highest office in the company. In addition we find that in his will he was appointed by George Whitefield to be one of two trustees of the Two Tabernacles: a post that he held from 1770 until his death in 1796. Furthermore, along with Thomas Wilson [II] his brother, Joseph Wilson and John Wilson we find that Daniel West was zealous in his support in the formation of a foreign mission and the founding of an academy for the training of Dissenting Ministers.

Above all, however we should not overlook the key role that he played in the lives of the Wilson and in particular the lives of his son in laws, Stephen and William Wilson. Exactly when or where he and his family made the acquaintance of the Wilsons is not known. Even though they were all engaged in the silk trade it is more than likely that it was through Whitefield's Tabernacle that the links between the Wests and the Wilsons were first forged when as young men both he and Thomas Wilson [I] took their children and their apprentices to listen to the greatest orator of the age, whose sermons were all life and fire.[39]

Clearly this link with the Wilsons forged as early as 1755 is one of the most distinctive features concerning Daniel West: a link that was to be consolidated by marriage and reinforced even further by his grandson who went on to become Bishop of Calcutta.

Yet, whatever the influence that Daniel West might have had on the lives of the Wilsons there is one person whose influence on the life of Daniel West cannot be overestimated and that is George Whitefield. Whether it was through his parents or indeed his sister, Elizabeth West, or for that matter through the influence of the Revd Samuel Brewer that he initially came under the influence of George Whitefield, we shall probably never know. Nevertheless, whatever the circumstance there is no denying the significance of Whitefield upon the life of Daniel West. Not for nothing was Whitefield described as the greatest orator of the 18th century arousing people from all walks of life from their moral and spiritual torpor, and amongst those that he aroused and challenged, lifting him out of his own moral and spiritual indifference, was Daniel West, who in his own quiet way went on to promote the glory of Jesus Christ and the spiritual interest of the congregation of the two Tabernacles.[40]

As a tribute to this unsung hero of the Christian faith and in accordance with the terms of his will Daniel West was buried in the vault under the Communion Table in Tottenham Court Road Chapel: an appropriate place for a morally upright and devout person who, in the words of Matthew Wilkes "not only lived well but died rejoicing in his Saviour."[41]

*Notes and References:*

(i)   *This is a modified version of an article originally published under the same title in the Journal of the United Reformed Church Historical Society: June, 2006.*

1.   See: Tyerman, Revd L. (1890) The Life of George Whitefield. 2nd ed. London: Hodder and Stoughton. Also: Bateman, J. (1860) The Life of the Right Revd Daniel Wilson, D.D.: Late Lord Bishop of Calcutta and Metropolitan of India. London: John Murray. 2 vols.

2.   The House is illustrated in, Ison, Walter & P.A. Bezodis. eds, (1957) Spitalfields and Mile End New Town. London: The Athlone Press. Vol. xxvii. See also: Blain, D. ed, (1989) The Saving of Spitalfields. London: The Spitalfields Trust. Byrne, A. (1986) London's Georgian Houses. London: The Georgian Press. Also: Girouard, M (1979) The East End's Streets of Silk: Spitalfields I, in Country Life. Nov 15. 1979. in which he considers that these houses are as grand as any in Mayfair.

3.   See: Cruikshank, D. No.2. Fournier Street: the Minister house' of Spitalfields: in, Blain, D. ed. (1989) The Saving of Spitalfields. London: The Spitalfields Trust, p.49-66.

4.   See: Bateman, J. (1860) ibid. p.7. where Bateman refers to the staircase down which Daniel Wilson would slide.
     There is an illustration of the staircase in : Blain, D. (1989) ibid, p.19: See also: Byrne, A.1986) ibid, p.166-167.

5.   See: Ison, W. & P.A. Bezodis. eds. (1957) Spitalfields and Mile End New Town. London: The Athlone Press. Vol xxvii.

6.   Thomas Wilson [I] was the uncle of Stephen Wilson [II], son in law to Daniel West. Thomas Wilson [I] was a partner in the firm of Thomas [I], John and Thomas Wilson [II] at 121 Wood Street, Cheapside founded in 1754 by Stephen Wilson [I] Apart from George Whitefield and John Newton we find that the Revd John Eyre, Revd Samuel Brewer and Benjamin Mills were along with Daniel West and Thomas Wilson[I] involved in the formation of the Hoxton Dissenting Academy in 1778. Later Thomas Wilson [II] Daniel West, Benjamin Mills and Thomas Haweis served as Directors of the London Missionary Society in 1795. On the Hoxton Academy see: Evangelical Magazine: ( 1796) vol.iv, p.47; Congregation Magazine (1825) vol.1. (n.s.) Historical account of Dissenting Academies: no v Hoxton Academy, p.524-527. See also: Wilson, J. (1846) Memoir of Thomas Wilson. London. also Bogue, D. & J.Bennett. (1812) History of Dissenters from the Revolution in 1688 to 1808. London. Peel, A. (1931) These Hundred Years. London.
     On the London Missionary Society: see: Morrison, J. (1839) The Fathers and Founders of the London Missionary Society. London. Also, Lovell, R. (1899) The History of the London Missionary Society. London. Ellis, (1844) The History of the London Missionary Society. London.
     See also: Martin, R. H. (1983) Evangelicals United: Ecumenical stirrings in Pre Victorian Britain, 1795-1830. London: Methuen. See also: Martin, R.H. (1980) The Place of the London Missionary Society in the Ecumenical Movement. Journal of Ecclesiastical History. Vol.31. no.3 July.

See also: letter to the Coutness of Huntingdon: 25 November 1773 from Daniel West: A4/7/8 The Cheshunt Foundation @ Westminster College, Cambridge.

7.  See: Girouard, M. (1979) The East End's Streets of Silk: Spitalfields I Country Life. Nov 15. Bateman, J, (1860) Life of Daniel Wilson. London.

8.  See: Girouard, M (1979) The East End's Streets of Silk: Country Life. May 15 1979.

9.  GUILDHALL LIBRARY. Gld Mss. Court Minute Books: Weavers Company: 4655/12/1721-1729. Also Gld Mss. Freedom Admission Books: Weavers Company: 4656/vol 6/1721-1737.

10. See: Byrne, A. (1989): London's Georgian Houses. London: The Georgian Press, where he notes that the houses in Wilkes Street (originally Wood Street, Spitalfields) represent the more modest houses of the period. Wood Street was nonetheless considered to be a desirable area in which to live.

11. GUILDHALL LIBRARY: Gld Mss. Apprentice Bindings: Weavers Company: 4657/vol 1/1694-1765, 2nd Feb. 1740.

12. GUILDHALL LIBRARY. Gld Mss: Court Minute Books: Weavers Company: 4655/15/1737-1750: and vol 16: 1750-1765, where he is cited as having been made good by servitude on the testimony of the said father, July 20 1752. Exactly why Daniel West should have deferred taking up his freedom in 1752 is not known but it may well be that he worked for his father, though not as a full partner.

Compleat Guide (1758) where Daniel West is cited as being a satin Weaver of Wood Street, Spitalfields. Later renamed Wilkes Street the houses are typically Georgian Spitalfield houses with integral mansards or garrets. See: Byrne, A. (1986) London's Georgian Houses. London: The Georgian Press, p.65.

13. Anne West: (née Brooke) was the eldest daughter of Captain Robert Brooke of Goodman Fields, Whitechapel who is cited in the Will of Captain Thomas Collett as being a Maritime Captain. See: PCC/Prob/11/726/1743. According to Boyles Marriage Index, 1738-1837 an Anne Brooke is listed as having married Daniel West in St Paul's Cathedral in 1750. It is from Captain Robert Brooke and Elizabeth, (née Collet) that the Brookes of Sarawak are descended. See Burke's Landed Gentry.(1931) See also: Jacobs, G.L. (1876) The Raja of Sarawak. London. 2 vols. also: Runciman, Sir. S. (1960) The White Rajahs. Cambridge in which he perpetuates the same genealogical errors found in Jacobs, G.L. where she states that Elizabeth Collet, daughter of Captain Thomas Collett was a descendent of Edye Viner, daughter of Sir Thomas Vyner, Bt; Lord Mayor of London, 1653 when in fact she was his sister by their father's second marriage. See: Vyner, C.J. (1885) The Vyners: a History. London.

See also: Farrington,A. (1999) Biographical Index of the East India Company: Maritime Service Officers: 1600-1834. London, where Captain Thomas Collet, is cited as being in the service of the HEIC maritime section.

14. See Burkes Landed Gentry. (1921) entry Brooke of Horton where a Captain Richard Brooke is cited as being the grandfather of James Brooke, Rajah of Sarawak. See Brooke, G.E. (1918) Brooke of Horton of the Cotswold. K&I.

Singapore: Methodist Publishing House where he states that his grandfather, Thomas Richard Brooke (1811-1889) always said that "he was a cousin of the Rajah." However, later editions of Burkes Landed Gentry deleted the reference to Richard Brooke of Horton as being the grandfather of James Brooke. Notwithstanding entries under Brooke of Sarawak state that Captain Robert Brooke of Goodman Fields, Whitechapel is believed to be a member of the family of Brooke of Warwick and Horton. In fact the two families are quite distinct as Gilbert Edward Brooke points out in his study on the Brookes of Horton.

15. It is interesting to note that although Bateman refers to Daniel Wilson visiting Sarawak to consecrate the new Church Bateman does not refer to the fact that Daniel Wilson, James Brooke and the Pattles were cousins. Likewise none of the biographies on James Brooke or the Pattles make this point. See: Wilson, Stephen. (1795-1803) Private Calendar where Stephen Wilson refers to Thomas Pattle, father of James Pattle, Aunt Brooke, and Cousin Thomas Brooke of Calcutta. Aunt Brooke was the grandmother to James Brooke and Cousin Thomas was James Brooke's father.

16. GUILDHALL LIBRARY: Gld Mss. Court Minute Books: Weavers Company. 4655/16/1750-1765, Dec. 20th 1758.

17. London Directory 1763: This is probably the same Mr Wren who is cited in the Court Minute Books of the Worshipful Company of Weavers as being the son of John Wren, deceased who was made free by patrimony 18 Mar. 1754. See GUILDHALL LIBRARY: Gld Mss. Court Minute Books: Weavers Company: 4657/1/1694-1765. Also: Gld Mss. Court Minute Books: Weavers Company: 4655/16/1750-1765.

18. London Directory: 1775. Stephen Wilson was the second son of Stephen Wilson deceased of Coventry and 121 Wood Street, Cheapside: See Table 4. See also: Bateman, J. (1860) Life of Daniel Wilson. London. vol.1. In 1774 Stephen Wilson married Anne Collett West, eldest daughter of Daniel and Anne West. See: Table 7. Stephen Wilson of Church Street, Spitalfields.

19. GUILDHALL LIBRARY: Gld Mss. Court Minute Books: Weavers Company: 4655/17/1765-1785: 2 vols. Also: Gld Mss. Court Minute Books: Weavers Company: 4655/18/1785-1795, where he is cited as having been elected Auditor, (1774) Renter Bailiff (1775) Upper Bailiff, (1776-77). Later Daniel West is listed as serving on a committee with Richard Lea of Old Jewry to investigate the importation of Bengali silk organized in Italy and passed off as Italian silk.

20. Daniel West and Robert Keene were executors to George Whitefield's will in which he left the Two Tabernacles and Ministers House to his Executors and Trustees of the Two chapels. See: E.M (1796) vol.iv. Obituary of Daniel West: p.518-521: See also E.M. (1803) Letter to the Editor from E. Parsons who refers to the late Daniel West and Robert Keene, the Revd Mr George Whitefield's executors. See also: Tyerman, Revd L. (1889) The Life of George Whitefield. 2nd edition. London: Hodder and Stoughton.

21. See MS. B.G. 105. (1757) Rules and Orders of a Friendly Society: Tower Hamlets Local History Library, in which we find that a Daniel West is a signatory to the

Rules of the Society: 7 Sept. 1757. The society met weekly to study the Bible and was one of the earliest friendly societies to meet at Hurley Street, Bethnal Green. See also: Welch, E. (1975) Two Calvinistic Methodist Chapels: 1743-1811: The London Tabernacle and Spa Fields; London: London Record Society where there is a reference to a Sister West in the Minutes of the London Tabernacle.

22. On the Evangelical revival see: Bebbington, D. (1989) Evangelicalism in Modern Britain: A History from the 1730s to the 1980s. London: Routledge. Hylson-Smith, K. (1988) Evangelicals in the Church of England: 1734-1984. Edinburgh: T&T. Clark. Noll, M.A. (2004.) The Rise of Evangelicalism: The Age of Edwards, Whitefield and the Wesleys. Leicester: IVP. Reynolds, J.S. (1953) The Evangelicals at Oxford: 1732-1871. Oxford. Wood, A. Skevington. (1967) The Inextinguishable Blaze Spiritual Renewal and Advance in the Eighteenth Century. London: Paternoster Press. Vol.viii The Paternoster Church History. See also: Ryle, J.C. (1978) Christian Leaders of the 18th century. Edinburgh: Banner of Truth Trust.

23. The temporary building that George Whitefield referred to as a tabernacle was replaced by a permanent building in 1753. Further developments took place in 1868: the foundation stone was laid by John Remington Mills the grandson of Benjamin Mills and Thomas Wilson. The inscription read: "Near this spot stood the Tabernacle built by Revd G. Whitefield in 1753. 115 years later it was taken down and in it's place this building was erected. This stone was laid by J.Remington Mills. Esq. MP on 11 September 1868." The Tabernacle in Tottenham court road was built in 1756 partly as a counter attraction to the Foundery that lay near by the Moorfields Tabernacle.

24. Replying to a correspondent Thomas Haweis says: "you ask of what Church we profess ourselves: We desire to be esteemed as members of Christ's Catholic and Apostolic Church and essentially one with the Church of England." See: Wood, A. Skevington: (1967) ibid. p.201 citing from Overton, John. H. (1886) The Evangelical Revival in the 18th century. London. p.185-186. See also: Bebbington, D. (1989) ibid. p.66 in which he points out that what Whitefield called a Catholic spirit was generated among Evangelicals.

The Two Chapels continued to follow the office of the Church of England right up until the time that J.C. Campbell moved them into the Congregational Union. See: K.Brownell, (1982) Voluntary Saints: English Congregationalism and the Voluntary Principle: 1825-1862. Unpublished PhD. University of St Andrews in which he quotes from a letter written by J.Pye Smith who states that the Whitefieldian Churches used the Book of Common Prayer in worship which many Congregationalists considered unscriptural. See also: Martin, B. (1960) An Ancient Mariner. London: Epworth where he cites Newton who says that when he attended Worship at the Tabernacle Revd Mr G. Whitefield made use of the office of the Church of England interspersed with exhortations, encouragements and the singing of Hymns: the service lasting about 3 hours.

25. Converted independently of the Evangelical Revival it is generally considered that Romaine was the first real leader of the Anglican Evangelicals in London. He was appointed lecturer at St Botolph's in 1748, lecturer: St Dunstan's in the West 1749;

a post that he held for a period of forty six years: Assistant minister; St George's Hanover Square, 1750-1755: Morning Preacher, St Olave's, Southwark and St Bartholomew's the Great, 1759-1761, Rector, St Anne's Blackfriars, 1766-1795. Following his conversion he attracted many fine preachers to the City, some of whom were foremost in the formation of the Eclectic Society. Of these Revd Henry Foster was appointed Curate to Romaine in 1767, Richard Cecil, St John's Bedford Row, 1780, John Newton, Rector of St Mary Woolnoth, 1779, Basil Woodd, Bentinck Chapel, 1785. See: Reynolds, J.S. (1953) The Evangelicals at Oxford: 1735-1871. Oxford; in which John Reynolds provides a thorough account of the contribution that the Oxford Anglican Evangelical Clergy made to the Anglican Church in London. See also: Ryle, J.C. (1978) Christian Leaders of the 18th Century. Edinburgh: Banner of Truth Trust.

26.  See: Bebbington, D. (1999) ibid, p.1-19. See also: Noll, M.A. (2004) ibid, p.13-18.

27.  It is interesting to note that John Wesley thought that the Tabernacle had a richer clientele . . . the Tabernacle beating the Foundery for riches, whilst Whitefield thought that the foundery had members who were very wealthy. It is probable that the affluent craftsmen, artisans masters and merchants attended the Tabernacle of whom Daniel West, Thomas Wilson, John Wilson, Stephen Wilson, not forgetting his son in law, William Bateman are good examples of people who were amongst the socially and economically elite in the City Guilds.

28.  The standard works on the life of George Whitefield are: Dallimore, A.A. (1970) George Whitefield: the Life and Times of the Great Evangelist of the 18th century Revival. Wetchester, IL. 2 vols. Tyerman, L. (1876) The Life of George Whitefield. London: Hodder and Stoughton. See also: Pollock, J. (1986) George Whitefield and the Great Awakening. Tring: Lion.Publications.

29.  See: Noll, M (2004) The Rise of Evangelicalism: the Age of Edwards, Whitefield and the Wesleys. Leicester, IVP, p.152. in which he comments on the fact that because Whitefield devoted less energy than Wesley to founding societies the two Tabernacles built by Whitefield were easily transformed in Dissenting Chapels. See also Welch, E. (1975) Two Calvinistic Chapels: 1743-1811: The London Tabernacle and Spa Fields. London: The London Record Society, where he states that the Two Tabernacles broke their links with the Church of England after Whitefield's death in 1770. In fact it was not until the ministry of J. C. Campbell, successor to Matthew Wilks that the Two Tabernacles were forced by some of its members amongst whom was William Bateman, brother in law to Daniel Wilson, (Bishop of Calcutta) in the Congregational Union despite attempts by some members such as Thomas Wilson (II) to prevent Campbell from undoing the Trust. See: C.L. Mss II; c.34: Item 11: J.C. Campbell to Thomas Wilson, May 22, 1834: Michael Cruttenden to Thomas Wilson, 22 Sept, 1834. See also n. 23.

30.  Evangelical Magazine. (1796) Obituary of Daniel West. vol. iv. p.518-521.

31.  Wilson, J. (1846) Memoir of Thomas Wilson. London.

32.  See: Wilson, J. (1846) ibid p.146: See also: Peel, A. (1931) These Hundred Years. London: p.10. See also: E.M. (1796) vol.iv. p.47. C.M. (1825) vol.1. (n.s.)

Historical Account of Dissenting Academies: no.v. Hoxton Academy. p.524-527. founded in 1778 it was later moved to Highbury in 1825. Nuttall, G.F. (1977) New College London and its Library. London: Dr Williams's Trust.

33. The standard works on the London Missionary Society include: Morrison, J. (1839) The Fathers and Founders of the London Missionary Society. London. Ellis, W. (1844) The History of the London Missionary Society. London. Lovett, R. (1899) The History of the London Missionary Society. London. See: also: Evangelical Magazine, 1796. also: Wilson, J (1846) Memoirs of Thomas Wilson. London, p.147-149. See also: A.N. Porter (2005) The London Missionary Society. Oxford DNB. www.oxforddnb.

34. According to the memoir of Thomas Wilson a small chapel was built at Stanford Rivers, near Ongar where David Livingstone preached while a student at Chipping Ongar. See: Wilson, J. (1846) Memoir of Thomas Wilson. London. also Binfield, C. (1967) The Threads of Disruption. T.CH.S vol.xx., no. 5. May. p.156-165. See also: Victoria County History: Essex: (1956) vol. vi. Ongar Hundred, p.218. ed., W.R.Powell.

35. GUILDHALL LIBRARY: Gld Mss: 4648b. Linborough Lecture Trust. Account Book: 1783-1813. See also: Christ Church Vestry Minute Books. Step. 82. Tower Hamlets Local History Library. By the terms of his Will James Linborough left a capital sum of £3,000 invested in 3% consolidated Bank Annuities for the purpose of establishing an annual course of lectures to be known as the Linborough Trust lectures. The first two trustees to be elected were Daniel West and Benjamin Mills. Amongst those who preached were: Henry Foster, Richard Cecil, Josiah Pratt and Thomas Scott. See: Scott, J.H. (n.d.) Spitalfields: Past and Present: 1197-1894: See also: Plummer, A. (1972) The London Weavers Company: 1600-1760. London. See also: Bateman, J. (1860) Life of Daniel Wilson. London: J. Murray. p.7.

36. See: Reynolds, J.S. The Evangelicals at Oxford: 1731-1871. Oxford.

37. E.M. (1796) iv. p.518-521. Obituary: Daniel West. See: Best, G; Evangelicalism and the Victorians in., The Victorian Crisis of Faith: ed. Anthony Symondson. London: SPCK, 1974 in which Best comments on the importance of the death bed scene recounted in the Evangelical Magazine in providing comfort and confidence for the believer in the face of death. At the same time they provided a model for the reader. Howbeit the account given by Stephen Wilson in his Private Calendar offers us a different picture. The only person present at his death was his son in law, Stephen Wilson who "sat up with him till 20 minutes past one o Clock this morning when he died aged 70." (30 Sept, 1796) Wilson, Stephen: Private Calendar: 1795-1802. (Privately owned)

38. E.M 1796. p.518-521: Obituary of Daniel Wilson. It is probable that the obituary was written by John Eyre, Editor of the Evangelical Magazine and a close friend of the family.

39. See: Leifchild, J. (1843) Piety the Best Patriotism London. p.18-19: who states that Thomas Wilson [II] was carried in his nurse's arms . . . to gaze upon George Whitefield.

40. See The Times: Oct. 27, 1989: "On this day:" Oct. 27 1922. In a speech made by

Lloyd George at the Tabernacle, Tottenham Court Road, he said of Whitefield that "there had been no oratory like his in the pulpit, that great power of preaching to tens of thousand of people moving tem in highways and byways." See also: Hazlitt, W. Lectures on English Poets & The Spirit of the Age. London. J.M.Dent. 1916. Everyman Edition. Referring to Cowper he says that: "Cowper's character of Whitefield in the poem on Hope is one of his most spirited and striking things. It is written Con Amore."

41.  E.M. 1796. p.518-521. Obituary of Daniel West. In his account of the funeral Stephen Wilson records that in addition to the Hearse and 4 and the four coaches and pair there were six other coaches bearing members of the family: with 8 Tabernacle Brethren who were Bearers. Stephen Wilson: (1795-1802) Private Calendar. (Privately owned)

# 5. Thomas Wilson of Highbury, Islington (1731-1794)*(i)*

Born in 1731 Thomas Wilson was a member of a family that came from Stenson, near Barrow upon Trent where they owned the free hold of their land in addition to renting land from the Harpurs of Calke Abbey.[1]

As successful farmers with one eye on the market and the other on what cash crop and livestock combination would make the greatest profit, the Wilsons obviously recognized the importance of commerce as a way of ensuring that their younger sons made their way in the world. In 1747, his father took Thomas to London with the aim of settling him in a suitable business. While they were in London, his father fell ill and so they cut short their visit. Before they could reach Stenson, his father died at Leicester. He was aged 51. Two years after his father's death, Thomas embarked on a ship for St Kitts, a centre noted for its slave plantations. (It was at St Kitts that James Stephens practiced as a lawyer before returning to England where he supported Wilberforce and others in the abolition of the slave trade.) After staying there for three years and escaping many dangers, he returned to England where he settled in Coventry. It was here that his elder brother, Stephen had a successful silk weaving company. Thomas chose however to enter into partnership with his younger brother William, but this enterprise proved to be a failure. It was during his time in Coventry that he probably attended the West Orchard Meeting House where he met Mary Remington the only daughter of John Remington, a wealthy merchant and Alderman of the City of Coventry.[2]

Soon after his marriage to Mary Remington, in the June of 1754 Thomas was invited by his brother Stephen, to become a partner in his silk manufacturing business. By the terms of the partnership it was agreed that Thomas should remain in Coventry whilst Stephen went to London to manage the branch of the business that he had recently opened.[3] London was an important centre for the purchase of raw silk, credit and capital. In addition, it was also an important centre for the marketing of finished silk goods. In 1755 whilst managing the London business in Wood Street Cheapside, Stephen contracted a fever from which he died. He was aged 32.

Two months after his death his widow Mary, renegotiated the terms of partnership with her brother in law. Under the new terms it was agreed that Thomas was to supervise the London branch leaving her to manage the Coventry business and look after her four children, all of whom were under the age of five. (See: Fig. 2)

On their arrival in London Thomas and his wife resided at St Peter's Precinct where he is listed as paying a rent of £2.10s for property in St Peter's Street,

Cheapside off Wood Street. Later, he is listed in the London Directory as living at 124 Wood Street, Cheapside that was to be the family home for the next fifteen years. It was here in this branch of the family business that succeeding members of the Wilson family were apprenticed before setting up in business on their own.

Looking back on the decision by his sister in law to send them to London, Thomas Wilson considered this to be an act of providence catering for their temporal and spiritual needs. On their arrival in London they attended the Old Meetinghouse at Old Jewry where the minister was the Revd Dr. Samuel Chandler whose preaching according to Thomas Wilson was of a kind little adapted to produce spiritual effect in the lives of the congregation. They had been advised by the Revd Ebenezer Fletcher of the Grand Meetinghouse in Smithfield Street to avoid the preaching of Methodists, no doubt a reference to the preaching of George Whitefield.[4]

They had not been long in London before his wife, whilst out with a friend came across Whitefield's Tabernacle which they chose to attend, there being a meeting on at the time. The speaker that night was the Revd Andrew Kinsman of Plymouth, one of Whitefield's first converts. So impressed was Mary Wilson by the preaching that she said that if she went again to hear such preaching she would indeed become a Methodist. Her husband who had not been with her that night suggested that they should go together to hear the preaching of George Whitefield, the next time that he was in London. Although they attended the Tabernacle on numerous occasions, notwithstanding their loyalties remained with the Dissenting movement in which Mary Remington had been brought up as a child. In 1760, they entered into fellowship with the congregation at the Old Meeting that met in Haberdashers Hall. The minister, the Revd Dr Thomas Gibbons was a close friend of Johnson and George Whitefield to whom he gave great support in his ministry.[5]

Although Gibbons belonged to the regular dissenters, it is significant to note that he held the post of Lecturer at St Helen's Bishopsgate and at Homerton College. Unlike other Dissenters who were, in the words of Thomas Wilson cold and stiff, Gibbons by contrast was a warm, lively and earnest preacher.

They had not long been at the Meeting before Thomas Wilson was appointed a Deacon, though this did not seem to prevent him being appointed Church Warden at St Peter's Cheapside, a post that he accepted with some degree of reluctance but, one that he fulfilled with great vigour.

Whilst there can be no doubting that it was through his wife's influence that Thomas Wilson chose to become a Dissenter, what cannot be overlooked is that in him Dissent had a powerful and wealthy benefactor, who according to his grandson devoted 1/10th of his personal wealth to the building of chapels and the supplying and training of ministers in the Congregational Church.[6]

By this stage Dissent, in particular, older Dissent, in the form of Presbyterianism was either in a state of decline or shifting towards Unitarianism.[7] Many like Thomas Wilson were concerned about the indifference to religion within dissent and so in response to the failure of the Dissenting movement to respond positively to the challenge of the Evangelical revival the Evangelical Society was formed in 1776. Amongst those connected with its foundation, several were associated with Moorfields Tabernacle; and Lady Huntingdon's chapel, Spa Fields, whilst at least one was a member of the Church of England. This was Benjamin Mills, later father in law to Thomas Wilson's only daughter, Mary Mills, (née Wilson).

Formed in 1776, the primary aim of the Society was to promote the preaching of the Gospel through itinerant preaching, to defray the expenses of ministers in the Congregational Church and to encourage the spread of the Gospel in the dark and neglected parts of the land.

According to Thomas Wilson, the formation of the Society in 1776 was an important event in the history of the country. Notwithstanding, finding suitable people for the ministry proved to be a formidable task and so it was that along with a number of like-minded Evangelicals Thomas Wilson took an active part in the formation of the New English Academy for the training of ministers in the Congregational Church. Amongst those involved were: Thomas Wilson of Highbury (1st treasurer), Benjamin Mills (1st Secretary), Daniel West and Robert Keene, Trustees of Whitefields Tabernacle, Revd Messrs Barber, Brewer, Clayton, Rogers, Towers, Trotman and Webb.[8] Tutors included, the Revd Samuel Brewer of Stepney Green Independent Chapel, Revd J Barbor, formerly of Brentwood and the Revd Mr Kello who taught Logic and Grammar.

In 1782, the Academy moved from Gracechurch to Grove House, Mile End where it remained until 1793 when the committee obtained from the Trustees of the Coward Trust the lease of a house originally owned by Dr Williams.

In addition to all this Thomas Wilson worked in close conjunction with the Countess of Huntingdon when he took an active role in the funding and supporting of chapels in Derbyshire, many of which had either been closed or fallen into disrepair. At Derby the arrival in 1778 of Thomas Jones, (one of Lady Huntingdon's preachers) and Joseph Griffiths had led to a revival amongst older Dissent resulting in the need for the founding of chapels and the funding and supporting of ministers.[9] And so in response to the ministry of Thomas Jones and Joseph Griffiths, the congregation had hired rooms in the old school at the rear of the Town Hall in Derby. In order however to meet the needs of a growing congregation Thomas Wilson undertook at his own expense to provide the congregation with a regular supply of ministers. Later in 1783, he purchased at his own expense the freehold of land at Brookside where a chapel was built. This was opened in 1784 and the Revd John Smith, formerly of Melbourne was appointed its first minister.[10]

Other Chapels in Derbyshire that benefited from his support were at Alveston, Ashbourne, Belper, Bakewell and Melbourne. Nearer to his birthplace in Stenson, Thomas Wilson gave financial support to the Independent Chapel in Barrow upon Trent, which had been founded in 1790. It was at this Chapel that his nephew, John Wilson [IV] attended.[11]

However, Thomas Wilson did not restrict his support to his native Derbyshire. Other parts of the country that benefited from his support included Coventry where he contributed to the refurbishment of the West Orchard Meeting House, Coventry. The original chapel had been built in 1777 following secession from the Old meetinghouse in Vicar Lane. Amongst those involved in the secession was John Remington, junior, brother in law to Thomas Wilson. The Remingtons were an established family of Dissenters who had originally worshipped at the Old Meeting House in Great Smithford Street. However, following the appointment of Ebenezer Fletcher, known for his Socinian or Unitarian views, a group of members led a secession and set up their own meetinghouse in Vicar Lane, which then split in 1777 to form a new meetinghouse in West Orchard.[12] The second minister of West Orchard meetinghouse was the Revd George Burder, one of the founders of the Religious Tract Society and later the London Missionary Society.[13] Thomas Wilson never lived to see the formation in 1796 of the London Missionary Society. He died in 1794 and was buried in Bunhill Fields: a fitting tribute to a person who had dedicated his life to the cause of the Gospel.[14]

During his married life, Thomas Wilson had been privileged to have the support of his wife Mary, the only daughter of John Remington of Coventry. In addition to assisting in the affairs of the trade, she took an active part in the management of the household. Family prayers were held every morning at seven and every evening at eight p.m. According to her grandson Joshua, her main delight was found in watching over the spiritual interests of her three children, Thomas (1764-1843), Joseph (1766-1851) and Mary (1769-1847), and "making their home happy to them and attaching to them by every prudent and winning method to the house of God." She died in 1816 at the age of 87 having outlived her husband by twenty-two years.[15]

In considering the contribution that Thomas Wilson [I] made to English Congregationalism it needs to be recognized that his achievements are all the more remarkable given that he was devoting his time to the family silk business of which he was a partner from 1755 to 1794. To what extent he may be described as a figure of the enlightenment is open to question. Nonetheless, his attitude towards slavery, the care of the poor, his desire to spread the Gospel and his assurance of salvation all serve to show that he did share in many of the principles expressed by the Enlightenment.[16]

Thomas Wilson, [I] was succeeded in his work in the Congregational Church by his son, also called Thomas Wilson [II], the seventh of nine children born to Thomas and Mary Wilson (née Remington). At the age of ten his parents sent him to a Dissenting academy in Newington Green where he received a commercial as opposed to a classical education. In 1778, he became apprenticed to his father, aunt Mary Wilson (née Fullalove) and cousin John Wilson in the family business at Foleshill, Coventry and Wood Street, Cheapside. As an apprentice, he spent most of his time in Coventry where the silk ribbons and other fancy goods were manufactured before being sent to London to be used in the making of dresses for the fashionable London society.

It was during his time in Coventry that he attended the West Orchard Meetinghouse with which his father and uncle John Remington, had been associated. Later he was to provide the minister Jonathan Evans, with funds enabling the congregation to erect a permanent place of worship at Little Heath, Foleshill.

On completing his apprenticeship in 1785, he was made a partner in the family business where he remained until 1798 when he retired ostensibly on grounds of ill health. In fact the real reason for his early retirement at the age of thirty four was to enable him to devote himself to the cause of Congregationalism.[17] Chief amongst these was the Hoxton, later Highbury Academy, the purchasing and reopening of disused chapels and the encouraging and establishing of those causes that he considered were worthy of his support.[18]

By this stage he had married on the 31st March, 1791 Elizabeth Clegg, the younger daughter of Arthur Clegg of Manchester. Thomas and Elizabeth had three children, Joshua, Elizabeth and Rebekah. (See Table 9)

One of the earliest causes to benefit from his support was at Foleshill, a place with which he was familiar, having spent his time there as an apprentice. In 1784 a group of independents had obtained the use of a disused boat house alongside the canal as a place of worship. With financial support from Thomas Wilson the congregation moved in 1794/5 to a permanent building at Little Heath, Foleshill.[19]

Nearer to home Thomas Wilson became involved with the conversion of a small building into a chapel at Hoxton Academy. By 1799 the chapel had proved to be too small for the needs of the Academy and so a new chapel was built to which was attached a Sunday School. At the time of the building of the Chapel Thomas Wilson had been advised to underwrite the project with an insurance policy. After six months of paying into the policy, he wound it up making a profit of £700.[20] Closely related to chapel building were his efforts to purchase and re-open chapels that had fallen into disuse. In 1798 he reopened at his own expense two chapels in Brentwood to which he sent David Smith a student at the Academy with the promise of £60. In 1800, David Smith was ordained minister of the Congregational chapel in Brentwood where he remained as the minister until his retirement in 1846.[21] Elsewhere in Essex he purchased and rebuilt at his own expense a Chapel in George Street Harwich, to which in 1799 he sent William Hordle, a Hoxton student, as its first pastor.[22]

He was also responsible for rebuilding, purchasing and sending students from Hoxton Academy to Lincolnshire where for many years Congregationalism had been weak.[23] In addition to all this he continued to build on the work that his father had commenced in Derbyshire. In 1790, he obtained access to the old Presbyterian Chapel in Ashbourne for Thomas Jones, one of the Countess of Huntingdon's preachers. Later he opened the chapel at Alveston for his use. Elsewhere in Derbyshire, he was involved with the building of a new chapel in Bakewell, which was built in 1804 to replace an old barn that had been converted in 1791. It is probable that he was involved with the chapel in Buxton, built on land purchased by his father in law, Arthur Clegg of Manchester and with the chapel built in Middleton by Youlgrave by his brother in law, Thomas Bateman in Middleton by Youlgrave, Derbyshire.[24] Other places that benefited from his support included: Dereham (Norfolk 1816), Epsom, Guildford, Liskeard, Portsmouth, Reigate and Wells (Somerset 1816), many of which had either fallen into disrepair or had been abandoned.[25]

In some cases, Wilson also undertook to provide a place of worship in areas that he considered were in need of a chapel. Thus we find that in 1819 in the small village of Stanford Rivers, Essex he converted his small cottage that he had purchased in 1796 into a place of worship to which was attached a Sunday School. Two years later he gave £200 towards the building of a new chapel built to seat up to 300 people. Today all that remains of the site at Stanford Rivers is the graveyard: the chapel having been burnt down in 1927.[26]

In addition to giving support to the Congregational Church in other parts of the country Wilson, like many of those in the Church of England was concerned with the lack of Churches in the rapidly growing suburbs of London. Amongst the numerous chapels built in London for use by Congregationalists from funds provided by Thomas Wilson, the first was Paddington Chapel, Marylebone Road opened in 1813 at the cost of £7,000. In so doing, he incurred the anger of the Evangelical minister, Basil Woodd, Vicar of Bentinck Chapel off the Edgware Road.[27]

This was followed in 1818 by the opening of Claremont Chapel, Pentonville. The first minister was the Revd John Blackburn, one time pastor of the Congregational chapel in Finchingfield, Essex.[28] The third chapel that benefited from his personal financial support was Craven Chapel. This proved to be the most expensive, costing over £11,000.[29] It was here that John Leifchild; author of *Piety the Best Patriotism* was the minister.

However, the cause that was closest to his heart was Hoxton Academy of which he was its second treasurer having succeeded to the post following the death of his father in 1794. It was from here that students were sent to fill the many vacancies that existed in Congregational chapels all over the country. In 1825, the Academy moved to a new building in Highbury that had been designed by John Davies.[30] Thomas Wilson donated 2,000 guineas to the cost of the building of the College.

By this stage, Thomas Wilson was getting old and increasingly he looked to his son, Joshua for assistance in Chapel building, funding ministers and the formation of the Congregational Union and its library.

Following the death of his father in 1843 Joshua Wilson continued the work to which his father had devoted over fifty years of his life.

Having originally been called to the Bar in 1832, Joshua chose instead to devote his life to the Congregational cause.[31]

Apart from chapel building and the formation of the Congregational Union, a commitment that he shared with his father, Joshua was also involved in the creation of the Congregational library. Amongst those present at the first meeting was his father Thomas Wilson [II], the Revd John Blackburn of Claremont Chapel, Benjamin Hanbury and the Revd John Pye Smith. Even though the trustees had managed in 1830 to obtain the lease of a building in Blomfield Street, off Liverpool Street, it was in fact not until 1832 that the Library was officially opened.[32]

The other major project to which Joshua was committed was the creation of a memorial hall to commemorate the bi-centenerary of the ejection of nearly 2,000 Puritan clergy from the Church of England in 1662. He was also eager that new Chapels should be built as a monument to this event. One area that benefited from this was Islington. For many years, Claremont Chapel had been the main base in Islington for Congregationalism. During his lifetime at least six more chapels were built: many with funds from the London Congregational Chapel Building Society.[33]

Supporting him in this work was that great benefactor to the Congregational cause, his cousin, John Remington Mills, grandson of the late Thomas Wilson, senior. As a young man, he had originally been apprenticed to his uncle, Joseph Wilson of Milk Street and Highbury Hill. In 1840, he retired from the silk trade in order to pursue a career in public affairs, eventually contesting the seat in Leeds as an MP.[34] A leading figure in the Congregational Church he served on numerous committees including the Congregational Union, the Memorial Library, Hoxton Academy and the Colonial Missionary Society. He is also credited with paying for the rebuilding of Whitefield's Tabernacle,

Moorefields and contributing the largest donation to the funds for the building of the Memorial Hall which he opened on 19th January 1875. Joshua Wilson never lived to see the opening of the Commemoration Hall and new library with which he had been closely involved with: he died on August 14th 1874. Nor did he live to see the opening of the Union Chapel in Islington that was completed in 1876 and opened in the presence of W.E. Gladstone. This was a real preaching chapel embracing all those qualities that meant a great deal to nonconformists for whom the preaching of the word of God was at the centre of the life of the worshipping community.

Congregations' other great benefactor was Samuel Morley, great nephew to Thomas Wilson (I) through his marriage to Rebekah Hope, daughter of Samuel and Rebekah Hope (née Clegg).[35] Like his cousins Joshua and John Remington Mills, Samuel Morley was keen to press ahead with the building of chapels: seeing this as a way of spreading the Gospel and advancing the cause of Congregationalism. During the period 1864 to 1870, it is estimated that he spent over £14,000 in Chapel building throughout the country.

Commenting on the death of his friend, Edwin Hodder writes: In the August of 1874 Samuel Morley lost his old and beloved friend, Joshua Wilson with whom for over 30 years he had been associated with in every kind of Christian and philanthropic work. A gentleman and a scholar Mr Morley found pleasure in his companionship and rarely entered upon any real enterprise without taking counsel with him: a remarkable tribute to a very self effacing person who deserves to be honoured as the founder of the Congregational Library.[36]

*Notes and References:*
(i)  *This is a modified paper entitled Patrons and Church Builders: The Wilsons of Highbury and Islington given at a Seminar organized by the Friends of Union Chapel and The Victorian Society, September 24th 2005.*
1.   Wilson, J. (1846) Memoir of the Life and Character of Thomas Wilson. Esq., by his son. London, hereafter: Memoir of Thomas Wilson. See also: Harrison, M. J. Patrons and Church Builders: The Wilsons of Highbury and Islington. A paper given at a seminar by the Friends of Union Chapel and the Victorian Society. Saturday September 24th 2005: Forthcoming publication: 2008.
2.   The Remingtons were a well established family in Coventry. Mary Remington was the only daughter of John Remington, Mercer and Sheriff of Coventry and a member of the Grand Meetinghouse in Smithfield Street, Coventry. There was a branch of the family in Northampton who attended the ministry of Dr Doddridge. The Remingtons of Coventry were also related to the Fullaloves and other leading members of the ruling elite of Coventry by marriage. See: Hinman, M.J. (1988) Men Who Rule Coventry: 1725-1780. Coventry: Coventry Historical Association. No. 14.
3.   Wilson, J. (1846) Memoir of Thomas Wilson. London. Stephen Wilson is recorded

as being the first member of the Wilsons of Stenson to enter the silk trade in Coventry. In 1754, he established a branch of the business at 121 Wood Street, Cheapside. See: Rothstein, NKA. (1961) The Silk Industry in London: 1702-1792. London: London University: M.A. In her study, she records a Stephen Wilson of Aldermanbury. (1755-1793). Wood Street, Cheapside was in the Ward of Aldermanbury. Although Stephen had died in 1755, it seems that the firm continued to practice under his name. See also: Rothstein, NKA. (1990) Silk Designs in the Collection of the Victoria and Albert Museum, London. London: Thames & Hudson. See also: London Directory, 1754 where he is recorded as being of Coventry and 121 Wood Street, Cheapside.

4.  Sibree, J & Caston, M. (1885) Independency in Warwickshire. Coventry. Ebenezer Fletcher is recorded as being Unitarian in his beliefs and taking the congregation with him down that line. See also: Stephens, W.B. Protestant Nonconformity in Coventry in: A History of Warwick. vol. viii. The Victoria County History. London: Oxford University Press, 1969. See also: Wilson, J. (1846) Memoir of Thomas Wilson. London. Chandler had been Minister of Bunyan's church in Bedford from 1690-1747. See: Tibbutt, H.G. Pattern of change. TRCHS. Vol xx no 5. May 1967.

5.  Dr Thomas Gibbons, along with the Revd Samuel Brewer and Doddridge were amongst the few notable Dissenters to give support to George Whitefield. It was Samuel Brewer who introduced John Newton to George Whitefield. On Thomas Gibbons see: DNB. vol. vii. Entry by E.C. Cruttenden. See also: Bebbington, D. (1989) Evangelicalism in Modern Britain: a History from the 1730s to the 1980s. London: Routledge. Nuttall, G. (1981) Methodism and old Dissent. JURCHS. vol. 2. no. 8.

6.  Wilson, J. (1846) Memoir of Thomas Wilson. London. There is no evidence that the Wilsons of Stenson were Dissenters: or that their sons were educated at the Dissenting Academy in Findern kept by Revd Dr Ebenezer Latham. It is important to note that although they were yeomen farmers who had far greater religious freedom than tenant farmers they remained members of the Church of England. Only later do we learn that Thomas Wilson's nephew, John Wilson [IV] entertained Methodists in his home and was a member of the congregation at Barrow upon Trent. See: Wilson, J. (1846) Memoir of Thomas Wilson. London.

7.  See: Bebbington, D. (1989) Evangelicalism in Modern Britain: a History from the 1730s to the 1980s. London: Routledge. Also: Noll, M (2004) The Rise of Evangelicalism: the Age of Edwards, Whitefield and the Wesleys. Leicester: Apollos.

8.  The Evangelical Academy was founded in 1778 but it was not until 1782 that the Committee secured a residential house in Mile End. In 1791, the Academy moved to Hoxton Square where it remained until 1825 when a new site was chosen in Highbury, Islington. See: Wilson, J. (1846) Memoir of Thomas Wilson. London.

9.  See: Reynolds, J.S. (1953) The Evangelicals at Oxford: 1735-1870. Oxford: Oxford University Press. Reynolds records that Thomas Jones later married the sister of Lady Austen, a close friend of William Cowper, the poet. Thomas Jones went on to become Curate at Clifton Reynes, near Olney where he established a Sunday School.

10. Wilson, J. (1846) Memoir of Thomas Wilson. London. The Revd John Smith is recorded as being the first minister at Barrow upon Trent. Prior to this, he had been at Melbourne then from 1787-1792 minister at Brookside Chapel, Derby. One of the Trustees was Thomas Wilson's nephew, John Wilson [IV], farmer of Stenson:
(1753-1835)

11. Wilson, J. (1846) Memoir of Thomas Wilson. London. John Wilson of Stenson, (1753-1835) is not to be confused with John and Mary Wilson, (née Buckley) of Derby from whom Ronal Bynge, the composer and musician is descended. They are two distinct and unrelated families. John Wilson of Stenson died unmarried and the farm passed to his niece, Mary Wayte, (née Moore). [See Table 3]

12. See: Sibree, J & Caston, M. (1885) Independency in Warwickshire. Coventry. They record that many of those who left Vicar Lane Meetinghouse had in fact been members of the Grand Meetinghouse, Smithfield Street, until the appointment in 1742 of the Unitarian minister, Ebenezer Fletcher.

13. George Burder played a significant role in 1793 in the formation of the Warwickshire Association of Ministers, considered to be the forerunner of the London Missionary Society. See: Fletcher, Irene, M. The Fundamental Principle of the London Missionary Society. part iii. Transactions of the Congregational Historical Society. vol. 19. 1963. See also: Skevington Wood, A. (1960) The Inextinguishable Blaze: Spiritual Renewal and Advancement in the 18th century. London: Paternoster Press.

14. Wilson, J. (1846) Memoir of Thomas Wilson. London. The epitaph on his vault reads: In this vault lies interred the remains of Mr Thomas Wilson late of Highbury Place. Obiit March 31st 1794 Aetat 64. He excelled in true friendship relative affection and zeal in the service of Christ.

15. Wilson, J. (1846) Memoir of Thomas Wilson. London. Mary Remington is described as being the subject of serious impressions from her youth. She was catechised at an early age but did not become a child of God by faith in Jesus Christ till after her marriage and removal to London. She was regular in public worship and family religion and would not allow guests and in particular ministers to leave without desiring them to pray with the family. She died on July 26th 1816 having suffered much from infirmities that made walking painful and laborious. See: Wilson, H.A, (1901) Private Sketch. (Privately owned) Letter to Mrs Moore, her niece: Dec 13th 1790.

16. See: Bebbington, D. (1989) Evangelicalism in Modern Britain: a History from the 1730s to the 1980s. London: Routledge. See: Wilson, J. (1846) Memoir of Thomas Wilson. London, in which he records that his grandfather, Thomas Wilson senior was a strict observer of the Lord's Day, gave generously to the poor, showed great concern for Negroes and gave support to the ill fated scheme in Sierra Leone. Although Thomas Wilson claimed to be a Nonconformist of the good old school of Puritans there is no evidence in support of this claim.

17. Wilson, J. (1846) Memoir of Thomas Wilson. London. See also: Wilson, T. Autobiographical Notes. Dr Williams's Library. C.L. Mss d.3. on completing his apprenticeship in 1785 the Weavers Company summoned him to be admitted as a

Freeman of the Company. Thomas Wilson chose instead to pay the statutory fine of £5 in lieu of being made a Freeman. GUILDHALL LIBRARY. Gld Mss. Court Minute Books: Weavers Company: 4655/17/1765-1785.

18. See: Wilson, J. (1846) Memoir of Thomas Wilson. London. See also: Brown, F.K. (1961) Fathers of the Victorians: the Age of Wilberforce. Cambridge: CUP.

19. The first minister of Foleshill Chapel was the Revd Jonathan Evans, (1796-1808) who had in 1784 secured the use of a former boat shed alongside the canal in Foleshill before moving to a permanent building at Little Heath, Foleshill in 1795 to which Thomas Wilson [II] gave financial support. See: Sibree, J & Caston, M. 91885) Independency in Warwick. Coventry.

20. Wilson, J. (1846) Memoir of Thomas Wilson. London. See also: London Borough of Hackney Archives: D/E/248/Hox. Hoxton Academy Sunday School Minutes.

21. On the history of Brentwood Congregational Chapel see: Quinn. W.T. (n.d.) Brentwood Congregational Church: a Brief History, 1672-1972. On Dissent in Essex, See: Davids, T.W. (1863) Annals of Nonconformity in the County of Essex. London.

22. On the Congregational Church at Harwich: see: E.R.O. (Colchester and North East Essex Branch) Acc. No. C.257: Church of Christ at Harwich. Acc. No. C 1032. Nonconformist Churches and Chapels: Harwich.

23. Nuttall, G.F. (1987) The Rise of Independency in Lincolnshire: Thomas Wilson and the students. JURCHS. vol.4. no.1.

24. Wilson, J. (1846) Memoir of Thomas Wilson. London. The Batemans of Middleton by Youlgrave are not to be confused with the Batemans of Bunhill Fields. They are two quite distinct families. See: Derby Record Office: Bateman pedigree: 1765M/F7. See also: Stell, C. (1976) Architects of Dissent: some Nonconformist Patrons and their Architects. London: Dr Williams's Trust. On the Batemans of Bunhill see: Lever, C. (1975) Goldsmiths and Silversmiths of London. London: Hutchinson. Also: Shure, David, (1959) Hester Bateman, Queen of English Silversmiths. London: W. H. Allen

25. Wilson, J. (1846) Memoir of Thomas Wilson. London.

26. See: Wilson, J. Autobiographical Notes. C.L Mss. d.3. Dr Williams's Library. See also: The Victoria County History of Essex. vol.

27. Wilson, J. (1846) Memoir of Thomas Wilson. The second minister was James Stratten, who married Rebecca Wilson, eldest daughter of Thomas and Elizabeth Wilson.

28. See: Surman, J. (1955) The Revd John Blackburn: Pioneer Statistician of English Congregationalism. The Congregational Quarterly. Vol.33. See also: Stell, C. (2002) An Inventory of Nonconformist Chapels and Meeting Houses in Eastern England. London: English Heritage.

29. Stell, C. (2002) An Inventory of Nonconformist Chapels and Meeting Houses in Eastern England. London: English Heritage.

30. Wilson, J (1846) Memoir of Thomas Wilson. London. See also: Lewis, S. (1842) The History and Topography of the Parish of St Mary, Islington in the County of Middlesex. London: J.M. Jackson.

31. The only son of Thomas Wilson of Islington, Middlesex, Joshua was admitted a

member of the honourable society of the Inner Temple in 1817: and was admitted to the Bar in 1832. He never practiced as a barrister.

32. Creasey, J. (1992) The Congregational Library. London: The Congregational Memorial Trust. See also: Halley, R. (1875) Recollections of Old Dissent. The Congregationalist. 1875.

33. Temple, P (1992) Islington Chapels: an Architectural Guide to Nonconformist and Roman Catholic Places of Worship in the London Borough of Islington. London: RCHM. See also: Stell, C. (2002) An Inventory of Nonconformist Chapels and Meeting Places in Eastern England. London: English Heritage.

34. Burkes Landed Gentry. 1882. Remington Mills of Tolmers Park, Herts.

35. Thomas Wilson's brother in law, Thomas Bateman of Middleton in Youlgrave, Derbyshire married Rebekah Clegg, eldest sister of Elizabeth Clegg. They were the daughters and co heiress to Arthur Clegg of Manchester. Thomas and Rebekah had one daughter, Rebekah who married Samuel Hope of Liverpool. It was one of their daughters, Rebekah Maria Hope whom Samuel Morley married. See: Hodder, E. (1887) The Life of Samuel Morley. London. p.69-70.

36. Hodder, E. (1887) The Life of Samuel Morley. London.

*Egyptian Hall, Mansion House. The Wilson Banquet.*

# 6. John Wilson of Upper Street, Islington and the Lea Wilsons

John Wilson the eldest son of Stephen and Mary Wilson (née Fullalove) of Coventry was born in 1751. His father, Stephen Wilson originally came from Stenson in South Derbyshire where his parents John and Ann Wilson (née Henshaw) owned a small farm that remained in the possession of the Wilsons until the end of the 19th century.[1]

As the second son of John and Ann Wilson Stephen was sent in 1737 to Coventry, where he entered into the Silk industry. By 1754, Stephen had established a successful business in Coventry enabling him to open a branch of the family business in Wood Street, Cheapside, City of London.[2] In the same year, he entered into a partnership with his younger brother Thomas, in which it was agreed that Thomas should remain in Coventry whilst Stephen moved to London.[3] The following year Stephen contracted a fever from which he died. By the terms of his will he left the business to his wife, Mary Wilson (née Fullalove) who then re-negotiated a new partnership with her brother in law, Thomas Wilson. This time Thomas agreed to go to London to supervise the Wood Street branch of the business whilst Mary and her four children, all of whom were under the age of five remained in Coventry.[4]

On reaching the age of 14 or thereabouts John was sent to London where he resided with his uncle, Thomas and his wife, Mary Wilson (née Remington).[5] Later, in 1767, his brother Stephen (1753-1813) joined the family business followed three years later by their cousin, William Wilson, the second son of John and Ann Wilson (née Cocks) of Stenson who went on to establish a silk business at 31 Milk Street.[6] As to John's younger brother Stephen, on completing his apprenticeship in 1774 he then entered into partnership with Daniel West, a wealthy satin manufacturer of Church Street, Spitalfields, and in the time honoured fashion married his partner's eldest daughter, Ann Collett West.[7]

But to return to John Wilson. Although there are very few details about this very quiet and private person we do know that in 1765 at the age of fourteen or thereabouts he was sent by his mother from Coventry to London to be apprenticed in the family business.[8] Even though there is no evidence in the records of the Weavers Company that he was bound an apprentice to his mother and uncle, Thomas Wilson this did not prevent John from being made a partner in 1772 in the business at 121 Wood Street, Cheapside where he remained until his death in 1826. Two years later he married in the February of 1774 Elizabeth Wight, the daughter of William Wight a merchant of the City of London. In an entry in his family Bible, he records that he and his wife lived first at 125 Wood Street, Cheapside where he resided for the next two years before taking up residence in Charles Square, Hoxton.[9] Amongst those resident in the Square was the Revd John Newton who in 1779 had recently been appointed Rector of St Mary Woolnoth in the City of London. This marked the beginning of a close friendship between the two men that was to last until Newton's death in 1808.

In 1787, John Wilson and his large family moved to 8 Highbury Place, not far from where his uncle, Thomas Wilson and his wife, Mary resided. It was here in this grand house that Samuel Wilson, later Lord Mayor Samuel Wilson was born, an event witnessed by Mary Wilson, (née Remington). Five years later John Wilson moved to Upper Street where he remained until his death in 1826.

From 1772 until the death of his mother in 1786 the business remained a co-partnership between Mary Wilson, Thomas Wilson and John Wilson, and then from 1786 until the death of Thomas Wilson in 1794 the business became a co-partnership between Thomas Wilson, John Wilson and Thomas Wilson, junior.[10]

In the meantime Thomas Wilson's younger son, Joseph had joined the family business. However unlike his elder brother, Thomas who became a partner in the business Joseph chose instead to enter into partnership with his uncle, John Remington, one time Lord Mayor of Coventry and Master of the Weavers Company in Coventry.

In 1798, Thomas Wilson retired from the business ostensibly on the grounds of ill health leaving the business as a co-partnership between John Wilson and his eldest son, also called John, until 1814 when they were joined by Josiah, the fifth son of John and Elizabeth Wilson (née Wight).

By this stage, John had effectively retired from the family business leaving it in the hands of his two sons, John and Josiah where it remained until 1840.

During his long and successful career in the silk industry, John Wilson never stood for office in the Weavers Company. Instead, he devoted his life to the family business that had originally been founded by his father, the late Stephen Wilson of Coventry in 1754.

Given the volatile nature of the silk business this was a remarkable achievement.

As a wealthy businessman, John also devoted a great deal of his time and money to a number of philanthropic and religious causes.

In 1795, he was elected a Lay member of the committee and Lay Examiner of Candidates for the mission field of the London Missionary Society. Other family members who served on the committee were his cousins, Thomas and Joseph Wilson, sons of Thomas Wilson senior.[11] Also on the lay committee was Daniel West, Whitefield's trustee and manager of the two tabernacles, a position that John Wilson was to hold after the death of Daniel West in 1796.

In addition to serving on the Lay Committee of the LMS John Wilson also subscribed to the British and Foreign Bible Society. He was also an active member of Whitefield's Tabernacle which he attended whilst serving his apprenticeship with his uncle, Thomas Wilson, senior.

Such was his standing at Whitefield's Tabernacle that on more than one occasion he was invited to serve as a trustee of the two tabernacles: a post that he declined. However, we learn that by the terms of the will of Daniel West he was appointed a trustee and manager of the two tabernacles: a post that he held until his death in 1826.

By the terms of his will John Wilson requested that he should be buried in the family vault in Bunhill Fields, a fitting tribute to a man who in the words of the Revd Matthew Wilks (minister of the two tabernacles) "carried Godliness into all things."[12]

Apart from John and Josiah, who went on to become partners in the family business, the only other two sons of whom there is any information that is of significance are Stephen (1777-1860) and Samuel (1791-1881).

From the few details known about Stephen, he is listed in the records of the Weavers Company as having been apprenticed to Richard Lea of Old Jewry a close friend of John Newton and a supporter of the British and Foreign Bible Society.[13]

Eighteen months before obtaining his freedom Stephen Wilson married Sarah Lea at the Church of St Olave's Old Jewry, the service being conducted by the Revd John Newton.[14] Following the completion of his apprenticeship in 1800 Stephen was made a partner in his father in law's firm. Three years later Stephen Wilson went to France with his cousin, Robert Brooke Wilson where we learn that between 1803 and 1807 they were held prisoners in a French prison. This would account for the reason why he failed to appear before the Court of Weavers on June 28th 1803.

Exactly why Stephen Wilson should have gone to France at a time when England was once more at war with the French is not known. Was it to obtain French silks and patterns or was it to obtain the secrets of the Jacquard apparatus that had been invented by John Marie Jacquard? Whatever the reasons for Stephen being incarcerated in a French Prison for a period of at least four years along with his cousin, Robert Brooke Wilson, they kept that secret to themselves.[15]

Following his return in 1807 the next entry in the Court Records of the Weavers Company relating to Stephen Wilson is for 1811 where he is listed as having been nominated as fit to hold the office of Upper Bailiff, a position he held on two further occasions. We also learn from the records of the Weavers Company that in 1821 he served as Auditor of the Company.

As a successful and innovative businessman, he was an advocate for the repeal of the Spitalfields Act, which he considered a relic of barbarism and an interference with capital and political economy. In his evidence before the Select Committee of the House of Commons, he voiced his objections to the Act on the grounds that because of its rigidity over wages the Act had driven the crepe, bombazine, gauze and handkerchief trade out of Spitalfields.[16]

However, his most important contribution to the silk industry was the introduction of the Jacquard machine into England some time in 1820.

In 1820, Stephen Wilson sent one of his servants, Thomas Smith to France with the instructions of obtaining drawings and if possible, a hook, a paste-board and some patterns and ribbons.[17]

Having obtained the necessary details Stephen Wilson then established a factory in Streatham in which he installed the Jacquard looms.

Even though the Jacquard machine was more advanced than the original draw-loom machine not all weavers took advantage of the new and more efficient invention.[18]

By this stage, Stephen had been joined by his youngest brother Samuel who like himself had also served his apprenticeship under Richard Lea of Old Jewry.

Soon after obtaining his freedom by redemption in 1813, Samuel married Jemima, the ninth child of Richard and Mary Lea a person of great piety who showed great concern throughout her married life over her husband's lack of interest in being a spiritual and domestic helpmeet to her and their only surviving son, Cornelius.

By the time of their marriage in 1813, Samuel was working with his elder brother, Stephen, probably in Old Jewry and then after 1820 in the Streatham firm which his brother had set up to house the Jacquard machine. Whilst working for his brother, Samuel wrote a book of pattern designs for the Jacquard machine of which two leaves were discovered in a Pattern book now in the possession of Vanners Silks, Ltd. Suffolk.[19]

After holding a variety of offices in the Weavers Company including that of Upper Bailiff, Samuel Wilson then went on to hold office in the Corporation of the City of London, much to the anguish of his long suffering wife. In 1831, he stood for office as Alderman for Castle Baynard, then from 1833-4 as Sheriff before being elected as Lord Mayor in 1838.[20]

During his mayoralty, Lord Mayor Samuel Wilson held a banquet in the Egyptian room of Mansion House to which he invited 117 members of the Wilson family; the youngest of whom, Harriet Ann Moore, daughter of Ambrose and Harriet Moore (née Fox) wrote a description of the event in her Family sketch in 1901. In her diary she records that during the mayoralty of Samuel Wilson her father had been 'quite his right hand man, but had no desire to serve as a sheriff.'[21]

At some point during his term of office as Lord Mayor Samuel Wilson was also responsible for the donation of a window in the Church of St Helen's Bishopsgate dedicated to the memory of Martin Bond, Citizen and Haberdasher of the City of London and Commander of the City Trained Bands at Tilbury in 1588. The window depicted St Edmund, St Michael and St Alban.[22]

For many years after his mayoralty he continued to take an active role in the affairs of the Weavers Company and the City of London, standing as Alderman of Bridge Without from 1853 to 1871 and Colonel of the Royal London Militia: a duty that he took very seriously. Unfortunately, his otherwise distinguished career as an Alderman Colonel came to a sad end in 1867 when his troops became caught up in a mob riot in Hyde Park. Following an enquiry by the City Aldermen, he handed over the command of his troops to Colonel Sir William Rose finally retiring at the age of 86 from all Civic duties in 1878 on the grounds of ill health.[23]

By this stage, he had taken up residence in his home The Cedars, Beckenham which he had inherited from his father in law, Richard Lea. There he remained until his death in 1881.[24] A plaque to his memory and that of his wife, Jemima and family was erected in the Church of St George's Beckenham.[25]

*Notes and References:*

1. Wilson, Joshua. (1846) Memoir of Thomas Wilson. London.
2. See: Rothstein, N.K.A. (1961) The Silk Industry in London: 1702-1766. London: unpub MA thesis; where she cites a Stephen Wilson of Aldermanbury: 1755-1793. This is probably a reference to Stephen Wilson of Coventry who established a branch of the family business in Wood Street, Cheapside as a co-partnership with his brother, Thomas Wilson. Although Stephen died in 1755, it is more than probable that the branch continued to remain listed under his name in the London Directory.
3. Wilson, J. (1846) Memoir of Thomas Wilson. London.
4. Wilson, J. (1846) Memoir of Thomas Wilson. London. See also: London Trade Directory, 1760 where Thomas Wilson is listed as being a ribbon weaver of Wood Street, Cheapside. According to the Land Register Rates, 1758-1759 Thomas Wilson is cited as living at St Peter's precinct and then in 1759 at 124 Wood Street Cheapside.
5. Wilson, J. (1846) Memoir of Thomas Wilson. London.
6. See: Bateman, J. (1860) Life of Daniel Wilson. London: John Murray. 2 vols. See also: Suffolk Record Office: Bury St Edmunds branch: HA/530/4/14: Certificate of Redemption: Land Tax Register: 1798. also: HA/530/4/1-9/7/1795: Purchase Deed: John Remington.
7. See: Bateman, J. (1860) Life of Daniel Wilson. London: John Murray. 2 vols.
8. Wilson, J. (1846) Memoir of Thomas Wilson. London.

9. John Wilson's Family Bible. (Privately owned).
10. Wilson, J. (1846) Memoir of Thomas Wilson. London.
11. Wilson, J. (1846) Memoir of Thomas Wilson. London.
12. Morrison, J. (1839) The Fathers and Founders of the London Missionary Society. London: Fisher and Son. 2 vols. *The Memoir of John Wilson* (p.569-582).
13. GUILDHALL LIBRARY: Gld Mss. Court Minute Books: Weavers Company Apprentice Binding Book: 4657/B54/5/vol.2.1765-1865: in which Stephen Wilson is listed as being apprenticed to Richard Lea of Old Jewry 2nd Aug 1791. He is not to be confused with his uncle, Stephen Wilson of Church Street, Spitalfields, father of Daniel Wilson and writer of the Private Calendar, 1795-1802.
14. Wilson, Stephen. Private Calendar. 1795-1802 in which Stephen Wilson of Church Street, records that the Revd John Newton officiated at the marriage of Stephen Wilson and Sarah Lea, daughter of Richard Lea of Old Jewry and later of Beckenham. In his book on the life of Newton, Richard Cecil records that Richard Lea used to convey Newton from his residence in Charles Square, Hoxton to St Mary Woolnoth in his personal carriage.

   As a close friend of John Wilson and his brother Stephen, we learn from the diary of Stephen Wilson that John Newton also officiated at the marriage of Ann Wilson (eldest daughter of Stephen and Ann Collett Wilson) and William Bateman, grandson of Hester Bateman, Queen of 18th century English silversmiths. The Batemans were also related to William Bull, a close friend of Newton and Cowper.
15. Wilson, H.A. (1901) A Family Sketch: (Privately owned) in which she records that both Stephen Wilson and Robert Brooke Wilson had been prisoners in the Bastille. See also: P.P. (House of Commons) Select Committee on the silk trade: 1818, in which Stephen Wilson states that he had been held a prisoner in the Bastille.
16. H.L. 1820-1821: House of Lords Report on Foreign Trade: 2nd report relative to silk and the wine trade. (vi) in which he states that he was an advocate for the repeal of the Spitalfields Acts.
17. Letter from Thomas Smith to Stephen Wilson of Lea, Wilson and Co, 26 Old Jewry, London: 3 Aug 1820 in Royal Society of Arts. vol. cvii, no. 5041: 1950-1960.
18. Rothstein, N.K.A. (1977) The Introduction of the Jacquard Loom to Great Britain, in, Studies in Textile History: in memory of Harold B. Burnham. ed by Veronika Gervers. Ontario: Royal Ontario Museum.
19. See Rothstein, NKA. Silk Designs of the 18th century. London: Thames and Hudson.
20. Plummer, A. (1972) The London Weavers Company: 1600-1970. London: Routledge, Kegan and Paul.
21. Wilson, J. (1846) Memoir of Thomas Wilson. London. See also: Wilson, H.A. (1901) Family Sketch. (Privately owned) in which Harriet Wilson (née Moore) provides a more detailed account of the event than that provided by Joshua Wilson in his memoir of his father, Thomas Wilson junior. See also: Plummer, A. (1972) The London Weavers Company: 1600-1970. London: Routledge Kegan and Paul.
22. The window was damaged in the late 1960s and replaced with plain glass. For a description of the window: see: The 1961 edition of A short guide to St Helen

Bishopsgate by John S.C. Miller and Gordon H. Jones.
23. Plummer, A. (1972) The London Weavers Company: 1600-1970. London: Rout-ledge, Kegan and Paul. See also: Arnold, Matthew. 1978. Culture and Anarchy. Edited by J. Dover Wilson. Cambridge: Cambridge University Press in which Arnold refers to an incident in 1867 in which Colonel Alderman Samuel Wilson whilst parading with his militia in Hyde Park became embroiled with a group of rioters. In his edition of Arnold's Culture and Anarchy John Dover Wilson comes to the defence of Samuel Wilson.
24. According to the 1851 census Samuel Wilson is recorded as living at 3 Sussex Square, Brighton with his wife, Jemima, his sister in law, Amelia Wilson (née Collins (aged 50) the wife of his brother, Josiah, their servants and a cousin, Ernest Francis Wilson (aged 17) who is described as a scholar. He was the son of the Revd William and Mary Wilson (née Garratt) Vicar of Walthamstow. After the death of Jemima in 1865, Samuel moved to his Beckenham residence, The Cedars that he inherited from his father in law, Richard Lea.
25. See: Borrowman, R. (1910) Beckenham Past and Present. Beckenham.
See also: Notley, Rachel, Lendon. (1985) A Historical Guide to St George's Parish Church Beckenham: written to mark the centenary 1885-1985. Beckenham: Beckenham Parish Church.

# 7. Stephen and Ann Collett Wilson of Church Street, Spitalfields

Stephen Wilson[II] who was born in 1753 in Coventry was sent to London to live with his uncle, Thomas Wilson [I] and his wife, Mary Wilson (née Remington), of Wood Street, Cheapside in 1767.[1]

He was the younger son of the late Stephen Wilson [I] and Mary Wilson (née Fullalove), silk manufacturers of Coventry and Wood Street, Cheapside, and a member of a family that came from Stenson, a small hamlet in the parish of Barrow cum Twyford, South Derbyshire where the Wilsons owned a small farm.[2]

Little is known about Stephen Wilson [I] apart from the fact that he was the second son of John and Ann Wilson (née Henshaw) of Stenson. As the first member of the Wilson family to enter the silk trade Stephen was married to a Mary Fullalove, member of a family of silk weavers in Coventry that were connected by marriage to the Remingtons and the Whitewells thus putting them amongst the ruling families in Coventry. By marrying Mary Fullalove it is clear that Stephen married well, leading to useful family and business connections within the principal families of Coventry. Thus we find that his brother Thomas, married Mary Remington whilst Stephen and Mary's eldest daughter Elizabeth, married William Freeman and Ann married Thomas Oldham. And then there was Stephen's son, also called Stephen, whose sister in law, Catherine West, youngest daughter of Daniel and Ann West, (née Brooke) married William Whitewell, son of Alderman John Whitewell of Coventry.[3]

All this however was in the future. As a prosperous and farsighted businessman, Stephen established in 1754 a branch of the family business in London. In the same year, he invited his younger brother Thomas, who had recently married Mary Remington, the only daughter of John Remington of Coventry to be a partner.[4] The agreement was that Thomas and his wife were to remain in Coventry whilst Stephen was to manage the London branch of the business.[5] In 1755, almost one year after opening the branch Stephen died from a fever leaving his widow, Mary, to manage both branches of the business and bring up four children, all of whom were under the age of five. These were: John (1751-1826), Elizabeth (n.d.), Ann (n.d.) and Stephen (1753-1813). (See Tables 2 & 4)

Two months after her husband's death Mary re-negotiated the terms of the partnership with her brother in law, Thomas Wilson [I] in which it was agreed that she should remain in Coventry whilst Thomas should supervise the London branch of the business.[6] It was to this branch of the family business that future generations of Wilsons were sent to receive their training in the silk trade before making their way in the world of commerce. The first two members of the Wilson family to follow in their late father's footsteps were his two sons, John (1751-1821) and Stephen (1753-1813). Following the completion of their apprenticeship John became a partner in the family business with his mother, Mary Wilson, and his uncle, Thomas Wilson.[7]

In 1774, Stephen entered into partnership with Daniel West, a wealthy and well-established silk manufacturer of Church Street, Spitalfields and Upper Bailiff of the Weavers Company.[8]

Soon after becoming a partner, Stephen Wilson married Ann Collett West, the eldest daughter of Daniel and Ann West (née Brooke).[9]

Exactly where Stephen Wilson met Ann Collett West is not known but it is more than probable that it was at Whitefield's Tabernacle Moorefields, where her father was one of the Trustees that they were first introduced. Apprenticed to his uncle Thomas Wilson [I], Stephen would have attended services at the Tabernacle where at this stage Matthew Wilks was the minister.

By marrying Ann Collett West, the eldest daughter of Daniel and Ann West (née Brooke) Stephen was marrying into a family that had prestigious links not only in the Weavers Company but also in the East India Company, a point totally overlooked or ignored by Josiah Bateman, son in law to Daniel Wilson.[10]

Ann Collett Wilson's father, Daniel West was a member of a family of silk weavers whilst her mother, Ann West (née Brooke) came from a family of maritime Captains and merchants in the East India Company. She was the eldest daughter of Robert and Elizabeth Brooke (née Collett) and is cited in the will of her father, Captain Robert Brooke as being married to Daniel West.[11]

The Colletts and the Brookes had a long history of serving as maritime Captains in the services of the East India Company. In the will of his father in law, Thomas Collett (d.1743), Robert Brooke is listed as being a mariner of Goodmanfields, Whitechapel, which at this time was a desirable and popular residence for merchants and captains in the East India Company.[12] Thomas Collett had been a Captain in the maritime services of the East India Company whilst his brother, Jonathan Collett had been a ship builder and part owner of the Blackwall docks used by the East India Company.[13] Robert married Elizabeth Collett, the second daughter of Thomas and Isabella Collett.

Robert and Elizabeth Brooke (née Collett) had five children: Ann (1722), Elizabeth (1725), Robert (1727), Thomas (1731) and Jonathan (1733) The only children to survive to adulthood were Ann, Elizabeth and Robert.

From the will of Robert Brooke senior, we learn that Ann married Daniel West. They had seven children of whom four survived to adulthood. These were Ann Collett who married Stephen Wilson, Elizabeth, who married William Wilson, (first cousin to Stephen Wilson) and Charlotte who remained unmarried whilst Catherine their youngest daughter, married William Whitewell, a merchant of Coventry.[14]

Of Robert and Elizabeth's other children, Elizabeth married Thomas Pattle, the eldest son of Edward and Ruth Pattle (née Casson). They had three children of whom only Ruth and Thomas survived to adulthood. Ruth married her uncle, Robert Brooke, the only surviving son of Robert and Elizabeth Brooke (née Pattle) whilst Thomas (1748-1818) married Sarah Hasleby.[15]

In his Private Calendar, Stephen Wilson mentions that in 1795 Thomas Pattle returned to India having been recalled by the East India Company to take up the post of Senior Judge in the Court of Appeal in the district of Murshidabad. Then sometime after 1802 he was transferred to the judgeship of the district of Cawnpore. In 1810, he retired from this post and returned to England. After the death of his wife, Sarah in 1812 or thereabouts he married Suzanne Wilson by whom he had a daughter.

Thomas and Sarah Pattle (née Hasleby) were the parents of James Pattle who had married Adeline De L'etang, second daughter of the Chevalier de L'etang and his wife, Therese Josephe Blin de Grincourt.[16] James and Adeline were the parents of seven beautiful daughters of whom Julia Margaret Cameron (née Pattle), the photographer and great aunt of Vanessa and Virginia Stephen is probably the most famous.[17]

Turning to Ruth Casson Pattle, the only surviving daughter of Thomas and Elizabeth Pattle (née Brooke), as we have already noted she married her uncle, Robert Brooke, by whom she had a son, Thomas Brooke, referred to in the Private Calendar of Stephen Wilson as Cousin Thomas Brooke of Calcutta. He was the father of James Brooke, 1st White Rajah of Sarawak.[18]

From the Private Calendar of Stephen Wilson we learn that his wife Ann Collett Wilson (née West) was a regular visitor to the home of Aunt Brooke, the mother of Thomas Brooke of Calcutta. We also learn that Ann Collett Wilson (née West) regularly corresponded with her cousin, Thomas Brooke of Calcutta, the only son of Robert and Ruth Casson Brooke (née Pattle).[19]

Aunt Brooke (Mrs Ruth Brooke) lived in Mortlake with her three Anglo-Indian grandchildren, Charles William, Sophia and Julia. They were the children of Thomas Brooke by his Indian Companion or Bibi.[20] As was the custom with the children of Anglo Indian families the three children had been sent to England for their education. From an entry in his Private Calendar Stephen Wilson records that Sophia and Julia attended the private school of Miss Jones in Stepney Green along with their cousins, the younger daughters of Stephen and Ann Collett Wilson (née West).[21]

In 1801, both Charles William and his sister Sophia returned to India where Charles entered the Bengal Native Army as a cadet. He eventually rose to the rank of Brevet Colonel but died in battle in 1836. To what extent his advancement in the Indian Army was due to his father's position is a moot point, but Charles William Brooke and his son, James Cheape Brooke are good examples of Anglo-Indians who were not socially ostracised.[22] Likewise his sister, Sophia who married David Morrieson a Writer in the East India Company did not suffer the risk of social isolation. As to Julia, it is probable that she remained in England with her grandmother.[23]

In the meantime their father, Thomas Brooke had in 1793 married Anna Maria Stuart, by whom he had eight children of whom only four survived to adulthood.[24] The eldest, Harriet Grace, was unmarried at the time of her father's death in 1835. Of the other three, Emma who married the Revd Charles Francis Johnson, provided Sarawak with the next generation of White Rajahs. James, who was his only surviving son, went on to become the first White Rajah of Sarawak. Before his death in 1868 James Brooke appointed his nephew, Charles Anthoni, the second son of Emma and the Revd Charles Francis Johnson, as the second Rajah of Sarawak, much to the anger of his sister, Emma.

Thomas and Anna Maria's last surviving daughter Margaret, married the Revd Anthony Savage, minister of a church in Brighton. During his life, James regularly corresponded with his sister Margaret, particularly over the mission that he had helped establish in Sarawak under the auspices of the Borneo Church Mission Institute in 1848.[25]

From this brief summary, we are able to see that Ann Collett West was a member of a family that had made and continued to make their mark in India. Amongst these was her son, Daniel Wilson, who went on to become the 5th Bishop of Calcutta, a post that he held from 1832 until his death in 1858.[26]

For the first twenty-five years of their marriage Stephen and Ann Collett Wilson lived at 6/7 Church Street, Spitalfields, one of the most imposing houses in the area. This was one of those grand roomy houses in a highly desirable and fashionable part of Spitalfields, popular with the Merchants and Masters. That they were able to afford to live in such a splendid house indicates that they were persons of substance.

As we have already noted before his marriage in 1774 to Ann Collett West Stephen had entered into partnership with her father, Daniel West, but in 1793 or thereabouts the partnership ended. By this stage, Daniel West had moved to Southampton Row where he lived with his daughter Charlotte until his death in 1796. In the meantime, we learn that in 1793 Stephen had entered into partnership for a short period of time with Harvey, Perigal and Ham of Spital Square, Spitalfields.[27] Thereafter Stephen seems to have acted as a merchant supplying raw and organzine silk for other manufacturers including his cousin William Wilson of Goldsmith Street, then of Milk Street, Cheapside. As a merchant Stephen would have been a frequent visitor to the warehouses of the

East India Company where the raw and organzine silk from India was stored. At this stage, the warehouses were in the East India Docks in Blackwall but later in 1806, new warehouses were built in Fenchurch Street.[28]

In addition to being a Freeman of the Weavers Company, we also learn from his private calendar that Stephen also served on the Court of the Company of Weavers as a member of the Livery and as an auditor. He is also listed as being a member of a committee responsible for the fixing of prices for silk and satin and a member of a Committee for poor weavers in Spitalfields.[29]

According to an entry in his private calendar, we also learn that he served as auditor to the Fishmongers Company to which he had been elected as a Freeman along with John Remington in 1793.[30]

In addition to his London business activities Stephen made regular trips to Coventry where he and his brother John, had property in the Foleshill district, the Coventry Canal Company and the Nuneaton Coal mines where he had shares.

From 1795 until his death in 1813, Stephen Wilson is listed as being a silk manufacturer of 6 Church Street, Spitalfields, and then at 12 Goldsmith Street Cheapside. After his death in 1813, the business passed into the hands of his sons, Robert Brooke Wilson, Stephen and Thomas Wilson where it remained until 1829.[31]

As we have had occasion to note, for the first twenty years of their married life Stephen and Ann lived at 6 Church Street, which they shared with Ann's parents and her younger sisters.[32] It was here in this grand house that Ann and Stephen's nine children were born: Mary (1775-1790), Ann (1776-1842), Daniel (1778-1858), Robert Brooke (1779-1829), Ruth (1782-1844), Elizabeth (1784-c.1858/9), Stephen (1787-1826), Thomas (1790-1826) and George (1793-1846) (See Table 7).

Apart from Mary who was baptized by the Revd William Romaine at Christ Church, Spitalfields, the remaining eight children were baptized by the Revd Samuel Brewer at Stepney Green Independent Chapel.[33]

As was the convention with families of their status Stephen and Ann's daughters along with their two Anglo-Indian cousins, Sophia and Julia, attended a private school in Stepney Green managed by a Miss Jones. Here they would have received an education appropriate to their social status enabling them to take their place in society as well educated young ladies.[34] As to their sons they were sent to Mr Searle's school in Eltham returning only for the holidays and the occasional weekend. Whereas their daughters remained at home until they married, their sons on reaching the age of fourteen or thereabouts were expected to follow in the family footsteps and serve an apprenticeship in the silk trade. Apart from George, the youngest of their sons, only Daniel, Robert Brooke, Stephen and Thomas are listed as being engaged in the silk trade. But whereas the latter three sons remained in the business, by contrast in 1798 Daniel was released from his indentures in order for him to train for the Anglican ministry. Contrary to what Bateman states there is in fact no evidence that Stephen showed any opposition to his son's decision when the subject was first raised by the Revd John Eyre in the October of 1797. All that Stephen urged was that his son should shelve the matter for the moment. Any suggestion that his father had closed his mind on the matter is incorrect. In fact, as the Private Calendar of Stephen Wilson makes quite clear we find that when Stephen raised the matter with his son in the March of 1798 Stephen actually went out of his way to support his son in his calling to the Church.[35]

To what extent Ann Collett acted as a mollifying force is not clear but there is very clear evidence that Daniel was very close to his mother and had in fact written to her expressing his desire to enter the ministry. There is no doubting the fact that she was a remarkable person in whom her children were able to confide knowing that she would act in their best interest.

Yet, at the same time it is clear that she could be very forthright and firm even to the extent of ensuring that on decisions of importance they spoke to their father. In the case of Daniel, it is more than probable that by the time that Daniel's father had raised the subject with him on that Wednesday afternoon (March 17th 1798) his mother had already prepared the ground, thereby ensuring that any decision her husband reached was in the best interest of her son and one to which she was able to give her support.

In so doing it could be said that she never lost sight of the importance of her role: a role that she probably learnt early in life when, following the death of her mother sometime after 1775 Ann Collett would have been left to care not only for her children, but also for her younger sisters until such times as they married.

From the few details that we have about her, she was a warm and affectionate person who showed great concern over her children's spiritual and moral welfare even to a wayward son. In addition to her role as a mother, she was a regular visitor to the homes of her relatives, including Aunt Brooke. She also took her duties of visiting the sick very seriously. Above all, she was regular in attending the prayer meetings and missionary meetings at the Tabernacle accompanied by her daughters.

Of Ann and Stephen's children, Mary who was the eldest died soon after her fifteenth birthday and was buried in the family crypt at Christ Church, Spitalfields.[36] The next eldest daughter, Ann, married William Bateman, the grandson of Hester Bateman, considered to be the Queen of English Silversmiths.[37] They were the parents of Josiah, later Chaplain to Daniel Wilson. Whilst in India Josiah married Eliza Emma, the only surviving daughter of Daniel Wilson.[38]

As to Stephen and Ann's other children, Robert Brooke Wilson who had entered into partnership with his father and younger brothers, Stephen and Thomas died five months after his mother in 1829 from a stroke. He never married. His two brothers, Stephen and Thomas had died three years earlier in 1826. According to the Private Calendar of Stephen Wilson, there is an entry which records that Thomas died from a stroke or apoplexy.

Ruth, their third daughter, married a Major Blundell and lived in France where she died in 1844 from a throat infection, probably diphtheria.[39]

George, the youngest member of the family was the only son not to have been engaged in the silk trade. Instead, he became a stationer and publisher in Fleet Street. He died of a stroke in 1846. He had married a Harriet Wilson by whom he had three children: Christopher, Eleanor, who married the Revd Professor Hart, and Margaret who married the Revd Professor Drew.

Daniel and Elizabeth were the last surviving children of Ann and Stephen Wilson. From letters written by Daniel to his sister Elizabeth whilst he was in India it seems that she had married a Percival White who died some time in 1851. Exactly how or when the private calendar written by her father Stephen Wilson [II] came into her possession is not known but it is clear that the source of the early information of Stephen and Ann's family was written by Elizabeth who signs herself as E.W. According to Elizabeth, the register was taken from a family Bible by her brother George and was in the handwriting of her dear father. (E.W. June 30 1831.)

However, it is clear that Elizabeth has added the additional details after the death of her younger brother, George. Elizabeth also wrote the inscription in the prayer book given by her mother to Daniel Wilson junior on his ordination.[40]

In the private calendar Elizabeth writes: "My dear mother, Ann Collett Wilson died at her son, Daniel's House in Barnsbury Court, Islington, June 3 1829, aged 79 years and three months of apoplexy."

She also records that "my dear father, Stephen Wilson died in New Ormond Street, December 7 1813, aged 60 years and one month of asthma."

As a wealthy and prosperous businessman Stephen gave generously to a number of charitable and religious societies: not only in terms of financial giving but also in terms of his time. From his private calendar, we learn that he was on the Board of the Charity school in Wood Street, Spitalfields, and a member of the Committee along with Richard Lea of St Anne's School, Peckham. We also learn that he served on the Vestry Committee of Christ Church Spitalfields, and on the committee for the poor sick weavers of Spitalfields. In addition to all this, he is listed as being on the committee for fixing prices for journeymen weavers in the Weavers Company and of the SPCK.[41] In many of these engagements, his wife and children supported him.

Commenting on his grandparents Bateman says that Stephen was a gentleman, a true Christian, a kind father and a good master: whilst of Ann Collett he says that in early life she had chosen the better part and subsequently became an exemplary wife and an affectionate mother.[42]

*Notes and References:*

1.  Stephen Wilson of Church Street, Spitalfields is not to be confused with his nephew, Stephen Wilson of Lea and Wilson who introduced into England the Jacquard machine. See: Rothstein, NKA. (1990) Silk designs of the 18th century in the Collection of the Victoria and Albert Museum. London: Thames and Hudson.

2.  See: Wilson, J. (1846) The Memoir of Thomas Wilson. London. This is the source of the early history of the Wilson of Wilson. The Wilsons of Stenson are not to be confused with John and Mary Wilson, (née Bucknell) of Derby from who Ronald Binge the jazz musician was descended.

3.  See: Wilson, J. (1846) The Memoir of Thomas Wilson. London. See also: Hinman. M.J. Men who Rule Coventry 1725-1780. Coventry: Coventry and Warwickshire Historical Society. Pamphlet no. 14. Amongst these were the Remingtons, Freemans, Whitewells and Oldhams. See also: App. A. Table 4 and App. B, Table 6.

4.  John Remington senior, father of Mary Remington, was a Master of the Coventry Weavers Company and an Alderman of the city. His son, also called John Remington, was Mayor of the city and a member of the Weavers Company. He moved to London where he purchased property in Milk Street which he then left to his two nephews, Thomas and Joseph Wilson, sons of Thomas and Mary Wilson, née Remington. See: PCC/Prob/11/1543/1813. See also: Harrison, M.J. Patrons and Church Builders: The Wilsons of Highbury and Islington. Paper given at a seminar: September 2005 to the Friends of the Union Chapel and the Victorian Society. (to be published in 2008.). See also: Wilson, J. (1846) Memoir of Thomas Wilson. London.

5.  Wilson, J. (1846) Memoir of Thomas Wilson. London. See also: Rothstein, N.K.A. (1960) The Silk Industry in London: 1702-1793. London University: unpub. MA thesis in which she refers to a Stephen Wilson of Aldermanbury, Cheapside: (1753-1793) Although Stephen Wilson died in 1755 it appears that his name was still listed in the trade directories as late as 1793. See also: Compleat Pocket Companion: 1741-1760: in which Stephen and Thomas Wilson are listed as being Silk Weavers.

6.  Wilson, J. (1846) Memoir of Thomas Wilson. London.

7.  Wilson, J. (1946) Memoir of Thomas Wilson. London.

8.  See: Bateman, J. (1860) Life of Daniel Wilson. London. John Murray. 2 vols.

9.  Bateman, J. (1860) Life of Daniel Wilson. London: John Murray. 2 vols. See also: Harrison, M.J. Daniel West: Whitefield's Forgotten Trustee. JURCHS. June 2006.

10. To what extent Bateman chose either to ignore or deliberately omitted Wilson's Anglo-Indian connections on his mother's side is a moot point: nonetheless to the

Victorians such a relationship was something not to be mentioned. See for example: James, Lawrence. (1997) Raj: the Making and Unmaking of British India. London: Little Brown & Co. See also: Olsen, V. (2003) From Life: Julia Margaret Cameron & Victorian Photography. London: Aurum Press.

11. On Daniel West: See Harrison, M.J. Daniel West: Whitefield's Forgotten Trustee. JURCHS. June 2006.

12. Thomas Collett: PCC/Prob/11/726/1743.

13. See: Hobhouse, H. ed., Survey of London: vol xliv. Poplar, Blackwall and the Isle Of Dogs: the Parish of All Hallows. London: The Athlone Press, 1949. See also: Farrington, A. (2002) Trading Places: the East India Company and Asia 1600-1834. London: The British Library.

14. See: Harrison, M.J. Daniel West: Whitefield's Forgotten Trustee. JURCHS. June, 2006.

15. British Library: OIOC: Biographical File: m Sarah Hasleby 10 June 1770 Cossimbazar, India. N/1/2/f.175.

16. In addition to James, Thomas and Sarah had eight other children of whom only Thomas Charles, Sophie, Sarah and William survived to adulthood.

17. On James Pattle and his daughters: See: Hill, Brian. (1973) Julia Margaret Cameron: a Victorian Family Portrait. London: Peter Owen. also: Boyd, Elizabeth French. (1976) Bloomsbury Heritage: Their Mothers and Their Aunts. London: Hamish Hamilton. See also: Olsen, Victoria. (2003) From Life: Julia Margaret Cameron and Victorian Photography. London: Aurum Press.

18. In addition to their son James, who went on after his father's death to become the 1st White Rajah of Sarawak, Thomas and Anna Maria Brooke (née Stuart) had 7 other children of whom apart from James the only others who survived their father were Emma who married the Revd F. C. Johnson and Margaret who married the Revd A. Savage by whom she had one daughter.

19. Stephen Wilson: 1795-1802: Private Calendar: (privately owned) in which Stephen refers to the correspondence between his wife and her cousin, Thomas Brooke of Calcutta.

20. See: Dalrymple, W. (2001) The White Mughals. London: Flamingo, in which he points out that in the second half of the eighteenth century the majority of Company servants, took a Bibi or Companion. See: Thomas Brooke: PCC/Prob/11/1854/1835: in which he leaves £1,000 to be paid by his son, Charles William Brooke, to the Mohar Bibi of Arah in Bihar. See: Brooke, Gilbert. (1911) The Brookes of Horton in the Cotswolds. Singapore: Methodist Publishing House who incorrectly states that Charles William Brooke was descended from the Brookes of Cavan. Charles William Brooke was the son of Thomas Brooke, by his Bibi. In his will Thomas Brooke also left £1,000 to his daughter, Sarah Morrieson (née Brooke) She was the eldest daughter of Thomas Brooke by his Companion or Bibi. In his Will Thomas Brooke makes no mention of Julia which would indicate that by the time of his death she had died: probably about the same time as her grandmother, Ruth Brooke (née Casson Pattle).

21. Stephen Wilson: 1795-1802: Private Calendar, in which he records that they attended Miss Jones' Private School in Stepney Green (Mile End Green), a small

hamlet in the Parish of St Dunstan's Stepney, a popular residential area for merchants and maritime Captains. It is probable that during term time Sophia and Julia Brooke resided either with their aunt, Ann Collett Wilson or at the School with Ann Collett Wilson's daughters.

22. See: Olsen, Victoria. (2003) From Life: Julia Margaret Cameron and Victorian Photography. London: Aurum Press on the attitudes of Victorians to people of mixed blood. See also Isabella Fane. (1985) Miss Fane in India. Gloucester: Alan Sutton: also the letters of Emily Metcalfe and Emily Eden neither of whom shared the same prejudices as those in England when it came to socializing with people of mixed parentage.

23. According to the Private Calendar of Stephen Wilson both Charles William Brooke and his sister Sophia, returned to India On the question of changing attitudes towards children of Anglo-Indian parentage see: Olsen, Victoria. (2003) From Life: Julia Margaret Cameron and Victorian Photography. London: Aurum Press: see also: James, L. (1997) Raj: the Making and Unmaking of British India. London: Little Brown & Co. Neither Charles William Brooke or his sister, Sophia or, for that matter, their cousins the Pattle sisters were affected by changing attitudes either in India or in England. All of them married well and in the case of Charles Brooke he rose to a rank of distinction in the Bengal Native Army. It is probable that Julia died sometime before 1836 there being no mention of her in the Will of Thomas Brooke.

24. See: Barley, N. (2003) White Rajah: a Biography of Sir James Brooke. London: Abacus. He is incorrect when he states that Anna Maria Stuart was herself almost certainly illegitimate. In fact, she was the daughter of Colonel the Hon, William Stuart. On his death she was adopted by her uncle, Lt Col. James Stuart. Likewise, Barley is incorrect in stating that Margaret Savage (née Brooke) died without issue. She had one daughter.

25. On the Borneo Mission in Sarawak see: Runciman, S. (1960) The White Rajahs. Cambridge.

26. It is significant that Bateman makes no mention of the fact that Daniel Wilson was through his mother a member of a family that had an Anglo Indian ancestry. On Daniel Wilson and his love of India see: Harrison, M.J. From Spitalfields to Calcutta: Daniel Wilson's Love of India. Indian Church History Review June 2006.

27. See: Rothstein, N.K.A. (1990) Silk Designs of the 18th century in the Collection of the Victoria and Albert Museum. London: Thames and Hudson.

28. Stephen Wilson: Private Calendar. 1795-1802. (Privately owned). On the East India Company docks and warehouses: see: Farrington, A. (2002) Trading Places: the East India Company and Asia: 1600-1834. London: British Library.

29. Stephen Wilson: Private Calendar. 1795-1802. (Privately owned). See also: Tower Hamlets Local History Library: Christ Church Vestry Minutes.

30. Stephen Wilson: Private Calendar, 1795-1802. (Privately owned)

31. See: GUILDHALL LIBRARY: Gld Mss. Court Minute Books. Weavers Company: 4655/19/1798-1825. Stephen and Thomas Wilson were made free by redemption

on 5th Nov 1816. By this time, they were in partnership with their eldest brother, Robert Brooke Wilson.

32. This was a house they shared with Daniel West, until 1793. See, Bateman, J. (1860) Life of Daniel Wilson. London: John Murray.

33. Stephen Wilson: Private Calendar: 1795-1802. See also Bateman, J. (1860) ibid in which he described Daniel Wilson's parents as being a kind of loose church people attending in the morning Mr Romaine and in the evening the Tabernacle. It is significant to note that Bateman makes no mention of the fact that apart from Mary Wilson, the Revd Mr Samuel Brewer of Stepney Green Independent Chapel baptized all of their remaining children. Samuel Brewer was one of the few Independent Ministers to support George Whitefield.

34. Although Spitalfields was quintessentially a French-speaking enclave, it is more than probable that Stephen and Ann Collett Wilson's children were conversant in French as indicated by the fact that after her marriage Ruth lived in Paris. Daniel's letters to his sister, Elizabeth, contain numerous lengthy quotes in French. We also learn that Robert Brooke Wilson went to France with his cousin, Stephen Wilson. This was essentially a well-educated and cultured family.

35. Stephen Wilson: Private Calendar: 1795-1802. Contrary to what Bateman and others following him state there is no evidence from the private calendar of Stephen Wilson to indicate that Daniel's father initially disapproved of his decision to enter the Church.

36. Stephen Wilson: Private Calendar: 1795-1802. (Privately owned)

37. On Hester Bateman see: Lever, Christopher. (1975) Goldsmiths and Silversmiths of London. London: Hutchinson. See also: Shure, David. (1959) Hester Bateman, Queen of English Silversmiths. London: W.H. Allen. The Batemans of Bunhill Fields are not to be confused with the Batemans of Middleton by Youlgrave in Derbyshire. They are two quite distinct and unrelated families. See also: Harrison, M.J. The Wilsons of Derbyshire: a note: JURCHS, Jan. 2008.

38. Bateman, J. (1860) Life of Daniel Wilson. London: John Murray. 2 vols.

39. There is a reference to Ruth Blundell (née Wilson), in the Family Sketch written by Harriet Ann Wilson (née Moore) (Privately owned) in which she is listed as living in Paris with her children.

40. Stephen Wilson: Private Calendar: 1795-1802. (Privately owned) The Prayer Book given to Daniel Wilson junior is in the archives of St Mary Islington.

41. Stephen Wilson: Private Calendar: 1795-1802. (Privately owned)

42. Bateman, J. (1860) Life of Daniel Wilson. London: John Murray. 2 vols.

# 8. William Wilson (1756-1821) of Milk Street and The Wortons: Oxfordshire

Family tradition has it that William Wilson, the second son of John and Ann Wilson (née Cocks) of Stenson, Derbyshire, accompanied by a friend walked from Derbyshire to London arriving barefooted and with only a few shillings in their pocket with the aim of making their fortune.[1]

This is the stuff of a family history and one not restricted to the Wilsons of Stenson, Derbyshire.[2]

Fascinating though this story about William Wilson might be there is in fact no foundation to this account.

Born in 1756 William Wilson came from a relatively prosperous family that did not expect their children to walk any distance let alone walk to London in search of a job. After all this was a family that had links in London that went back to 1754 when his uncle, Stephen Wilson, set up a branch of the family silk business in Wood Street, Cheapside to which the younger members of the family were sent.[3]

By the time that William entered the business in 1770 where he served his apprenticeship it was a co-partnership between Mary Wilson (née Fullalove), Thomas Wilson senior and John Wilson.[4]

During his time as an apprentice, William's father paid for his apparel, board and lodgings and laundry as well as any tools that were required. From a letter written by William to his eldest sister, Ann, we learn that she made his shirts.[5]

Although there is no reference in the records of the Weavers Company to his being apprenticed to his aunt, Mary Wilson (née Fullalove) and her brother in law, Thomas Wilson, it is more than likely that he fulfilled the requirements laid down by the company enabling him to obtain in 1778 his freedom by redemption for the sum of £5.[6] This enabled him to play an active role in the Weavers Company and enjoy the privileges that came with it including being able to stand for office both in the Company and in the City and train apprenticeships.[7]

In the same year that he obtained his freedom, William was elected to the Court of the Company of Weavers enabling him to take up his livery.[8] The following year he married Elizabeth West, the second daughter of Daniel and Ann West (née Brooke).[9] Elizabeth's sister, Ann Collett West had married Stephen Wilson, first cousin to William and a partner with her father, Daniel West of Church Street Spitalfields.

By marrying Elizabeth West, he married into a family that enjoyed a very comfortable and prosperous lifestyle. Her father, Daniel West, was a wealthy

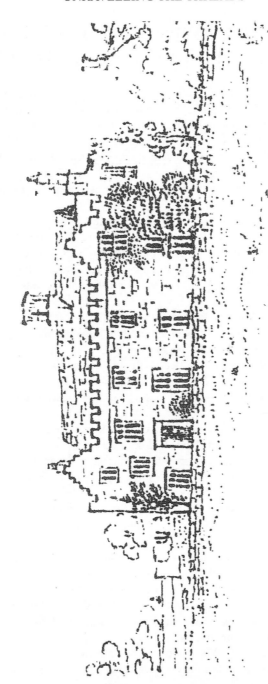

*Manor House, Nether Worton, Oxfordshire. Drawn by Harriet Ann Wilson, 1845. (Privately owned)*

silk manufacturer who had in 1774 been elected Upper Bailiff of the Weavers Company: a post normally restricted to the economic and socially elite in the Company.[10]

Her mother, Ann West, (née Brooke) was the eldest of three daughters of Robert Brooke, a maritime Captain in the EIC and his wife, Elizabeth Brooke (née Collett), the second daughter of Thomas and Isabella Collett.[11] It was from Robert and Elizabeth Brooke (née Collett) that the Brookes of Sarawak, Daniel Wilson, 5th Bishop of Calcutta, and the seven beautiful Pattle sisters were descended.[12]

For the first eleven years of their marriage, William and Elizabeth lived in Goldsmith Street, Cheapside, but in 1790, William Wilson and his family moved to 31 Milk Street, Cheapside, which he rented from Thomas Flight and then in 1791 from John Remington.[13]

The premises in Milk Street consisted of a warehouse and counting house on the ground floor. On the first floor was the dining room, breakfast room and kitchens, whilst on the second floor was the Drawing room and the principal bedrooms. Above these were the garret rooms.[14] As a successful; businessman he is said to have employed 500 people of all ages, many of whom were probably engaged in the production of broad loom silk. That he was able to employ such a large working force in his premises was made possible by the fact that his looms were driven by waterpower.[15] In addition to this he would have farmed out a great deal of his work to journeymen weavers in other parts of the City including Spitalfields.

By this stage, William and Elizabeth had four children, Ann (1785-1827), Joseph (1786-1855), Selina (1788-1863) and Charlotte. Other children soon followed William (1791), Sophia (1792), and Eliza (1793).[16]

Life within William's household which by 1795 consisted of 7 children, servants and apprentices was highly regimented: a practice that he learnt from his uncle and aunt, Thomas and Mary Wilson (née Remington), and one that remained with him through out his life.[17]

Each day began and concluded with Family Prayers led either by William or by a member of the family to which the whole household including servants were expected to attend. Commenting on the family prayers Daniel Wilson is recorded as saying that he lived entirely without prayer on the grounds that they rose no further than the ceiling. Later, in a letter to Francis Thomas McDougal he commented on the fact that what he objected to as a young person was the use of written prayers, which as far as he was concerned left his soul quite impoverished.[18]

Within five years of William and Elizabeth moving to Milk Street Elizabeth died as a result of a miscarriage.[19] Following her death on Thursday, 27th February, 1795 his three eldest daughters, Ann, Selina and Charlotte, along with their younger brother, William, went to live with their aunt and uncle, Ann Collett and Stephen Wilson in Spitalfields.[20]

One year after his wife's death William Wilson along with his son, Joseph and his younger children moved to Clapham where he resided until 1810 before moving permanently to his estate at Nether Worton, Oxfordshire which he had purchased in 1797.[21] Two years later, he purchased the neighbouring estate of Over Worton from William Ralph Cartwright, MP of Aynho, Northamptonshire. Although Nether Worton was his preferred place of residence, it was not until 1810 that he finally retired to Oxfordshire leaving the business in the hands of his eldest son, Joseph and his nephew, Ambrose Moore.[22]

As a freeman and master of the Weavers Company William Wilson was eligible to take on apprentices who were indentured to him for a period of not less than seven years. Under the terms of the Weavers Company he would have been responsible for providing them with board and lodging and training. In his private calendar, Stephen Wilson records that William Wilson charged £2.2 shillings (2 guineas) per quarter for Daniel Wilson's laundry.[23]

During his long and successful career in the silk industry William took an active role in the Weavers Company serving as Auditor, Renter Bailiff and finally as Upper Bailiff. In addition, we find that in 1788 he is listed along with Daniel West as serving on a committee to investigate the price of silk.[24]

Later, in 1793 he served on a committee to provide relief for the poor in Spitalfields. Amongst those on the committee was Thomas Fowell Buxton who became successor to William Wilberforce for the abolition of slavery, John Remington and Joseph Wilson of Remington, Wilson and Co.[25]

With the fortune that he made from the silk industry, William Wilson senior purchased two large country houses and estates in Oxfordshire. The first estate that he purchased in 1797 was the manor of Nether Worton from Colonel William Draper, whose family had held the estate since 1641. This included the living and patronage of St James, Nether Worton that remained a separate living until 1864. Two years later, he purchased the manor and estate of Over Worton, a small parish that lay south of Nether Worton. The estate at Over Worton originally belonged to the Cartwrights of Aynho from 1649.[26] Exactly what part his cousin and brother in law, Stephen Wilson played in finding and purchasing these properties is not clear, but according to an entry in his Private Calendar we learn that Stephen Wilson made a trip with his cousin William to the Wortons, probably to advise him on the suitability of the property.[27]

In addition to purchasing the livings of Over and Nether Worton, William Wilson senior also purchased the livings of St Mary Islington, St Mary's Walthamstow, Lower Tooting, Hampton Gay and Deddington.[28]

As an Anglican Evangelical of Calvinistic tendency William Wilson was a member of the wider circle of the Clapham sect. This movement had its origins in Clapham and is largely associated with William Wilberforce, the Thorntons and the Venns.[29] Thus, we find that on April 12th 1799 he is listed as being present at the first meeting of the CMS when he was elected as a member of the Lay Committee.[30] Although he is not listed as being a member of the committee of the British and Foreign Bible society, he was none the less an active supporter of the Society. We also learn that he chaired the first meeting of the Oxford Auxiliary Society of the BFBS on the 25th June 1813 when Daniel Wilson and Charles Simeon gave after dinner speeches.[31]

As well as supporting the two main causes dear to the heart of the Clapham movement William Wilson was responsible for the establishment of Sunday Schools and Day Schools in and around The Wortons, many of which he financed personally.[32]

As we have already noted William married Elizabeth West, the second daughter of Daniel and Ann West (née Brooke). There were seven children by his marriage: five daughters and two sons. Of these, his eldest daughter, Ann married her cousin, Daniel Wilson who went on in 1832 to become the Bishop of Calcutta.[33] Selina (1788-1863) married the Revd John Davies. They were the grand parents of Charlotte Wilson (née Martin) the feminist radical of DNB status.[34] William and Elizabeth's third daughter Sophia, married the Revd Richard Greaves.[35] Whether it was through business connections in the city that the Wilsons encountered the Greaves is a moot point. It is more than likely that it was whilst William Wilson junior was at Wadham College, Oxford, which at this time was the bastion of Evangelicalism, that he first met Richard Greaves whom he introduced to his sister Sophia.[36] As to William's third daughter Charlotte, she married the Revd Charles Wetherall. The only daughter not married was Eliza who remained at home to care for her elderly father. Eliza died in 1817, aged 24 and was buried at Nether Worton on December the 27th, 1817.[37] In a letter to the Revd Thomas and Mrs Lancaster of Banbury, William Wilson writes "with her death he had lost a beloved child and in her an affectionate and amiable companion and friend." Although her death was to him a heavy affliction, probably something unexpected nonetheless, it is he writes "a great source of comfort for me to reflect that my dear child died in peace trusting to the mercy of God through her Saviour looking and longing for Glory." (See: Addendum 3)

Commenting on William Wilson senior's daughters Bateman says that they were admirable women taught of God, "who laid themselves out with unbounded charity and unwearied diligence to teach others and to render permanent the work of Grace that was going on". Furthermore they were he says, "very successful in establishing small schools in the surrounding villages". and providing the whole neighbourhood with Bibles and Prayer

*Over Worton House (n.d.).*

*Over Worton Church (n.d.).*

books. Bateman goes on to state that his daughters were also active in providing education for gypsies, and it was whilst one of his daughters was busy in conversation with a group of gypsies that William Wilson rode by in his carriage. He was about to disperse them when he noted that one of his daughters was in their midst and so he left them knowing that they were safe.[38]

As to his two sons Joseph (1786-1855) and William (1791-1867), even though they had been apprenticed to their father in the silk manufacturing industry only Joseph who was born in 1786 completed his apprenticeship under his father, receiving his freedom by servitude on the 21st of July 1807.[39]

In the same year he was made a partner in the business of Wilson and Robinson of 31 Milk Street. Later in 1810, he was joined by his cousin, Ambrose, the only surviving son of Ambrose and Ann Moore (née Wilson) who had been an apprentice in the family business.[40]

Although Joseph was legally a partner in the family business he had by the time of his marriage to Emma Aplin in 1808 withdrawn from the business and left the management of the firm to his cousin Ambrose Moore, in order to devote his time more fully to a variety of philanthropic, religious and educational causes.[41]

Amongst these was the Lord's Observance Society of which Joseph Wilson of Clapham was the founder and first Secretary: a post that he held until his death in 1851.[42] Those present at its first meeting in 1832 included his first cousin and brother in law, Daniel Wilson, (recently appointed as the 5th Bishop of Calcutta) who had prepared the Primary Address which was then included in the Annual Reports of the Society.

Like his father and brother, Joseph took an interest in educational matters. Thus we find that in addition to being on the Committee of the Westminster Infant School he is listed as being one of the founders of the Spitalfields National School, which was founded in 1819 and Patron of the Quaker Street Infant School Spitalfields (1821). The first teacher to be appointed at the Quaker Infant School was Samuel Wilderspin who had been recommended to him by James Buchanan.[43] At a later stage, Joseph introduced Samuel Wilderspin to his brother William Wilson Vicar of St Mary's Walthamstow, who had in 1824 opened what was probably the first Infant School in the Church of England.[44]

During his lifetime Joseph is listed as being a member of at least 22 societies, president of one, on the committee of 5, governor of 6, member of the Vice Society, Treasurer of the Prayer Book and Homily Society, and on the Committee of the BFBS, CMS and Evangelical Alliance.[45] Along with his brother, William Wilson junior, he is also listed as being a benefactor to Francis Close of Cheltenham as well as playing a part in the formation of the Home and Colonial School Society. In addition, he also served as High Sheriff for the

County of Oxfordshire.

Even though the name of Joseph Wilson is not included with the 10 on the plaque at Clapham Parish Church, nonetheless he maybe considered as being a member of the Clapham sect in its widest sense and on close terms with such people as Sir Thomas Fowell Buxton.

At some stage in his lifetime Joseph extended and rebuilt the house at Nether Worton, (which he had inherited in 1821), transforming it into a Gothic pile complete with castellations. The house was later remodelled in 1920 with the addition of two wings and a porch and passage creating an inner courtyard. Shortly after Joseph's death in 1851 the property was divided into two parts: one part of the estate was sold to the Boultons of Great Tew, the manor was sold to the Beauchamp Hayes who held onto the property until 1911 when it was sold to A.C. Thimbleby in 1911. The manor was later purchased by the Schusters in whose hands the property still remains.

Nearby is the Church of St James, containing the memorials of his father, William and of Joseph and Emma Wilson (née Aplin) by whom he had six children. Of these only three survived into adulthood, Nathaniel who married his cousin, Agnes Wilson, Cornelius who married Eliza Prinsep, a member of the Prinsep family and Joseph Henry who married Henricia Haigh. According to details in the family sketch of Harriet Ann Wilson, Nathaniel Wilson lived in Devonport where he had a brewery and was three times Mayor of Devonport.[46]

As to William Wilson's youngest son also called William (1791-1867), he was also apprenticed to his father as a silk weaver but never completed his indentures. Instead he was admitted as a Commoner to Wadham College, Oxford in 1810 where he graduated in 1814 with a 2nd class degree in Mathematics. He then obtained his MA in 1817 before proceeding to the degree of Bachelor of Divinity in 1827. According to an entry in the Register of Wadham College he was responsible for the installation of the Oriel window of the Hall which he paid for at his own expense in 1827.[47] Ordained a Priest in 1814 to a Church in Harrow he was then appointed a year later as Curate to Holy Trinity, Over Worton, which at this stage was in the patronage of his father, William Wilson senior. Following the death of his father in 1821 William Wilson junior inherited the manor of Over Worton and the patronage of the Church as well as the living and patronage of St Mary Walthamstow.

By this stage, the house had long since been demolished by his father and rebuilt between 1810 and 1816 in the style of a town house consisting of three bays and three floors and a basement that had been part of the original house.

Later, in 1850 or thereabouts, William Wilson junior added the two wings to the house and a swimming bath, 16 feet square and 6 feet deep lined with white glazed tiles. Two large coppers sited in the washhouse heated the water. In addition, he altered the hall or entrance hall. It is more than probable that he was responsible for the removal and re-building of the village so as not to spoil the view from the House.

During his lifetime, he was responsible for the building of the Lodge or Grove in 1826, which was further extended in the 1850s and then in 1873. This was the home of his daughter in law Ann Rodick Wilson. After William's death in 1867, the estate passed to his daughter in law, Ann Roddick Wilson who held it for life. It then passed to her son, Admiral William Wilson who held the estate until 1911 and it was eventually sold to A.C. Thimbleby in 1913.[48]

As a person of relatively independent means, William took an active role in Church building both in Walthamstow and in Oxfordshire as well Infant School Education on which he published many books.

During his time in Oxfordshire, he paid for the building of the Chapel of St John the Evangelist, Hempton and gave active support to numerous schools in the Wooton Hundred.

It was however his son, also called William, who was responsible for the rebuilding of the Church at Over Worton along Tractarian lines resulting in an altercation that was resolved by the intervention of the Bishop of Oxford leading to William Wilson's son being transferred to St Mary's Banbury. Although the rebuilding of the Church was never completed, it gained an outstanding organ built by J.C. Bishop of London.[49]

Like other members of his family and in particular his brother, William took an interest in education seeing it as a means to an end rather than an end in itself.

Inspired by the methods employed in the Quaker Street Charity School of which his brother Joseph of Clapham and Nether Worton was the Patron and founder, he too decided to establish in 1824 an Infant School at St Mary's Walthamstow. On the recommendation of his brother, he invited Samuel Wilderspin to organize and manage the school along the same lines that were used in the Quaker Street School. The school, which was originally housed in the Tithe Barn, was transferred to a purpose built school funded by William Wilson in 1828. According to Burgess, the Church Infant School was built in 1819 but it would seem that Burgess has confused this with the National School that was built nearby. The newly built Church Infant School was not built until 1828. Although Wilderspin claims to have been the originator of the Infant School system and the founder and opener of the Infant School in Spitalfields these claims are disputed by William Buchanan in correspondence to Lord Brougham. In a letter dated 2nd May 1851, Buchanan states that it was Joseph Wilson who established an infant school in Spitalfields and on the recommendation of James Buchanan engaged Samuel Wilderspin to manage the school. Likewise, Wilderspin's claim that he opened on his own account the

Church Infant School in Walthamstow is also incorrect. In fact, it was Joseph Wilson who introduced Samuel Wilderspin to his brother William who then went on to engage Wilderspin to manage his Church School.[50]

It is significant to note that it was to the Church school in Walthamstow that the three Fuegians received their education having been brought over to England in 1830 by Captain Fitzroy of the *Beagle*. It would seem that Fitzroy had written to the Revd J. L Harris, Vicar of Plymstock regarding a suitable place in which to place the Fuegians. Harris who at this stage was a minister in the Church of England wrote to the Secretary of the Church Missionary Society, Dandeson Coates, who then directed Fitzroy to the Revd Joseph Wigram, Secretary of the National Society, and brother of George Vicesimus Wigram. Their father was Sir Robert Wigram.[51]

Wigram who happened to live in Walthamstow referred Fitzroy to William Wilson who was pleased to oblige Fitzroy by settling them in his school where they came under the care of a Mr and Mrs Jenkins. After staying in Walthamstow for a year they returned to Tierra del Fuega aboard the *Beagle* with Charles Darwin.[52]

In addition to opening and funding of schools and the building of Churches in the Deddington and Worton area, he was also responsible for building district Churches in Walthamstow. Amongst them were St John's Chapel End (1829), St Peter's New End (1840), and St James, Marsh Street (1841/2).

Even though the Revd William Wilson came from an eminent Evangelical family and married into an equally distinguished mercantile and Evangelical family, there is no evidence to suggest that he was himself either Evangelical or a member of any of the leading Evangelical societies. Least of all did he share the same catholic spirit that was a feature of the earlier Evangelicals such as Romaine, Cecil or Eyre. As such, his values may be styled as Broad High Church Victorian, as opposed to Evangelicalism or Tractarian: a movement that he was opposed to, resulting in an altercation in 1849 between himself and his eldest son, the Revd William Wilson. This led to the Bishop of Oxford, Samuel Wilberforce intervening by arranging for an exchange of livings in 1849 between the Revd T.L. Lancaster, Vicar of Banbury and the Revd William Wilson's son, also called William, where he remained until his death in 1860.

As Vicar and patron of St Mary's Walthamstow, Wilson was also Chairman of the Workhouse, the motto of which was that if a person did not work they were not to be fed, a sentiment with which Wilson would have concurred. Paternalistic in outlook he believed that the poor should be content with their lot in life. This was in stark contrast to the attitude of his father, William Wilson senior who according to the epitaph erected to his memory in the Church of St James, Nether Worton, was "eyes to the blind, feet to the lame and father to the poor." In short, William Wilson junior personifies the hardening of the arteries that characterized certain aspects of Victorian Christianity with its emphasis on Church order, Sunday observance, family prayers and discipline in the home.

But to return to William Wilson senior. From 1810 until his death in 1821 his involvement in the silk trade and the Weavers Company had gradually declined so that in 1819 we find him writing a letter to the Clerk of the Company thanking him for the honour of inviting him to fulfil the duties of the Upper Bailiff but begging to be excused the honour on the grounds of ill health.[53] By this time, he had effectively withdrawn from the business leaving it to his son Joseph and his nephew Ambrose Moore who had been made a partner in the business in 1810.

In 1821, William Wilson senior died and was buried at Nether Worton where a plaque to his memory was erected by one of his descendants.[54] Commenting on the death of William Wilson senior, the Revd John Hill, Vice Principal of St Edmund Hall wrote in his diary for Thursday September 6th 1821 that he felt quite low today for which I can only account by the missing of my old and valuable friend with whom when here I used to take a regular morning ride.[55]

Today the only evidence that remains of the Wilsons of Over Worton and Nether Worton are the tombstones and plaques: such is the transitory nature of this life.

*Notes and References:*

1.  See Wilson, J.W. (n.d.) The Legend of the Wolfsons. See also: Wintringham, Elizabeth, (n.d.) mss: Parish Records: Holy Trinity Over Worton: Wilson, John Dover. (1969) Milestones Along the Dover Road. London: Faber.
2.  See: Forster, Margaret. (1998) Rich Desserts and Captains Thin: a Family and their Times: 1831-1931. London: Vintage.
3.  Wilson, J. (1846) Memoir of Thomas Wilson. London. See also: Rothstein, N.K.A. (1960) The Silk Industry in London: 1702-1793. London University MA thesis in which she refers to a Stephen Wilson 1755-1793 of Aldermanbury, Cheapside: and a Thomas Wilson of Aldermanbury. See also: Compleat Pocket Companion: 1741-1760 listing Stephen Wilson and Thomas Wilson as being Silk Weavers. Stephen and Mary Fullalove were the parents of Stephen Wilson of Church Street who married Ann Collett West.
4.  Wilson, J. (1840) Memoir of Thomas Wilson. London. Mary Wilson (née Fullalove), was the widow of Stephen Wilson (1723-1755), silk manufacturer of Coventry and Wood Street Cheapside. In his will, Stephen left the business to his wife. In December 1755 she entered into a new partnership with her brother in law, Thomas Wilson, senior. Later in 1772 her eldest son, John was made a partner in the family business.
5.  Letter: William Wilson: dated 11th May 1773. to his sister Ann (Nancy) Wilson.
6.  GUILDHALL LBIRARY: Gld Mss: Court Minute Books: Weavers Company: 4655/17/1765-1785: William Wilson is cited as being made free by redemption on

Feb 3rd 1778. In the Court Minute Books he is listed as being of Goldsmith Street, Cheapside.

7.  See: Gordon, C & W. Dewhirst. (1985) The Ward of Cripplegate in the City of London. London: Cripplegate Ward Club. See also: Plummer, A. (1972) The London Weavers Company: 1600-1970. London: Routledge Kegan and Paul.

8.  GUILDHALL LIBRARY: Gld MSS. Court Minute Books: Weavers Company 4655/17/1765-1785. Plummer, A. (1972) The London Weavers Company: 1600-1970. London.

9.  See: chapter. 3. Elizabeth Collett and her descendents: also Ch. 4: Daniel West: Whitefield's Forgotten Trustee. Also: Ch. 7. Stephen Wilson of Church Street Spitalfields. Elizabeth West's sister, Ann Collett West had married Stephen Wilson, first cousin to William and a partner with Daniel West of Church Street, Spitalfields. See also: Harrison, M.J. Daniel West: Whitefield's Forgotten Trustee. JURCHS. June 2006.

10. GUILDHALL LBIRARY: Gld Mss: Court Minute Books: Weavers Company. 4655/17/1765-1785, also vols 18: 1786-1798; vol 19, 1798-1825.

11. See: Harrison, M.J. Daniel West: Whitefield's Forgotten Trustee. JURCHS. June 2006. See also: Robert Brooke: PCC/Prob/11/873/1762: also Thomas Collett: PCC/Prob.11/725/1743. See also: Harrison, M.J. From Spitalfields to Calcutta: Daniel Wilson's Love of India. Indian Church History Review. June. 2006.

12. On the Pattles see: Hill, B. Julia Margaret Cameron: A Victorian Family Portrait. London: Peter Owen, 1973.

13. Thomas Flight is listed as of St Michael's Wood Street Precinct: 1760-1761: See also Indenture between Thomas Flight and John Remington: Suffolk Record Office (Bury St Edmunds Branch) HA: 530/4/1-9.

14. Wilson, H.A. (1901) Family Sketch. (privately owned.)

15. Suffolk Record Office. (Bury St Edmund's Branch). HA: 530/4/1-9/Indentures between Thomas Flight and John Remington. See also: Bateman, J. (1860) Life of Daniel Wilson. London: John Murray, 2. vols.

16. See: Table 8: William Wilson: Appendix.

17. Wilson, J. (1846) Memoir of Thomas Wilson. London.

18. See: Bateman, J. (1860) Life of Daniel Wilson. London: John Murray. 2 vols. See also: Bunyan, C. (1889) Memoir of Francis Thomas McDougall. London: Longman. p.75. See also: Forster, E.M. Two Cheers for Democracy. Harmondsworth: Penguin, 1974 p.193, in which he refers to the prayers that had been written by Henry Thornton which then circulated amongst his friends. Only later were they published by his friend Sir Robert Inglis.

19. Private Calendar: 1795-1802. Stephen Wilson, in which he states that Elizabeth was buried in the newly constructed family vault at Christ Church, Spitalfields that he purchased with his brother in law William Wilson.

20. Private Calendar: 1795-1802: Stephen Wilson. In his Private Calendar Stephen records that on Monday the 12th of March, Ann, Selina and Charlotte went to Miss Jones private residential school in Stepney Green with his younger daughters, having been removed the previous week from Mr Johnson's school in Bromley.

21. See: The Victorian History of the Counties of England, a History of the County of

Oxford, vol.11, ed. A. Crossley. London: Oxford University Press, 1983. In his Private Calendar: 1795-1802 Stephen Wilson refers to William purchasing Nether Worton in 1797. See also: Bateman, J. (1860) Life of Daniel Wilson. London: John Murray. vol.1.

22. Wilson, H.A. (1901) Family Sketch of the Wilsons, Moores, Foxes *et al.* (Privately owned.)

23. Stephen Wilson: Private Calendar: 1795-1802.

24. GUILDHALL LIBRARY: Gld Mss. Court Minute Books: Weavers Company 4655/17/1765-1785.

25. The Evangelical Magazine, 1798. Joseph Wilson was a partner with his uncle, John Remington and is not to be confused with William Wilson's son also called Joseph, founder of the LDOS.

26. See: The Victoria History of the Counties of England, a History of the County of Oxford, vol.11, ed. A. Crossley. London: Oxford University Press, 1983. See also: PCC/Prob/11/1649/1821, will of William Wilson of Nether Worton. On the Cartwrights of Aynho see: Cooper, N. (1984) Aynho: a Northamptonshire Village. Banbury: Leopard's Head Press.

27. Wilson, Stephen. 1795-1802. Private Calendar (privately owned)

28. See: The Victoria History of the Counties of England, a History of the County of Oxford, vol.11, ed. A. Crossley. London: Oxford University Press, 1983. See also: Bateman, J. (1860) The Life of Daniel Wilson. London: John Murray. 2 vols. See also: will of William Wilson: PCC/Prob/11/1649/proved 1821.

29. On the Clapham Sect: see: Howse, E.M. (1973) Saints in Politics: the Clapham Sect and the Growth of Freedom. London: George Unwin. Although 10 names are mentioned on the plaque the Clapham Sect was not restricted to those ten names but included many others including William Wilson senior and his son, Joseph of Clapham and Nether Worton amongst its members all of whom shared a common faith and a common interest.

30. Hole, C. (1896) History of the Church Missionary Society. London. William Wilson served on the Committee from April 12th 1799 to May 27th 1806.

31. Owen, J. (1816) History and Origin of the First Ten Years of the British and Foreign Bible Society. London. 2 vols. See also: Reynolds, J.S. (1953) The Evangelicals at Oxford: 1735-1871. Oxford. William Wilson was High Sheriff of Oxfordshire in 1813

32. See: The Victoria History of the Counties of England, a History of the County of Oxford, vol.11, ed. A. Crossley. London: Oxford University Press, 1983.
See also: Bateman, J. (1860) Life of Daniel Wilson. London: John Murray, 2 vols.

33. Bateman, J. (1860) Life of Daniel Wilson. London: John Murray. 2 vols. Ann and Daniel were first cousins. Their respective mothers were sisters whilst their respective fathers were first cousins.

34. On John Davies: see: Memorial Notices of Revd J. Davies ed. W.H. Havergal who preached his funeral service. John and Selina were the grand parents of Charlotte Martin, only daughter of Robert Martin, Surgeon: see The Medical Register, 1859: The Medical Directory, 1881 and 1896. On Charlotte Martin see: Hinely, Susan. Charlotte Wilson: Anarchist, Fabian and Feminist: PhD upub diss: Stanford

University, 1987. See also Oxford Dictionary of National Biography. Vol 59. p.513-515. Nicolas Walter.

35. On Richard Greaves: see: Latham, J.E.M. Notes and Queries: n.s. vol. 46. no.1. March 1999: also: Search For a New Eden. J. E. M Latham. London: Associated University Press, 1999. See also: Bodleian Library: Diaries of the Revd John Hill. Mss 67. See also comment made by Bp Wilson in his diary, p.8.Bodleian Library: MS Eng. Misc.e.9. It is significant to note that Bateman makes no mention of his father in law's personal comments.

36. Reynolds, J. (1953) The Evangelicals at Oxford 1735-1871: Oxford: Clarendon Press.

By the time that the Greaves resided in London the Wilsons had moved to Nether Worton. As such, there was no possibility of any social mixing: added to which daughters were not normally paraded in public until the eldest daughter had married or they had reached the age of 16. On the protocol of coming out see: Vickery, A. The Gentleman's Daughter: Womens Lives in Georgian England. Newhaven (USA) Yale University Press. 1998.

37. In a Letter written by William Wilson senior to Revd T. Lancaster in January 1818, William Wilson comments on the loss he felt on the death of his daughter who he described as being an affectionate loving and constant companion He also comments on her faith.

38. Bateman, J. (1860) Life of Daniel Wilson. London: John Murray. 2 vols.

39. GUILDHALL LIBRARY: Gld Mss. Court Minute Books: Weavers Company; 4655/19/1798-1825.

40. See: Wilson, Harriet Ann. (1901) Family Sketch . . . et al. (privately owned)

41. See: Brown, F.K. (1960) Father of the Victorians: the Age of Wilberforce: Cambridge: Cambridge University Press. See also McCann P. & F.A. Young. (1982) Samuel Wilderspin and the Infant School Movement. London & Canberra: Croom Helm, in which they mistakenly confuse Joseph Wilson of Clapham and the Wortons with his cousin, Joseph Wilson of Highbury.

42. See: Baylee, J.T. Statistics and Facts in Reference to the Lords Day. London who makes the point that it was Joseph Wilson of Clapham who came up with the idea of forming the society. After further consultations with his brother in law Daniel Wilson, he then went ahead with its formation.

43. UCL:26554: Brougham Letters: corr: William Buchanan to Lord Brougham 2nd May 1851. See also: McCann. P. & F.A. Young. (1982) Samuel Wilderspin and the Infant School Movement. London & Canberra: Croom Helm.

44. See also: McCann. P. & F.A. Young. (1982) Samuel Wilderspin and the Infant School Movement. London & Canberra: Croom Helm.

45. See: Brown, F.K. (1960) Fathers of the Victorians. Cambridge: CUP.

46. Wilson, H.A. (1901) Family Sketch. (privately owned)

47. Wadham Register: see also Al Oxon. Ed. J. Foster. According to the Index of Oxfordshire Clergy he is listed as being Curate of St Ebbe's Oxford. On this matter it would seem that he has been confused with William Wilson of Queen's College a point not noticed by Dianne McClatchy in her book on Oxfordshire Clergy or for that matter the editor of the entry in the VCH for the Wooton Hundred. He was

Vicar of St Mary, Walthamstow from 1822-1848. He is then listed as having been appointed Curate of Deddington, 1850, Vicar of Over Worton, 1855, then Rector of Over Worton, 1860-1862. In the Quarterly sessions for the County of Oxford he is listed as having been a Justice of the Peace for the periods, 1830, 1837 and 1842 At his death he left less than £8,000 to be divided between his children. No money was left to any society, both secular or religious.

48.  See: Harrison, M.J. New light on the organ at Holy Trinity, Over Worton. Bios Reporter. January 2005.

49.  See: Bodleian Library: Bodl: G. A. Oxon b 92 (40) Sale Catalogue: 4th September, 1913. See also: Victoria History of the Counties of England: a History of the County of Oxfordshire, vol.11, ed. A. Crossley. London: Oxford University Press for the Institute of Historical Research, 1983. p.296.

50.  See: McCann, P. & F.A. Young. (1982) Samuel Wilderspin and the Infant School Movement. London & Canberra: Croom Helm.

51.  Both Harris and Coates were to cede to the Plymouth Brethren where they were joined by Bulteel. See: Stunt, T. (2000) From Awakening to Secession: Radical Evangelicals in Switzerland and Britain, 1815-1835. Edinburgh: T&T Clark.

52.  See: Lucas Bridges. E. (1951) Uttermost Part of the Earth. London: Hodder & Stoughton. See also: Chatwin, B. (1998) In Patagonia. London: Vintage. Also: Hazlewood, N. (2000) Savage: the Life and Times of Jemmy Button. London: Hodder & Stoughton.

53.  GUIDLHALL LIBRARY: GLD Mss. Court Minute Books: Weavers Company. 4655/19/: 1798-1825.

54.  For an account of his death and a summary of the sermon preached at his funeral see: Diary of Revd John Hill, MSS 67/1 & 67/2 St Edmund Hall/Deposited in the Bodleian Library:
He was buried at the Parish Church of St James, Nether Worton. Daniel Wilson erected the plaque to his memory. October 9th 1821.
At his death, his estate was valued at £250,000 of which over £120,000 was left to relatives and various charities and religious societies. We also learn from the terms of William Wilson's will that he left the patronage of St Mary's Walthamstow to his second son, the Revd William Wilson, the patronage of St Mary Islington to his son in law Daniel Wilson, and Deddington to another son in law, Richard Greaves. See: PCC/Prob/11/1649, with two codicils: Proved 1821.

55.  Bodleian Library, Oxford: MS St Edmund Hall: Diary of Revd John Hill, Vice Principal of St Edmund Hall.

# Addendum

1.   Article by Elizabeth Wintringham (née Arkwright) later Elizabeth Dover Wilson.

The Wilsons of Worton: Oxfordshire.

The Wilson family were small farmers of the hamlet of Stenson in the Parish of Barrow cum Twyford in the County of Derby.

Many of the younger sons migrated to London and many of them prospered in the trade. Such a one was William Wilson the elder, born 1756 died 1821.

It is recorded that he and a friend walked all the way from Derbyshire to London arriving with only a few shillings in their pockets: he was then about sixteen.

He was not without friends in London: however: since he had three Uncles in London engaged in the ribbon trade: he appears to have served his apprenticeship with one of these and before long he was in business on his own as a silk manufacturer.

His warehouse was at 31 Milk Street and he and his wife and family lived over the warehouse.

He made a large fortune and in 1797 or thereabouts, he bought the Wortons as a county seat. From then on, his family spent the summer at Nether Worton Great House and William came for short visits whenever he could.

After his death, he left Nether Worton to his eldest son, Joseph, (said to be the founder of the LDOS) and Over Worton to his younger son Revd William Wilson, DD who was also Rector of the Parish and Vicar of St Mary Walthamstow, Essex.

The Revd William and his family had their home in Walthamstow and spent the summer months at Over Worton, Great House, which I believe no longer exists.

The parish of Worton was served by appointing a Curate, a fellow from one of the Colleges who drove out on a Sunday for the day and conducted three or four services driving rapidly from church to the other.

From 1804 to 1809 the office was filled by the Revd Daniel Wilson afterwards Bishop of Calcutta.

Bishop Wilson's life was written by his son in law and Chaplain, the Revd Josiah Bateman and published by John Murray in 1860.

In it there is a description of the wild and neglected state of the parish in those days and of the crowds that flocked to hear Daniel Wilson's sermons for he was a fiery and eloquent preacher in a parish where sermons were prized.

It is said that the Church and school room were filled to over flowing and people clustered around the windows to hear him often coming from miles around and following him from one service to another.

Signed by Elizabeth. Wintringham.

*(The original handwritten mss is lodged at Over Worton Parish Church. (n.d.)*

2.   Letter dated: London May 11 1773 from William Wilson to Ann Wilson.

Dear Sister,

I have been for some time waiting to receive my shirt you told me you would send which made me not write before. If I had known it would be so long before you sent it I would have answered your letter before.

I have received a letter from Cousin Gould in which he tells me he wrote to me before tho' I believe I never received any letter.

I hear one of my cousins in Bull and Moth Street is coming down into Derbyshire in about a week but do not know whether to see you at Stenson or her father. Relations should be glad you would let me know when you write again.

I hope to have a fulfilment of your promise with my shirt very soon.

This is a very long letter now don't let me be shuffled off with any trifling excuse for I must certainly expect a long letter.

I should be glad also to hear when we may expect my father in town. We hear nothing about it for a good while and we expect to see him in about a fortnight if he comes this spring. My uncle seems to think we shall see him.

I should be glad to hear also when my Aunt Joseph comes to town, my Aunt Thomas said a good while ago she would come so we shall be exceeding glad to see her.

And I have not heard of the certainty of my father coming so I cannot be certain whether I shall see you this summer or not.

Pray give my love to my brother John and tell him tho' he seems to have quite forgot me I have not forgotten him. I hope you will excuse all my faults as I am rather busy and also the sharpness. I long to receive my shirt as I expect so many letters with it.

My last stocks you made are much too large and the first is too small. They make me pay double price for washing them. If I come to Stenson I will bring them down and have them altered.

I have said nothing about what you devised. I would not but it is not for want of a will but an opportunity. I so far think it my duty that I don't know how I might clear my own conscience.

I hope to write a long letter to you soon but must first expect one from you.

Pray give my duty to my Father, love to Bro and sister and accept my best wishes from your loving brother, William Wilson.

*(The original handwritten letter is in the Diary written by Harriet Ann Wilson and is privately owned.)*

3.  Letter from William Wilson, Senior to Revd Mr Lancaster:

Worton House<br>January 3rd 1818

My Dear Sir,
   I sincerely thank you and Mrs Lancaster for your Christian sympathy. I have lost a beloved child and in her an affectionate and amiable companion and friend. I feel it a heavy affliction, but I calm my feelings in the will of God. I remember the many mercies I have enjoyed from Him and still enjoy.
   It is also a great source of comfort for me to reflect that my dear child uniformly lived in the Faith and obedience of the Gospel of our Lord Jesus Christ, and that she died in peace trusting to the mercy of God through her Saviour looking and longing for Glory and happiness of a better state.
   I am now most anxious that this affliction may be so sanctified of God that it may work on me and all parts of my family the peaceable fruits of righteousness; through the goodness of God we are all in better health and more comfortable than we could reasonably expect to be.
   I request to be kindly remembered to Mrs Lancaster.

I remain                              My Dear Sirs

Yours very sincerely<br>William Wilson

*Re the death of his daughter: Eliza: who died at Nether Worton House and was buried at Nether Worton Church: Dec 27th 1817.*

4.  Memorial Plaque: St James Church, Nether Worton.

   This monument is erected by his afflicted family as well asunder the influence of gratitude to the most high from the blessing which they received for this advice and examples in admiration of the many singular excellence of his eminently Christian character when the ear heard him, it gave witness to him, because he delivered the poor that cried and the fatherless and him that had none to help him, the blessing of him that was ready to perish came upon him and he caused the widows heart to sing for joy: he put on righteousness and it clothed him, his judgement was as a robe and a diadem: he was eyes to the blind and feet was he to the lame, he was a father to the poor and the cause which he knew not, he searched out.

*Stowlangtoft Hall, Suffolk (n.d.). Photo courtesy of Rosemary Jewers (née Brereton).*

# 9. Joseph Wilson of Highbury Hill House and Stowlangtoft(i)

Joseph Wilson who was born in London in 1766 was a member of a family that originally came from Stenson in South Derbyshire where the Wilsons owned the freehold of their land.[1] His father, Thomas Wilson [I] was the second member of the Wilson family of Derbyshire to enter the silk trade. In 1754, Thomas was invited by his brother Stephen to become a partner in his business. By the terms of the partnership it was agreed that Thomas and his wife, Mary, the only daughter of John Remington a wealthy merchant and Alderman of the city of Coventry were to supervise the business in Coventry whilst Stephen was to supervise the London branch of the business, which he had recently established. In 1755, one year after establishing the London branch Stephen contracted a fever from which he died. He was thirty-three years of age.

Three months after the death of Stephen, his widow, Mary Wilson (née Fullalove) re-negotiated the terms of the partnership with her brother in law, Thomas, in which it was agreed that Thomas and his wife were to manage the business in London whilst Mary Wilson, (née Fullalove) was to supervise the Coventry branch of the business.

On December the 15th 1755, Thomas and his wife moved to London where they resided first at St Peter's Precinct and then at 124 Wood Street, Cheapside. They had nine children of whom only three survived to adulthood, Thomas (1764-1843), Joseph (1766-1851) and Mary (n.d.).

At the age of seven or thereabouts Joseph was sent to a Dissenting academy in Stoke Newington where he received an education that was of a commercial as opposed to a classical education. On reaching the age of fourteen Joseph left school and was apprenticed to the partnership between his aunt, Mary Wilson (née Fullalove), and his father, Thomas Wilson [I] of Wood Street, Cheapside.[2] Although there is no reference in the records of the Weavers Company indicating that he had been bound to his father it is probable that he fulfilled the necessary requirements enabling him in 1791 to take up his freedom by redemption in the Weavers Company.[3] This coincided with his being taken into partnership with his uncle, John Remington, a wealthy merchant of Coventry.

The following year he married Mary Anne Maitland, the eldest daughter of Robert and Elizabeth Maitland (née Ridge).[4] Like Joseph Wilson's parents they too were members of a family well known in Evangelical circles. Her father, Robert Maitland and his brother, Ebenezer Maitland, were members of the Congregational Society and the British and Foreign Bible Society. As such, it was either through the Congregational Church or the Bible Society that Joseph was first introduced to Mary Maitland and her family.[5]

Mary's father was the eldest son of Robert Maitland and a member of the family of Maitlands who were descended from the Maitlands of Thirlstone, Berwickshire. The first Lord Maitland of Thirlstone was Sir John Maitland who was created Lord Maitland of Thirlstone in 1590 with remainders to the heirs: Earl of Lauderdale, Viscount Maitland.[6]

Robert and Mary had seven children, four sons and three daughters, of whom only two daughters, Mary and Frances, survived to adulthood. The third daughter, Elizabeth died in early childhood. Mary who was the eldest married Joseph Wilson of Highbury whilst her younger sister, Frances, married the Revd John Savill, member of a family that had at one time owned one of the largest cloth manufacturing businesses in the Braintree/Bocking area.[7] By the time that the Revd John Savill married Frances Maitland in 1808 the business had long since gone into decline. Any suggestion that he owed his wealth either to his family or to his wife is however incorrect. Likewise, any suggestion that it was through his brother in law that Joseph Wilson was drawn to the area where he set up a silk business in Braintree is also unfounded.

John Savill was a member of a family well known like his wife's own family in Non-Conformist circles. One year after their marriage the Revd John Savill was appointed minister at Lion Walk, Colchester, a position that he held until 1828. Because of dissatisfaction with his ministry and following discussions with the Deacons, he then tendered his resignation and in 1829 accepted an invitation from the Church at Halstead remaining there until 1832 when he finally retired to Colchester where he died in 1836.

Returning to Joseph and his wife Mary Wilson (née Maitland) they had four children of whom only three survived to adulthood. The first was Mary (1794-1865) who married Henry Grace Sperling (1792-1821). He was a member of a Swedish family of fur traders who had settled at Dynes Hall near Halstead sometime in the 18th century. Another branch of the Sperling family settled at Lattenbury Hill, St Ives, Hunts, whilst another branch from which Henry Grace Sperling was descended resided at Theydon Garnon near Epping.[8]

Following his education at Harrow then Trinity College, Cambridge obtaining a BA in 1815 and MA in 1818, Henry Grace Sperling was then ordained a Priest. From 1819 until his death in 1821, he was Rector of Papworth St Agnes, Cambridge. Soon after the death of her husband, Mary Sperling (née Wilson) and her infant son, Henry Maitland Sperling went to live with her father, Joseph Wilson who had by this stage married Emma Welford, the eldest daughter of John Welford of Blackheath. She was his second wife. In his will, Joseph left Highbury Place to his wife and daughter for life. On their death the estate at Highbury reverted to his heir Henry who then left it to his son and heir, Fuller Maitland Wilson (1825-1875) of Stowlangtoft, Suffolk.

Joseph and Mary Wilson's second daughter, Frances (1796-1890) married the Revd Charles David Brereton, member of a family that originally came from Cheshire. He was the second son of John and Anna Margaretta Brereton (née Lloyd) of Brinton Hall, Norfolk. In 1820, Joseph Wilson presented his son in law with the living of Little Massingham Church, which remained, in his care until 1867 when his son John Lloyd Brereton succeeded him.[9] In addition to taking an active interest in local affairs, Charles David Brereton also gave support to the founding of the Borneo Mission in 1846 that came under the patronage of James Brooke, the first White Rajah of Sarawak. Exactly why James Brooke should have sought the support of the Revd Charles D. Brereton, Vicar of such a remote parish as that of Little Massingham Norfolk, is not known. The most likely reason is that it was through the Revd Charles D. Brereton's fifth son, William Wilson Brereton, one time Midshipman in the Royal Navy, that James Brooke sought and obtained his help in such a venture. William Brereton's mother, Frances Brereton (née Wilson) was second cousin to Daniel Wilson, Bishop of Calcutta. Any claim however, that James Brooke was related to the Breretons as he stated in a letter to his mother (Mrs Anna Maria Brooke née Stuart) is incorrect. As to the circumstances under which James Brooke met William Brereton it was whilst William Brereton was serving as a midshipman aboard the *Semarang* under the command of Captain Sir Edward Belcher that Midshipman William Wilson Brereton found himself dumped unceremoniously on the shores of the River Sarawak near Kuching in 1843. During the short period of time that the crew of the *Semarang* were in Kuching, James Brooke established a friendship with William Brereton who was deeply impressed by the exploits of James Brooke. In fact such was the impression that Brooke made upon him that we learn that in 1848 William Brereton much to his father's anger resigned his post in the Royal Navy and joined the Rajah in Sarawak where he remained until his death in 1854. He was twenty-four years old.

Whether James Brooke ever discussed his proposal to found a mission with his cousin, Daniel Wilson Bishop of Calcutta is not clear though we do know from a letter written by Frances Brereton (née Wilson), to her sister, Mary Sperling (née Wilson), that whilst the Bishop was on furlough in England from 1845 to 1846 he had received a letter from James Brooke. No details are given about its content but it is more than probable that James Brooke had written to the Bishop sounding him out as to the feasibility of such a proposal and what progress if any had been made in obtaining the support of Christians in England. As events turned out in May 1846 the first committee under the chairmanship of Lord Ellesmere met to discuss the formation of a mission that would be under the protection of James Brooke.[10]

By the time that Bishop Wilson had returned to India on December the 18th

1846 Charles Brereton had already been in contact with the Revd Dr Francis McDougall to arrange an interview with him in the New Year with the purpose of making him an offer. As things turned out, by the April of 1847 we learn from a letter written by Frances Brereton (née Wilson), to her sister Mary, that McDougall had accepted the invitation to go out as leader of a group of missionaries.

Despite the death of William Brereton probably from dysentery, his mother continued to maintain a regular correspondence with the missionaries in Sarawak as well as organizing and raising funds for the mission.

Turning to Joseph and Mary's only son, Henry (1797-1866), after completing his education at Oriel College, Oxford, he then entered Lincoln's Inn as a student in 1819 but left in 1826 having decided not to enter the Bar. It is more than probable that it was during this time that he made the acquaintance of Richard Torin Kindersley, later Sir Richard, one that was to prove advantageous in later years. That however is to move ahead of ourselves. In the meantime, Henry married in 1824 his cousin, Mary Fuller Maitland (1802-1834), the eldest daughter of Ebenezer and Bethia Fuller Maitland.[11] There were eight children by their marriage all of whom survived to adulthood. Soon after the birth of their last child, Janet, his wife, Mary died, probably from puerperal fever. Five years after her death he married Caroline Fitzroy (1809-1891) the only daughter of Revd Lord Henry Fitzroy, son of the 3rd Duke of Grafton.[12] Her brother, The Revd Augustus Fitzroy, Rector of Great Fakenham married Emma Fuller Maitland, daughter of Ebenezer Fuller Maitland by his second marriage.[13]

Although Henry does not appear to have shared his parents' Non-Conformist Evangelical Churchmanship, notwithstanding we find that like his sisters he clearly took an active interest in the Borneo Mission and in particular the career of James Brooke.[14] Thus, we find that when in 1852 James Brooke attended a Dinner held in the City of London at which James Brooke received the Freedom of the City, amongst those on the guest list were Henry Wilson, his brother in law the Revd C.D. Brereton, and his son Charles Brereton. Also present at the dinner were Charles Bayley, C.J. Bunyon, brother of Harriette McDougall (née Bunyon), Thoby Prinsep and the Earl of Ellesmere. Of these Charles Bayley and Thoby Prinsep had served on the Supreme Council in India whilst Lord Ellesmere was one of the founding fathers of the Borneo Mission along with the Revd C.D. Brereton.

Equally interesting is the fact that in addition to taking an interest in the Borneo Mission we also learn that in 1851 Henry Wilson provided funds for the installation of a window dedicated to the Lords of the Manors of Cowley and Brampford Speke, North Devon.[15] Exactly how he became involved in this project is not known but the fact that his name should be linked with the Revd G.C. Gorham, well known for his Calvinistic Evangelical leanings is very interesting, especially when one takes into account Wilson's close friendship with the Revd Samuel Rickards, equally well known for his Tractarian leanings and one time friend of Newman until Newman's defection to the Church of Rome. Equally significant is that prior to the installation of the window at Brampford Speke the Rector, the Revd G.C. Gorham had been engaged in a lengthy altercation with Bishop Philpot, well known for his Tractarian views on Baptism.[16]

In addition to this, Henry Wilson was also responsible for the remodelling of the Church at Stowlangtoft. The architect responsible for the work was William White who had been responsible for the design and building of St Saviour's Aberdeen Park Highbury, the only Tractarian Church in a sea of Evangelicalism.

Henry was also responsible for the rebuilding of Stowlangtoft Hall on a new site probably for his eldest son and heir, Fuller Maitland Wilson who had in 1852 married Caroline Agnes Kindersley, the second daughter of Sir Richard T. Kindersley: whilst Henry's daughter, Frances married Edward Leigh Kindersley, eldest son and heir to Sir Richard T. Kindersley.[17]

As Lord of the manor of Stowlangtoft Henry took an active interest in local affairs serving as MP for West Suffolk from 1835-1837 and then as a Justice of the Peace and Deputy Lieutenant and High Sheriff.[18] On his death in 1866 he was succeeded by his son, Fuller Maitland Wilson.

To return to Joseph Wilson of Highbury Place, two years after the death of his wife Mary Ann in 1798, he married Emma Welford, the eldest daughter of John Welford of Blackheath. There were no children by this second marriage.[19] By this stage he had purchased the capital mansion of Highbury Estate, which remained his family home.[20]

Later, in 1820 he purchased the estate, rectory and advowson of Little Massingham, in Norfolk. Of these, the estate was entailed to his son Henry whilst the Rectory was given to his son in law, the Revd Charles David Brereton two years after his marriage in 1818 to Joseph's daughter, Frances Wilson. In 1826 after a bitter dispute over the price, Joseph purchased the property of Stowlangtoft Hall, near Bury St Edmunds, Suffolk, which remained in the hands of the Maitland Wilsons until 1914.[21] Of his descendants the most famous is Field Marshall Henry Maitland Wilson, 1st Baron of Libya and Stowlangtoft.

Throughout his long and distinguished career in the silk trade, Joseph Wilson remained an active member of the Company. According to the records of the Weavers Company, we learn that in 1795 he was elected auditor of the company along with his brother in law, Samuel Mills. In the same year, Joseph was elected Renter Bailiff of the Company, a post that he held for two years. Thereafter he rose steadily through the ranks of the Company rising eventually to the rank of Upper Bailiff the highest position in the company and one normally reserved for the economically and socially elite within the City.[22]

From 1791 to 1809, the main business was directed from 30 Milk Street, Cheapside but in 1809 Joseph expanded into Essex where he purchased an old flour mill in Chapel Lane, Braintree. With its own water supply, this was a silk manufacturer's dream. All that was required was for someone with the flair and skill to convert the old flourmill into a silk mill for the manufacture of crepe silk. That person was George Courtauld who had sometime between 1798 and 1799 converted a flourmill in Pebmarsh for the firm of Witt & Co of Friday Street, Cheapside.[23]

By the terms of the contract, it was agreed that George Courtauld should manage the mill for a period of fourteen years and to receive a share of the profits. In the event, the partnership proved to be ill fated, concluding in 1818 with a court decision that went against Joseph Wilson.[24] Despite losing the case it was not until 1843 that Joseph Wilson eventually sold his business in Braintree to Samuel Courtauld III. By this stage, Joseph Wilson who was 77 years of age had virtually withdrawn from the business and retired to his home in Highbury Place where he lived with his widowed daughter, Mary Sperling (née Wilson) and Emma, his second wife.[25]

In addition to his business activities, Joseph retained a life long interest in a number of religious and philanthropic causes. Thus, we find that along with other members of his family, including the Maitlands, he is listed as serving on the Board of the London Missionary Society, the British and Foreign Bible Society and the Congregational Union. Later, in 1846 encouraged by his two daughters and his grandson, William Wilson Brereton, he took a keen interest in the Borneo Church Mission Institution in Sarawak of which his son in law, the Revd Charles Brereton, Vicar of Little Massingham, was the first Honorary Secretary.

When Joseph died in the March of 1851, he was buried in the family tomb in Bunhill Fields along with members of his family including his first wife, Mary. His second wife, Emma who died in the December of 1851, was also buried in the family tomb at Bunhill Fields.[26]

To most people, especially Essex people, the story of the Braintree Silk Industry is synonymous with the Courtaulds and in particular George Courtauld and his son, Samuel Courtauld III.

However, contrary to popular belief the story of the silk industry in Braintree does not begin with the Courtaulds but with Joseph Wilson of Remington, Wilson and Co of 31 Milk Street, Cheapside, City of London.

Although the contribution of the Courtaulds to Braintree was significant, but for the altercation between Joseph Wilson and George Courtauld it might have been the name of Remington, Wilson and Co that people would have remembered, not the name of Courtauld. That however is another story.

*The Rectory, Little Massingham, Norfolk (n.d.). Photo courtesy of Rosemary Jewers (née Brereton).*

## Notes and References:

(i) Joseph Wilson, (1766-1851) the second son of Thomas and Mary Wilson, (née Remington) is not to be confused with Joseph Wilson, (1786-1855) eldest son of William and Elizabeth Wilson (née West) of 31 Milk Street and The Wortons, Oxfordshire. See: McCann, P & F. Young. (1992) Samuel Wilderspin & the Infant School Society. London: Croom Helm, where he makes this confusion.

1. Wilson, J. (1846) Memoir of Thomas Wilson. London.

2. Wilson, J. (1846) Memoir of Thomas Wilson. London.

3. GUILDHALL LIBRARY: Gld Mss. Court Minute Books: Weavers Company 4655/18/: 1786-1798, which records that on January 4th 1791 Joseph Wilson, of Milk Street was freed by redemption.

4. Mary Anne Maitland was a member of the family of Maitlands that were descended from the Maitlands of Thirlstone, Berwickshire. Her sister, Frances Maitland married the Revd John Savill member of the Savill Family of Bocking, cloth manufacturers. Joseph and Mary Anne Wilson (née Maitland) consolidated even further their position with the marriage of their only son, Henry to Mary Fuller Maitland, eldest daughter of Ebenezer Fuller Maitland of Stansted Hall, Stansted Mount Fitchet, Essex.

5. Robert Maitland and his brother, Ebenezer Maitland of Stansted Hall, Stansted Mountfitchet were members of the Congregational Church. Ebenezer Maitland is cited along with Joseph as being on the Committee of the Congregational Union, London Missionary Society and the British and Foreign Bible Society. Ebenezer Maitland added Fuller to his name following his marriage to Bethia Ellis: her mother was co-heir to Thomas Fuller. See: n.4.

6. On the Maitlands see: Harrison, George, Rogers-Harrison. Genealogical and Historical Account of the Maitland Family. London: privately printed. 1869.

7. On the Savills of Bocking: see: ERO: D/Cd: Savill Family Papers and Notebook. See also: Baker, Michael. (1992) The Book of Braintree and Bocking. Whittlebury: Baron Books.
On the Revd John Savill: see: Blaxill, E.A. (1938) History of Lion Walk: 1642-1937. Colchester.

8. On the Sperlings of Dynes Hall and Papworth St Agnes: see: Mrs Hurst Dancing: and Other Scenes from Regency Life: 1812-1823 with sketches by Diana Sperling and commentary by George Mingay, with an introduction by Elizabeth Longford. London: Victor Gollancz, 1981. I am grateful to Miss Diana Chardin, Librarian, Trinity College, Cambridge, for allowing me access to her personal copy of the book.

9. The Breretons of Norfolk were a branch of the Cheshire family of Breretons many of whom were executed during the reign of Henry VIII. See: Ives, E. (1986) Anne Boleyn. Oxford: Blackwell. See also Brereton Family Papers: Norfolk Record Office: Acc no 2001/276/Box22/f197. also: Revd R.F. McLeod. Massingham Parva: Past and Present. London, 1882. See also: R.L. Maitland Brereton. The Brereton Family of Cheshire: 1834-1911.

10. On his return to England Daniel Wilson addressed the SPG. Present at the meeting

was Bp. Stanley a close friend of C.D. Brereton and F.T. McDougall. On the Borneo Mission see: Bodleian Library: Rhodes House: SPG Pamphlets: Borneo Church Mission Institution; Ms. Ind. Ocn. S. 292, MSS: Pac.S. 104: on Francis McDougal: see: Bunyon, C.J. (1889) The Memoirs of Francis Thomas McDougall and Harriette his Wife. London. Contrary to what Brooke stated he was not related to the Breretons: he was however related to the Bishop's mother Ann Collett Wilson (née West). James Brooke's father, Thomas Brooke, was first cousin to the Bishop's mother. See also: Brereton Family Papers: Norfolk Record Office: Acc No. 2001/276/Box 22/f.201.

11. Henry Wilson married 1st, Mary Fuller Maitland eldest daughter of Ebenezer and Bethia Fuller Maitland of Stansted Hall, Stansted Mountfitchet, then 2nd Caroline Fitzroy only daughter of Revd Ld Henry and Caroline Fitzroy and niece to the 4th Duke of Grafton, Euston Hall, Suffolk.

12. Burkes Peerage: see also: Burkes Landed Gentry.

13. Harrison, G. & Rogers-Harrison. (1869) Genealogical and Historical Account of the Maitland Family. London: privately printed.

14. Norfolk Record Office: Brereton Family Papers: Acc no. 2001/276/Box22/fl97: letter from Henry Wilson to Charles David Brereton: Sept 1st 1851 in which Henry Wilson expressed his desire to meet Sir James Brooke before he returned to Sarawak. As events turned out he was invited to a civic dinner in London along with his brother in law, Charles David Brereton in 1852.

15. Orme, Nicholas. A Guide to St Peter's Church, Brampford Speke, Devon. In 1857 the Revd Richard Cockburn Kindersley, brother in law to Fuller Maitland Wilson was appointed Vicar of the combined parishes of Brampford Speke and Cowley. I am grateful to Angela Muzzlewhite, of Brampford Speke for this information.

16. Whether Wilson shared Rickard's Tractarian views is a moot point: it is more than probable that he was moderate in his Churchmanship, hence the fact that he gave a donation for the installation of a window in the Church of Brampford Speke, North Devon. On the Gorham Controversy see: Chadwick, O. (1971) The Victorian Church. 3rd edition. London: A&C Black.

17. Burkes Landed Gentry.

18. See: Burkes Peerage: Maitland Wilsons of Libya and Stowlangtoft, Suffolk.

19. Joseph Wilson's second wife, Emma was the eldest daughter of John Welford of Blackheath. She died in 1851 without issue and was buried in the family tomb at Bunhill Fields.

20. Joseph Wilson purchased the Capital Mansion of Highbury Estate in 1789. Highbury Hill House, which was designed by Daniel Asher Alexander, was demolished in 1928. See: Suffolk Record Office: Bury St Edmunds Office: Papers relating to Joseph Wilson: London Estate: HA 530/4/1-18.

21. In 1826 Joseph Wilson purchased Stowlangtoft Hall and its estates for his son, for which he paid £80,000. On Stowlangtoft see: Suffolk Record Office: Bury St Edmunds Office: HA/530: Papers relating to Joseph Wilson of Highbury Place.

22. GUILDHALL LIBRARY: Gld Mss: Court Minute Books: Weavers Company 4655/18-20. D. Possee is incorrect when he states in his book: The Weaver and the Throwster, (1998) that Joseph Wilson was Lord Mayor of the City of London. It

was Samuel Wilson of Lea and Wilsons of Old Jewry, a second cousin to Joseph Wilson who held this position from 1838-1839. See: Plummer, A. ((1972) The London Weavers Company: 1600-1760. London: Routledge, Kegan & Paul. ch. 16: An Early Victorian Lord Mayor. p.340-353. See also: Rothstein, N.K.A. (1990) Silk Designs of the 18th century in the Collection of the Victoria and Albert Museum. London: Thames and Hudson. It was Ld Mayor Samuel Wilson's brother, Stephen Wilson of Lea and Wilson who was responsible for introducing the Jacquard machine into England sometime between 1820 and 1821. See: Letter from Sir Ernest Goodale from the Warner Papers: dated Paris Aug 3rd 1820 from Thomas Smith to Stephen Wilson of Lea, Wilson & Co, 26 Old Jewry, London. Journal Royal Society of Arts. Vol. cviii, no. 5041, 1950-1960 p.374-376.

23. Joseph Wilson was first introduced by an unknown third party to George Courtauld in 1806. See: Essex Record Office: (ERO) Bocking: D/F.3/2/94; Letters, Papers & Deeds Relating to George Courtauld and Joseph Wilson: c.1809-1817, (12 pages). For later deeds of partnership see: D/F/3/1/18. See also: Booker, J. (1974) Essex and the Industrial Revolution. Chelmsford: Essex County Council in which he states that George Courtauld moved to Braintree and set up in another converted flourmill. This is not strictly accurate. He was invited by Joseph Wilson to convert and then manage the silk firm in Chapel Lane. Likewise Crosby A. & A. Corder-Birch are incorrect in stating that the Courtaulds dominated Braintree in 1809. See: Crosby, A. & A. Corder-Birch, The Courtauld Family & the Essex Landscape. Essex Journal, Autumn 2001. The standard and authoritative work on the Courtaulds is that by D.C. Coleman. The Courtaulds: an Economic and Social History. Oxford: Clarendon, 1969. 2 vols.

24. See: Coleman, D.C. (1969) Courtaulds: An Economic and Social History. Oxford: Clarendon Press. 2 vols. See also: ERO. Bocking. D/F.3/2/94: Letters, Papers & Deeds relating to George Courtauld and Joseph Wilson: c.1809-1817.

25. In his will Joseph left his house in Highbury Hill to his eldest daughter, Mary Sperling, (née Wilson) for life. Emma Wilson (née Welford) died in the December of 1851.

26. See: Burkes Peerage & Baronetcy who record that Emma died on March 11th 1851. On this matter they are incorrect. She died in the December of 1851. See also: Stockborough, D. Lords of the Manor of Stowlangtoft. (n.d.) who is incorrect when he states that Joseph died in the early 1840s; and was buried at Stowlangtoft. As a Nonconformist, he was buried in the family tomb in Bunhill Fields with other members of his family including his parents and two wives. Bunhill Fields in the City of London is an historic burial ground used by Nonconformists. It was here that notable Dissenters including John Bunyan, Henry Cromwell, Daniel Defoe, John Owen Isaac Watts, Susanna Wesley and Robert and Elizabeth Maitland were buried. See: Bunhill Fields: a guide by the Corporation of London. 1902.

# 10. From Spitalfield to Calcutta: Daniel Wilson 5th Bishop of Calcutta*(i)*

On June 19th 1832 Daniel Wilson, recently appointed as the 5th Bishop of Calcutta boarded the *"James Sibbald"* for Calcutta.[1] Accompanying him was his only surviving daughter, Eliza, his Assistant Chaplain, Josiah Bateman and a native servant.[2] Daniel Wilson was fifty-four years of age and the most unlikely of all people to be appointed to such a post.[3]

Born on July 2nd 1778 at 4.am, Daniel Wilson the third child of Stephen and Anne Collett Wilson (née West) was baptized by the Revd Samuel Brewer, Minister of Stepney Green Independent Meeting House on Sunday 23rd of July.[4] His father, Stephen Wilson [II] was the second son of Stephen and Mary Wilson, (née Fullalove) a silk manufacturer of Coventry and Wood Street, Cheapside, London.[5]

After serving his time in the family business, which at this stage was being managed by his mother, Mary Wilson (née Fullalove) and his uncle, Thomas Wilson, senior, Stephen entered into partnership in 1774 with Daniel West, a wealthy silk merchant who lived in Church Street, Spitalfields, considered to be one of the finest residences in the area.[6] As a married man with four unmarried daughters to provide for it must have been a cause of concern to Daniel West that he had no obvious heir to whom he could pass on the family business, his only son having died some time after 1764.[7] The situation that Daniel West found himself in was not unusual but by entering into partnership with a younger person, he was in a position of keeping the business on a firm footing and of providing for his family. Equally important was the fact he was able to leave the management of the business to his partner leaving himself free as the sleeping partner to carry out his duties as Renter Bailiff in the Weavers Company.[8]

In 1774, Stephen Wilson married Ann Collett West. She was the eldest daughter of Daniel and Ann West (née Brooke). Her father who was the only son of Daniel and Elizabeth West, of Vine Court, Wood Street Spitalfields[9] had married Anne Brooke the eldest daughter of Robert and Elizabeth Brooke (née Collett), of Goodman Fields, Whitechapel.[10]

From the little that we know about them her father, Robert Brooke was a wealthy maritime Captain, in the services of the East India Company whilst her mother, Elizabeth Brooke (née Collett) was the second daughter of Thomas Collett a maritime Captain in the services of the East India Company.[11] Robert and Elizabeth had five children of whom only three survived to adulthood. The two daughters were, Ann who married Daniel West from whom Daniel Wilson the 5th Bishop of Calcutta, was descended, and Elizabeth who married Thomas

*Holy Trinity, Over Worton, 1804.*

Pattle from whom the seven beautiful daughters of James Pattle were descended. Amongst these was Julia Margaret Cameron, the famous Victorian photographer and great aunt of Vanessa Bell (née Stephen) and Virginia Woolf (née Stephen).[12] Whether Daniel Wilson ever met any of James Pattle's daughters when he went to Calcutta in 1832 is not known but given Julia Cameron's position within the Calcutta society it is more than probable that they were to meet on numerous occasions.[13] We do know however that he was acquainted with Thoby Prinsep, who was married to Sara Pattle, and his brother, Charles Prinsep, both of whom served on a committee for the arrangement of the education scheme for the La Martiniere School in Calcutta.[14]

The youngest of Robert and Elizabeth's children was a son also called Robert from whom the 1st White Rajah of Sarawak James Brooke was descended.[12]

Later in 1851, on his return to Calcutta via Singapore from Sarawak, Daniel was to meet James Brooke, his third cousin whom he described as an "English Gentleman of benevolence, talent and singular wisdom."[15]

From early childhood Daniel Wilson would probably have heard his mother talk about India where her cousins, Thomas Brooke and Thomas Pattle, worked as employees in the services of the East India Company. Daniel's mother is recorded as being in regular receipt of letters from her cousin, Thomas Brooke, as well as being a regular visitor to the home of Mrs Ruth Brooke, her aunt in Mortlake, where she lived with her three Anglo Indian grandchildren, Charles, Sophia and Julia. They were the children of Thomas Brooke by his Indian companion or Bibi.[16] At what stage the three children were sent to England to live with their grandmother is not known, but during their time in England the two girls, along with Daniel's younger sisters, attended a school in Stepney Green that was managed by a Miss Jones.[17] There is no knowing how much Daniel absorbed as a young child about India from the various conversations he overheard or the numerous letters that his mother received from cousin Thomas, but it seems impossible that they did not make an impression upon him. India was in his blood but it would not be until he was aged fifty-four that he would eventually stand on the banks of the Hooghly River. In the meantime, all he could do was dream about India.[18]

As a child Daniel lived with his parents and grandfather, Daniel West, at 6 Church Street, Spitalfields, one of those grand roomy and comfortable houses, says Daniel Wilson, which abounded in the old fashioned parts of London.[19]

For a young child Spitalfields must have been an exciting and fascinating area in which to be brought up with its dazzling sights, its crowded streets bustling with trade and unabated noise and its overwhelming stench. Howbeit all this was to come to an end when at the age of seven Daniel was sent to a private school managed by a Mr Searle in Eltham which at this stage was still a pretty little village surrounded by beautiful countryside.[20] Under normal circumstances he would have remained at this school until he was fourteen years of age, but for reasons best known to themselves his parents removed him and placed him in a School at Homerton. This was a Dissenting academy managed by the Revd John Eyre, well known for his radical and pro-Whig ideas: a person with one foot placed decidedly in Dissent and the other planted in the left wing of the Anglican Church. Within late 18th century Evangelical circles, John Eyre was to say the least a remarkable person. Having originally trained at Trevecca College for the Dissenting Ministry, he chose instead to take Holy Orders in the Church of England. In 1778, he entered Emmanuel College, Oxford and on the 30th of May 1779, he was ordained first as a Deacon and later in the same year as a Priest. After serving first as a Curate to the Revd Richard Cecil and then with the Revd William B Cadogan of Reading, Eyre then moved to Homerton where he was appointed Pastor of a small Episcopal Chapel known as Ram's Chapel.[21]

By placing the education of her somewhat wayward son into the hands of John Eyre it seems that Ann Collett Wilson was taking a calculated risk: one however that she clearly considered justified in taking. From the few details that we have about her, she was a well-educated person and an accomplished letter writer: a habit or gift that Daniel seems to have inherited. Like many young women of her time, her life was devoted to charity and religious service. In his Private Calendar, her husband Stephen Wilson, records that she visited the sick, assisted in raising funds for the poor and for missionary societies as well as attending their meetings. In addition to all this, we find that along with her young daughters she attended the Prayer meeting held at the Tabernacle. Yet, in all this endless round of entertainment and being entertained, of visiting and being visited, Ann Collett Wilson never lost sight of her role as a wife and as a mother, even to a wayward son. Here indeed was a person of great piety and spiritual insight, who was possessed of a remarkable level of grace and determination.[22] By entrusting her son's education and welfare in the hands of John Eyre, she made an excellent choice. He was it seems "eminently qualified not more by his educational attainments than by his talents for serving the affections of the rising generation." In the words of one contemporary, "no preceptor of youth was more beloved by his pupils, some of whom are living today among whom may be named the highly respectable Bishop of Calcutta and the Revd Mr Wildbore of Cornwall who can bear testimony to the love and respect which reigned in this establishment." Whilst there he studied Latin, Greek and French, a language in which he excelled. He also studied English, Mathematics and probably Natural Philosophy: a popular subject at this stage. In addition, he studied the Old and New Testament and possibly the Articles of the Church of England and the Catechism to which Eyre attached great importance.[23]

Yet, as Daniel Wilson must have fully realized once he had reached the age of fourteen he would be expected to abandon his studies and follow the example of his father. Accordingly, we learn that on the 2nd of December, 1792 Daniel was bound an apprentice to his uncle, William Wilson of 31 Milk Street.[24] During his apprenticeship he resided with his uncle, who is depicted by Wilson's biographer as being "a cold and distant person, whose eyes were everywhere and in whose presence all was order and decorum."[25] For someone as sensitive as he was and who clearly resented being forced from his studies and from fulfilling his own ambtion of following in the footsteps of his Anglo-Indian cousins as a Writer in the services of the East India Company it is not surprising therefore that he should react in the manner that he did, even to the extent of rebelling against his religious upbringing.[26]

Although as we have noted all the signs were that he was destined to follow in the footsteps of his father and uncle as a silk merchant it seems that during his apprenticeship he underwent a religious experience that was to have a dramatic effect upon him altering the whole course of his life. Yet, as he himself records in his early days he showed no obvious interest in religious matter, believing that his prayers reached no higher than the ceiling.

In a letter written in 1853 to his children he reflects upon the fact that during his early childhood he was careless and glorified in his infidelity and godlessness: "full of sin to the very brim, set upon iniquity, sold to wickedness, Satan's bond slave." He also recalls his early life as an apprentice and the events that led up to his conversion. He states that, "I am entering the 58th year of my life (O wonder of mercy) since the words addressed to me in my father in law's warehouse were the means of awakening my soul from a state of rebellion and every vice, secret and open contempt of God and the Evangelical Doctrines in which I was nourished." He goes on to say, "my fellow servant was fond of theological disputes but with no proof of piety." He was arguing with me on some point the particulars of which I forget. I objected to his statement and said in levity: "You talk to me of Religious feelings but I have none such." He replied, " Pray for the feelings." At first, Daniel Wilson thought nothing of this but when he returned to his chamber, he states that he knelt down for the first time in sincerity in his whole life and prayed to God for the feelings.[27]

Even though Daniel Wilson often looked back to the 9th of March 1796 when in his words the first admonition of grace reached my feeling and my heart leading to personal prayer as a sinner it was not until Sunday October the 1st 1797 when he went to Ram's Chapel where he received Holy Communion that he obtained the joy and peace that had eluded him for so long.[28]

Undoubtedly, Ram's Chapel was a watershed in his life and yet, as his letters show he was not given to excessive hilarity of spirits or joy: his was a faith that combined activism with habitual penitence of the heart even to the extent of being over critical regarding his own personal state of holiness.[29]

Whereas before his conversion, he was destined for the silk trade after his conversion he professed a desire to enter the Church. Soon after receiving Holy Communion at Ram's Chapel Daniel Wilson shared the matter with the Revd John Eyre who then acting on Daniel's behalf visited Stephen Wilson on Monday October the 23rd to inform Stephen Wilson of Daniel's wishes. After consulting with Daniel on this matter, it was agreed by all concerned that the matter should be discouraged for the moment.[30]

According to Bateman it would seem that on the 5th of December 1797, he wrote, to his mother in which he stated that his desires were drawn to this object, but the Lord showed me that it was my duty to wait till He should see fit to give me a door of utterance. He goes on to state that, "at my age and under my relative obligations it was my duty to be implicitly obedient to the will of my parents and my master, it appeared my duty merely to open my mind to you, to make you acquainted with the state of my soul and then leave it to the Lord to influence your determination." Doubtless, he hoped that by sharing with his mother his desire to enter the Church she would then break the news gently to her husband, who according to Bateman was a remote and unapproachable person. Whether his mother ever divulged the contents of her son's letter to her husband is not known. Although Stephen in his private calendar makes no reference to this letter it is significant to note that contrary to what Bateman states in the biography of his father in law there is no evidence that Stephen refused to give Daniel his consent to terminate his indentures with his uncle William Wilson and enter the Church. In fact the very opposite. Contrary to what Bateman says it was on Wednesday March the 14th 1798 that Stephen asked his son which Church he preferred, "the Church of England or the Dissenting line?" Daniel replied, "the Church of England."[31]. Had Stephen been totally opposed to the wishes of his son he would not have raised the matter again let alone have gone out of his way to discuss the matter with members of the Dissenting and Anglican Church. As it was we find that on the following Sunday 18th March, between Dinner and the Evening Service Stephen records that he went to see the Revd I. Goode of White Row, Spitalfields and spoke to him about Daniel's desire to enter the Church of England. According to Stephen it would seem that not only did the Revd Mr Goode approve of Stephen's proposed plan that Daniel should be examined by a number of Ministers but we also learn that Mr Goode then proposed that Daniel should be seen by the Revd Mr Richard Cecil of St John's Bedford Row, the Revd Mr Ford and himself. Mr Goode then said he would discuss the matter with the Revd Mr Cecil the next day and let Stephen know Mr Cecil's decision on the Tuesday next. On the following Tuesday, March 20th Mr Goode dined with Stephen and informed him that the Revd Mr Richard Cecil approved of Stephen's proposal. However, on the following Monday, 26th March Stephen records that Daniel received a letter from the Revd Mr John Eyre in which he stated his disapproval of Stephen's proposal. In his opinion, he felt that it appeared to be a final and binding proposal both on Daniel and on Stephen. His concern was that if all the parties involved were of the opinion that Daniel should not enter the ministry then it left Stephen with no room to over-ride their decision and rule in his son's favour. On reading the letter, Stephen rode over to Homerton to discuss the matter with the Revd John Eyre. In his Private Calendar, he records that "Mr Eyre continued in that mind." Later that same day he went to see the Revd Mr Sabine who not only approved of Stephen's proposal but also considered that the Revd Mr John Eyre was quite wrong in what he had said.

The same week he records that on Thursday 29th March he went to see the Revd Mr Richard Cecil to hear his opinion of Daniel's call to the ministry. Cecil who had already discussed on Monday the 26th with Daniel his calling was clearly of the opinion that it was a real call and one that should be pursued. The following day Stephen went to see the Revd Mr W. Goode of Blackfriars to arrange an appointment for Daniel to see him that afternoon to discuss with him the matter of his calling.[32] In the afternoon of Friday March 30th Stephen went round to speak to the Revd Mr I. Goode of White Row, Spitalfields before riding over to Islington to speak to his brother, John Wilson of Upper Street. Although Stephen does not mention the content of his conversation with his brother it is more than probable that he wanted to sound him out regarding Daniel's desire to enter the ministry and possibly to re-assure himself that he himself was in fact acting in his son's best interests. As a Lay examiner for candidates for the missionary field John was an ideal person to discuss his son's calling to the ministry.[33]

On the 3rd of April, Stephen records that the Revd John Eyre came to dinner to discuss with Stephen what steps should be taken prior to Daniel going to College. That same afternoon they went over to the Revd Mr G. West of Lemon Street, who recommended that Daniel should be entered into St Edmund Hall, Oxford in the term previous to the long term in Lent. This, he said would give him six months before he arrived at St Edmunds during which time he should be placed in the care of the Revd Mr Josiah Pratt who would instruct him in Greek and prepare him for his examinations.[34] Acting on the Revd Mr West's advice Stephen records that on the 5th of April he rode over to see Mr Pratt at his residence in Doughty Street to discuss with him the terms of his tuition and what books Daniel would require. According to an entry in his Private

Calendar Stephen records that Mr Pratt's fees were £100 per annum, which would include accommodation and tuition. On the following Friday Josiah Pratt dined with the Wilsons ostensibly to meet Daniel and to explain what steps Stephen and Daniel would have to take regarding Daniel's admission to St Edmund's Hall. During his visit, Josiah Pratt selected thirty books from Stephen's library, which he considered would be appropriate for Daniel's studies. It was also agreed that Daniel should take up residence with the Revd Mr Josiah Pratt following Daniel's return from Oxford.[35]

Under Josiah Pratt's tuition, he studied the Bible and in particular, Scott's commentary on the Bible, which according to Bishop Sumner was Daniel Wilson's first great oracle and wherever he went some volumes were his constant companion. This short period under Josiah Pratt's guidance marked effectively the beginnings of Wilson's ecclesiastical career and in a sermon preached on the occasion of the Farewell to his Clergy in Calcutta in 1845 he stated on hearing the news of Josiah Pratt's death that, "he was the affectionate tutor who guided my youth and prepared me for the University in 1798 and continued my bosom friend from that time to the moment of his death."[36]

In November 1798, Daniel Wilson went up to St Edmund Hall, Oxford where in the words of Bishop Sumner he proved himself an able scholar gaining several prizes. Doctrinally his views were according to Sumner very much those of Thomas Scott whom he regarded as his first great oracle.[37]

After graduating from Oxford in 1801, he was ordained by the Bishop of Winchester, Dr Brownlow North at Farnham Castle on September the 20th before taking up his first curacy with the Revd Richard Cecil at Chobham and Bisley. It is significant to note that both John Eyre and Josiah Pratt had been Curates to Cecil, and Pratt was until 1804 Assistant to Cecil at St John's Bedford Row. Both of them were important influences in the life of Wilson but it was probably through Josiah Pratt that his interests in the Missionary Field and in particular India was further developed and re-awakened.[38] According to Bateman, it was in 1797 that Daniel Wilson felt his spirit stirred to go as a missionary to a heathen land, probably India, though Bateman does not actually state so in so many words. Nevertheless, it is more than possible that this was what he had in mind when he stated that it was to be another 30 years before he stood on the banks of the River Hooghly. Whilst this may be correct, what Bateman fails to disclose is the fact that from early childhood he had been nurtured upon India.[39] Any idea therefore that he had no knowledge of India is obviously incorrect so that when he says in a letter dated January 14th 1835 that he told the Rajah that "I came from England for love of India and had been interested in its welfare for forty years," he was in fact quite correct.[40] India was virtually in his blood. Whereas however he had only heard members of the family talk about India on that first Sunday in

October 1797 he chose to serve God by going out as a missionary to India. Even so there was to be a long period of just over 30 years before he entered the field of foreign missions when in 1832 he was appointed Bishop of Calcutta. In the meantime he was actively involved in deputation work for the CMS, as well as Home Missions and in proclaiming the Evangelical Truth and being a Shepherd to his flock: a lesson that he had learnt as a Curate under Richard Cecil.

Within late eighteenth and early nineteenth century Anglican Evangelicalism Richard Cecil was a key figure who sought to strive for what may be described as a form of "Catholic Evangelicalism" and in this context he was clearly an important influence in shaping Wilson's style of Churchmanship. In his sermons preached on the occasion of Richard Cecil's death Wilson admits that he freely owed his obligations to this early teaching. It would he said "be ungrateful in me not to profess that to his kindness, his advice, his instruction and his guidance I owe under God's blessing all I am, or ever may be . . . I never shall, I never can while I know my myself forget the advantages that I have derived from his eminent wisdom and experience."[41]

During his first Curacy at Chobham, he married Anne Wilson, his first cousin and childhood companion, thus strengthening even further his family connections within the business world and the Anglican Church. They had six children of whom only three survived to adulthood: Daniel (1805-1886), John (1807-1833) and Eliza Emma (1814-) who married Josiah Bateman, her first cousin.[42]

Throughout the twenty-five years in which Daniel and Anne were married, it was his wife who by nature was reserved, more than made up for her husband's formal nature. She was the devoted wife who by her warmth and courtesy enabled the students to feel at ease during the termly dinners: a tradition that Crouch had established when he was Vice Principal.[43] Above all she was a person of great piety for whom the home was the cradle of religious nurture; the place where she was able to devote her time to the spiritual. moral and material welfare of her children. This was a role she had learnt early in life when at the age of ten her mother died leaving her to care for her younger brothers and sisters. She was indeed a woman possessed of a remarkable level of wisdom, patience and grace: a person of great piety and spiritual insight who clearly never lost sight of her role as a mother and a wife. And yet, as Bateman says, "she neither murmured nor hesitated when the path of duty led from Worton and its quiet country scenes to Oxford, London and Islington."[44]

After two years at Chobham Daniel Wilson was invited by Isaac Crouch to assist him at St Edmund Hall with the view of taking up the post of Vice Principal. At the same time, he also assisted part time as a Curate at the Churches of Over and Nether Worton. They were in the patronage of his uncle and father in law, William Wilson. He was a shrewd businessman, a person possessed of great foresight and acumen who had purchased a number of livings as well as two estates in Oxfordshire to which he had retired in 1810.[45] Although Daniel Wilson took his duties seriously at St Edmund Hall, unlike Crouch or for that matter his successor, John Hill, he was never fully at ease with University life.[46] So, when in 1809 Cecil invited Wilson to succeed him at St John's Bedford Row London, Wilson did not hesitate in accepting the offer. However, it was to be another three years before the Revd John Hill was appointed to succeed Wilson as Vice Principal of St Edmund Hall, Oxford. In the meantime, Wilson divided his time between Oxford and London: a situation, which for a person of his temperament he found to be both frustrating and tiresome.

Once however that Daniel Wilson was free of his duties at Oxford, he was able to devote all his energies to the Chapel, which remained a fashionable centre of Evangelicalism attracting large congregations. Amongst those who attended were the Thorntons, the Grants, Ld Calthorpe, Sir Robert Inglis, Sir Thomas Blomefield, Ld Ryder, the Duchess of Beaufort and her daughters, the Macaulays and occasionally William Wilberforce and his two sons, Robert and Samuel.[47] During the time that Wilson was at St John's, he involved himself in a wide range of activities both within the Parish and also in London. Thus, we find that he was active in setting up a District Visiting Society linked to St John's, as well as the London Clerical Education Society of which he was its first Secretary. In addition, he took an active role in the Church Missionary Society, the Bible Society, the City of London Auxiliary Bible Society and the Eclectic Society. All was hustle and bustle with Wilson and as a result, he seems to have had a recurrence of a skin disorder from which he had suffered since childhood.[48] Consequently, he was forced to relinquish his duties in the Parish and on the advice of his doctor take a rest abroad. Whilst touring through Europe accompanied by his wife and family he wrote a journal entitled "Letters from an absent Brother," addressed mainly though not wholly to his sister, Eliza. This is a remarkable journal in which he describes the places they visited, the beautiful countryside and buildings and the people they met including a Mrs H who had lived so long in the very house in which he was born in Spitalfields.[49]

Following his return to England he seems to have suffered a further relapse of his skin disorder but by early April, 1824 he seems to have recovered sufficiently to take on a new challenge that had arisen as a result of the death of Dr Strachan, incumbent of St Mary's Islington. As Patron of the Church, he had to decide whether to appoint a new incumbent or resign his position at St John's and accept the living of St Mary, Islington.[50] To a person of Wilson's temperament, calibre and administrative ability Islington was an opportunity that he clearly could not ignore. It was after all a challenge of a life time allowing him to make use of all the talents that he had formed early in his life in promoting a Parish that would be a witness in the Metropolis and the Church of England. During the eight years in which he was the incumbent, he turned Islington from a run down Parish to one that was bustling with activity. With regard to his period of office as Incumbent of St Mary, Islington it is worth quoting from the speech made by the Church Warden, Charles Woodward, in which he stated that: "they were cheered with the pleasing prospects of an answer to our prayers for by you was our attention called to the want of our fellow Parishioners . . . and by your means were the new Churches erected and dedicated to the service of the Most High." He goes on to add that, "in order to render the great work most effective, you my Lord, made an avoidance before the Lord Bishop of the Diocese of the three district Churches, and presented as patrons of the Livings the Ministers of the three Churches to be Incumbents, at the same time with your accustomed liberality resigning in their favour all the Fees, Easter offerings and other Ecclesiastical dues, thus rendering the Ministers independent of yourself and carrying home the sacraments of the Church to the very threshold of the more distant inhabitants." Charles Woodward then went on to point out that "under your auspices my Lord, was yonder proprietary School erected, which has afforded the children of the higher classes those means of Religious Instruction that were previously principally confined to the children of the poor . . . by you numerous other Institutions and Societies have been formed."[51]

From this contemporary account it maybe observed that as incumbent Daniel Wilson's influence and activity in the Parish was considerable and although he was not successful in getting Smithfield Market changed from Monday to Tuesday there were according to the evidence of John Twells "only twenty or thirty shops out of four hundred that refused to close on the Sabbath."[52] To Wilson the observance of the Sabbath was next in importance to Education, Family Prayers and Public Worship, a point that he emphasized in a pastoral address he preached in 1826. Although he had paved the way on Sunday Observance in his Induction Sermon it was not until 1827 that he preached a series of sermons on the Divine and Perpetual Obligation of the Lord's Day. Prior to the publication of these sermons, Daniel Wilson had received a deputation led by Revd John Blackburn, Minister of Claremont Chapel, Islington and Secretary of the Christian Instruction Society.[53] The purpose of his visit was to seek the support of Daniel Wilson regarding the observance of the Sabbath: Wilson declined the invitation.[54] Undeterred by this John Blackburn then led a deputation to see the Bishop of London, C.J. Blomfield. Commenting on his visit John Blackburn states that they were warmly received by their Lordship with much courtesy. Encouraged by the

*Islington Parish Church.*

deputation the Bishop published a letter on the subject of Sunday Observance in which he acknowledged his indebtedness to the Christian Instruction Society whom he said "had borne a powerful testimony to the awful profanation of the Lord's Day."[55] It is significant to note that it was in response to the Bishop of London's Letter to the Clergy that Wilson decided to repeat his sermons on the Lord's Day, which were subsequently enlarged and published in 1831. In the same year, his cousin, Joseph Wilson of Clapham invited him to attend the first meeting of the Society for the Due Observance of the Lord's Day. Although Daniel Wilson was not the founder of the Society his influence and standing within Evangelical circles helped give the society a lead in the field of Sunday Observance, so inspiring a major assault upon the desecration of the English Sabbath.[56] Fired by the belief that a sign of vital religion was demonstrated in the observance of the Lord's Day and the attendance of Public Worship, Wilson was alert to any obstacle that might prevent his parishioners from attending Church. Amongst these was the system of pew rent that he had inherited from his predecessor. Wilson was of the opinion that such a system prevented the poor from attending public worship. He believed that the Gospel should be available to all regardless of class or wealth. After a lengthy meeting lasting four hours, it was agreed that the seats should be free at the evening service.[57]

Even though he took an active part in local and national affairs he did not neglect his pastoral duties. The notion of the Vicar as the Shepherd was one that Wilson had learnt whilst serving as a Curate under Richard Cecil. However, following the death of his wife in 1827 and then of his mother in 1829 we find that Wilson's attention turned more and more to India and in particular the appointment of a suitable candidate for the vacant Bishopric resulting from the death of Bishop Turner in 1831. Along with other members of the CMS Wilson was obviously concerned that not only was the right person appointed for such a demanding post but, that the Government should be seen to be acting responsibly. Afflicted by ill health for most of his life there seemed that there was very little chance that Wilson would be considered a suitable candidate for the now vacant See. However, given the absence of any other candidate being prepared to take up the challenge of this very demanding post it might seem that by putting himself forward as a candidate Wilson was acting impulsively without considering the consequences of his decision. But, in fact it is more than likely that it was on the advice of his Doctor that he decided to put himself forward having been informed by his Doctor that his skin condition would in fact improve in a hot climate.[58] To this should be added the fact not mentioned by Bateman and that was Wilson's Anglo-Indian credentials. As we have already observed Daniel Wilson came from a family whose links with India and the East India Company went back to the late 17th century. Through his mother, Ann Collett Wilson (née West) he could trace his links with India back to Thomas Collett, the father of Elizabeth Collett, his great grandmother and the wife of Robert Brooke from whom both James Brooke, the 1st White Rajah of Sarawak and James Pattle, father of the seven beautiful Pattle sisters were descended.[59] In addition to this, many of his mother's cousins were still serving on the Council of India. Amongst these were James Pattle, a senior member of the Board of Revenue and Senior Judge, and the husbands of four of his daughters who had returned to India where their respective husbands dominated the administrative circles of the HEIC and later the Supreme Council of India. These were Charles Hay Cameron, husband of Julia Margaret Cameron (née Pattle), Henry Thoby Prinsep, husband of Sara Pattle, and Henry V. Bayley who had married Louisa Pattle.[60] James Pattle's fourth daughter, Maria married Dr John Jackson a surgeon in the services of the HEIC and later Professor of the medical College. Maria and her husband did not however take an active part in the social life of the Calcutta Community as did her sisters, Julia, Sara or Louisa: all of whom were at the top of the Calcutta Society.[61]

All these details would probably have been common knowledge to Grant and possibly Grey: facts overlooked or ignored by his biographer and son in law, Josiah Bateman.

Although Wilson may have had his critics at home which would account for his never being appointed a Bishop in England, in the opinion of Grey and Grant it was clear that Wilson had all the right credentials for such a position.[62]

Three months after submitting his name to Charles Grant for the vacant position of Bishop of Calcutta Wilson received a letter dated March 27th 1832 asking him to accept the Bishopric of Calcutta.[63] A month later he was consecrated Bishop of Calcutta and after appointing his son, Daniel as Patron and Vicar of the living of St Mary Islington, Daniel Wilson senior took leave of his friends and sailed to India thus fulfilling an ambition of a lifetime when as a young child he could only dream of standing on the banks of the River Hooghly.[64]

*Notes and References:*

(i)    On Daniel Wilson and his reasons for going to India see: Harrison, M. J. From
       Spitalfields to Calcutta: Daniel Wilson's Love of India Indian Church History
       Review. June 2006.The standard work on the life of Daniel Wilson is that by his son
       in law and Chaplain, Josiah Bateman. Life of the Right Revd Daniel Wilson D.D.
       London: John Murray, 1860. 2 vols. All other writers follow this work. For further
       details, regarding the Wilsons of Stenson and their involvement in the silk trade
       reference should be made to Wilson, J. (1849) Memoirs of the Life and Character
       of Thomas Wilson by his Son. London. See also: Harrison, M.J. (2005) Patrons and

*Church Builders: The Wilsons of Highbury and Islington. Paper delivered on 24th September 2005 at a study day organized by the Friends of the Union Chapel in association with the Victorian Society. See also, Harrison, M.J. The Wilsons of Derbyshire: a note. JURCHS. Jan. 2008.*

1.  Farrington, A. (1999) Biographical Index of East India Ships, Journals and Logs: 1600-1834. London: British Library. There is no record that the *James Sibbald* had been wrecked. As such, it would seem that Bateman has exaggerated the account. See: Bateman, J. (1860) The Life of Daniel Wilson. London. 2 vols. Amongst those to see him off was Charles Simeon: any chance of Simeon passing his mantle on to Wilson was lost. Within 4 years of Wilson's departure the Evangelicals had lost two of its greatest stalwarts: Wilberforce and Simeon. See: Kings, G. Canal, River and Rapids; Contemporary Evangelicalism in the Church of England. The Anvil: vol.20. No.3, 2003.

2.  Eliza Emma Wilson was the only surviving daughter of Daniel and Anne Wilson who married her first cousin, Josiah Bateman, Assistant Chaplain to Bp Daniel Wilson.. See: McNally, S.J. (1976) Biographical Notes of East India Company Chaplains: 1600-1858. London: British Library. Also: Lewis, D.M. (1995) Blackwell's Dictionary of Evangelical Biography: 1730-1860. Oxford: Blackwells. 2 vols. Josiah was the 3rd son of William and Ann Bateman (née Wilson). William Bateman was the grandson of Hester Bateman, and considered to be the Queen of English silversmiths in the 18th century. Although the Batemans were on close terms with the Revd John Newton they chose to worship at Whitefields Tabernacle, a fact overlooked by Ian Rennie in his entry on Josiah Bateman in the Biographical Dictionary of Evangelicals. Oxford: Blackwell.

3.  See: Bateman, J. (1860) Life of Daniel Wilson. London. 2 vols in which he comments on Wilson being noted for his impulsive and prompt behaviour. See also: Roberts, W. (1832) Memoirs of the Correspondence of Hannah More. 2nd ed. London. 4 vols in which Wilson is described as being impetuous and imperious. The same points are noted in the Catholic Review: 1860, vol.lxix, September in the review of Bateman's Life of Daniel Wilson. This is a habit that he would probably have developed during his apprenticeship in the Silk industry and more appropriately his associations with the Weavers Company in which pomp and ceremony would have been an important part of the life of the Company.

4.  Stephen Wilson: (1795-1802) Private Calendar (privately owned.) In an entry in his Diary, we find that apart from Stephen and Anne Collett Wilson's eldest daughter Mary, the remaining children were all baptized by the Revd Samuel Brewer, Minister of the Independent Chapel in Stepney Green. Within the Dissenting movement Samuel Brewer was an important person who gave great support to the ministry of the Revd George Whitefield. Samuel Brewer in fact introduced John Newton to the Revd George Whitefield. There is no reference to the Wilsons close connections with Samuel Brewer in Bateman's life of Bishop Wilson. It is as if Bateman was embarrassed by his father in law's Dissenting upbringing as indeed he was of his own. Likewise, it would seem that Bateman has either ignored or deliberately omitted his father in law's Anglo Indian connection

5.  See: Wilson, J. (1846) Memoir of Thomas Wilson. London. See also: Bateman, J.

(1860) Life of Daniel Wilson. London. 2 vols. For further details, reference should be made to ch. 1. From small beginnings: The Wilsons of Stenson, Derbyshire and ch 2. Entering the Silk Trade. See also: Rothstein, N.K.A (1960) The London Silk Trade. London: London University: M.A. Thesis, in which she cites a Stephen Wilson and Co., of Aldermanbury, 1755-1793. This is probably a reference to the firm originally established by Stephen Wilson, [1] of Coventry and Wood Street, Cheapside, which remained in the family until 1840. See: Rothstein, N.K.A. (1990) Silk Designs of the 18th Century. London: Thames and Hudson. Although as she points out there were many Stephen Wilsons engaged in the silk industry they were in fact related. Stephen Wilson [I] originally came from South Derbyshire where his father, John Wilson owned the free hold of their land in Stenson, a small hamlet in the parish of Barrow cum Twyford. Stephen Wilson [I] was the first member of the Wilson family to enter the silk industry in Coventry, which at this stage was an important centre in the manufacture of silk ribbons.

6.  Bateman, J. (1860) Life of Daniel Wilson London: vol.1. The house in Church Street, later renamed Fournier Street is illustrated in: Ison, W.A. & Bezodis, P.A. 91957) The Survey of Spitalfields and Mile End New Town. London: The Athlone Press. See also: Blain, D. ed., (1989) The Saving of Spitalfields. London: The Spitalfields Trust.

7.  See: PCC/Prob/11/878/1762: Robert Brooke in which Daniel West's son, also called Daniel, is listed as being in receipt of £200 by the terms of the will of Robert Brooke. Other recipients included his two granddaughters, Ann Collett West and Catharine who died sometime between 1762-3. She is not to be confused with their youngest daughter also called Catherine who was born in 1764 and married a William Whitewell, son of Alderman John Whitewell of Coventry. It is probable that his grandson, Daniel died at the same time as Catherine. Anne Collett West's middle name was the surname of her grandmother, Elizabeth Collett, the 2nd daughter of Captain Thomas Collett, an officer in the maritime services of the East India Company. British Library: OIOC. Biographical File: Thomas Collet. See also: Farrington, A. (1990) Biographical Index of East India Company Maritime Service Officers: 1600-1834. London: British Library. Also: Farrington, A. (1990) Biographical Index of East India Company Ships: 1600-1834. London: British Library. A wealthy maritime officer Thomas Collett is cited as having left £100 to the parish of Barking with which to buy bread for the poor of the parish. In addition to this, he and his brother, Jonathan Collett left £210 to the Church with which to purchase land; the rent to be used to buy bread for the poor. See: PCC/Prob/726/1743: Thomas Collett. See also: VCH. (1965) Essex: vol v: Barking/Ilford. Oxley, J. The land was eventually sold in 1872.

8.  GUILDHALL LIBRARY: Gld Mss: Court Minute Books, Weavers Company 4655/17: pt 17: 1765-1785 in which Daniel West is cited as having been appointed the post of Upper Bailiff in 1775. This was a position normally reserved for the economic elite in the City and Weavers Company.

9.  See: Harrison M.J. Daniel West: Whitfield's Forgotten Trustee. JURCHS. June 2006.

10. Although attempts have been made to link Robert Brooke of Goodman Fields with

the Brookes of Horton in the Cotswolds there is no evidence that they are related. According to Burke's Landed Gentry, (1937) Robert Brooke is said to be descended from the Brookes of Horton. This is incorrect and is probably based on an error that arose in Burke's Landed Gentry, 1921 where it is stated that "Captain Richard Brooke was the grandfather of James Brooke, 1st White Rajah of Sarawak. Although the error was removed from later editions it is significant to note that the error was repeated by Runciman in his biography: The White Rajahs: a History of Sarawak from 1841 to 1946. Cambridge. 1960. There is in fact no connection between the two families. See: Brooke. G.E. (1918) The Brookes of Horton in the Cotswolds. Singapore: Methodist Publishing House; where he states that the two families are quite distinct and unrelated families. Likewise, there is no evidence to link Elizabeth Brooke (née Collett) with either Sir Thomas Vyner, Bt. Lord Mayor or his nephew, Sir Robert Vyner, Bt., and Lord Mayor. What we have here is a good example of the cultivation of a legend conjured up by the title of Rajah of Sarawak.

11.  See: Barley, N. (2003) White Rajah: A Biography of Sir James Brooke. London: Abacus Press. This is the most accurate biography regarding James Brookes pedigree. See also: Bodleian Library: Rhodes House, Basil Brooke Papers: MSS. Pac. S.90: Box 3/11 f.1/Margaret Noble: Pedigree of the Brookes of Sarawak. There are however two inaccuracies in the pedigree: It was Robert Brooke, son of Robert and Elizabeth Brooke who was part owner of the East Indiaman, *The Speke*. The other error pertains to Sophia Brooke. She was the daughter of Thomas Brooke by his Indian Companion, the Moher Bibi of Arah. She is referred to in the Private Calendar of Stephen Wilson (1795-1803) along with her brother and younger sister as living with their grandmother, Mrs Ruth Brooke. In 1801, Charles and Sophia returned to India where Charles enlisted as a Cadet in the Bengal Army whilst Sophia subsequently married David Morrieson a writer and later Judge in the services of the East India Company. Thomas Brooke was the only son of Robert and Ruth Brooke. (née Pattle). He was the first cousin of Anne Collett Wilson (née West), eldest daughter of Daniel and Anne West (née Brooke). See: PCC/Prob/873/1762: Robert Brooke of Goodmanfields, Whitechapel in which he left a legacy of £200 to his granddaughter, Anne Collett West. His will indicates that he was a substantial landowner with property in Epping, Parndon and Brentwood, Essex. In his will, he left his three children as tenants in common of these estates.

12.  On the Pattles see: Hill, Brian. (1973) Julia Margaret Cameron: A Victorian Family Portrait. London: Peter Owen. Boyd, Elizabeth, French. (1976) Bloomsbury Heritage: Their Mothers and their Aunts. London: Hamish Hamilton. Olsen, Victoria. (2003) From Life: Julia Margaret Cameron & Victorian Photography. London Aurum Press.

13.  See: Boyd, E F. (1976) Bloomsbury Heritage: Their Mothers and their Aunts. London: Hamish Hamilton; who states that in the absence of their being a Governor General's wife it was Julia Margaret Cameron upon whom devolved the role of entertaining the Calcutta society. See also Olsen, V. (2003) ibid and Hill, B. (1973) ibid. According to the letters of the Hon Emily Eden we learn that she undertook the role of entertaining the Calcutta Society during the time that her

brother, Lord Auckland was Governor General. Letters from India. Hon Emily Eden. London. 2 vols. 1872.

14. See: Bateman, J. (1860) Life of Daniel Wilson. London: J. Murray. See also: Olsen, Victoria, (2003) ibid who comments that the controversy over English Education was the biggest battle to be fought between Prinsep and Macaulay. It is significant to note that on the inclusion of Religious Education to follow the teaching of the Church of England Thoby Prinsep supported Wilson whilst Sir E. Ryan initially opposed such a decision. He eventually supported Wilson and Prinsep.

15. It is significant to note that although Bateman in his biography of Bp. Daniel Wilson refers to his father in law meeting James Brooke in Singapore he makes no mention of the fact that they were related. Likewise, in his letters to his mother and friends James Brooke makes no reference to this relationship. By this time James Brooke's grandmother and two of her grandchildren by the Moher Bibi of Arah in Bihar were dead and accordingly James Brooke most probably had no idea that he and the Bishop were in fact 3rd cousins. See: Keppel, H. (1853) A Visit to the Indian Archipelago in *HMS Maeander*. London. 2 vols in which he cites a letter dated Jan 24th 1851 written by Bp Daniel Wilson to the Revd Charles D. Brereton of Little Massingham, Norfolk.

16. Stephen Wilson. (1795-1802) Private Calendar where he refers to the three grandchildren of Mrs Brooke, also known as Aunt Brooke. The three children, Charles, Sophia and Julia were the children of Thomas Brooke by his companion, the Moher Bibi of Arah in Bihar to whom he left a pension of £1,000. See: PCC/Prob/11/1835: Thomas Brooke. The term Bibi is a Muslim one and is equivalent to the English terms of Mother or Wife. See: Dalrymple, W. (2003) White Mughals. London: Flamingo. in which he notes that it was not unusual for English Writers of the HEIC to leave their Bibi or Companion a bequest in their will.

17. The School was in Stepney Green (Mile End Green) a small hamlet in the Parish of St Dunstan's Stepney, a popular residential area for merchants and maritime Captains. See: Galinou, M. ed., (2004) City Merchants and the Arts: 1670-1720. Weatherby: Oblong Press for the Corporation of London.

18. Bateman, J. (1860) Life of Daniel Wilson. London: 2 vols.

19. Bateman, J. (1860) Life of Daniel Wilson. London. 2 vols See: Byrne, A. (1986) London's Georgian Houses. London: The Georgian Press where he notes that apart from the fleur-di-lis which was added at a later date the door case is the only one of its kind. He goes on to add that the door case is an incredibly incorrect marriage of an Ionic pedimented and console hooded door case. Interestingly the Ionic pillars to the door case are correctly reflected in the Ionic pillars and capitals that frame the entrance to the staircase compartment. Also: Blain, D. ed., (1989) The Saving of Spitalfields. London: The Spitalfields Trust that contains an illustration of the staircase down which Daniel Wilson would slide.

20. Stephen Wilson (1795-1803) Private Calendar in which he refers to his younger sons also attending Mr Searle's School at Eltham. See also: Bateman J. (1860) Life of Daniel Wilson. London: J. Murray. 2 vols.

21. See: Bateman, J. (1860) Life of Daniel Wilson. London. 2 vols. See also:

Robinson, J. (1842) The History and Antiquities of Hackney. London. also: Morrison, J. (1839) Fathers and Founders of the London Missionary Society. London: 2 vols. The Revd John Eyre was minister of Ram's Chapel Homerton that had been built by Stephen Ram in his back garden in 1722.

22. Stephen Wilson. (1795-1802) In his private calendar he refers to the regular visits his wife and children would make to the homes of the Revd S. Brewer and his family, the Revd and Mrs Newton, as well as visiting the sick. In addition, their home was a regular centre of entertainment. According to an entry in the Private Calendar of Stephen Wilson we learn that it was whilst she was visiting the Revd Samuel Brewer that he held her gently by the hand and said to her " God bless you my dear Mrs Wilson, and lead you the right way to the City of Habitation The same afternoon that the Revd Samuel Brewer died: She was the last person to have been blessed by him. This is piety at its best.

In his Private Calendar, there are frequent references to his wife and children attending the various Missionary Sermons, and charity events for the Wood Street Charity School and attending regularly the Prayer meeting at the Tabernacle.

23. Morrison, J. (1839) Fathers and Founders of the London Missionary Society. London. 2 vols. That the Wilsons should have placed Daniel under his care was probably on account of Daniel's poor behaviour and lack of progress. See: Bateman, J. (1860) Life of Daniel Wilson. London. 2.vols. See also: Evangelical Magazine. 1803. Obituary of John Eyre. p.223-230; 273-287. DNB. Vol VI. p.964-965.

24. GUILDHALL LIBRARY: Gld Mss. Court Minute Books: Weavers Company: 4655/18. pt.2. 1786-1798: also: Gld Mss: 4657/vol.2. 1765-1865. Apprentice Bindings. Dec.2nd 1792. William Wilson married Elizabeth West, second daughter of Daniel and Anne West (née Brooke)

25. Although William Wilson was an efficient businessman, it would seem that Bateman is being unduly harsh when he depicts him as being a cold and remote person. Likewise, he is incorrect when he states that at this time William Wilson was a widower. It was not until 1795 that his wife, Elizabeth Wilson (née West), died. The following year William Wilson moved to Clapham. See: Wilson, S. 1795-1802: Private Calendar (in private hands).

26. It would seem that what Daniel Wilson objected to and reacted to were the cold forms of prayer that left the soul quite dry and impoverished. See: Bunyon, C.J. (1889) Memoirs of Bishop McDougall and Harriette his Wife. London in which Bunyon cites a letter written by Daniel Wilson to Frances McDougall exhorting him not to use any book on family prayers or from the Liturgy a practice observed by Archbishop Howley, the Bishop of London, the Bishop of Exeter and elsewhere. See also: Forster, E.M. (1951) Two Cheers for Democracy. Harmondsworth: Penguin where he refers to the volumes of prayers that Henry Thornton composed. It may well have been a copy of these prayers and the Book of Common Prayer to which Wilson was referring

27. Bateman, J. (1860) Life of Daniel Wilson. London: J. Murray. 2 vols. However, according to an entry in the Private Calendar of Stephen Wilson, he records that Daniel spent the day with his parents, returning the following day to 31 Milk Street

where his uncle William Wilson carried out his business in the silk trade.

28. See: Wigley, J. (1980) The Rise and Fall of the Victorian Sunday. Manchester who incorrectly states that it was through Newton that Daniel Wilson was converted. In fact, it was as a result of the ministry of John Eyre and in particular a letter that he received the same week that he went to Ram's Chapel that proved to be the turning point in Daniel Wilson's life. It is significant to note that he received Holy Communion before he was confirmed by Bishop Cleaver on June 7th 1798 at Oxford and as such, it would appear to have been an irregularity in Church procedure, but on such matters, it would seem that John Eyre did not always conform to the rubrics of the Church of England. In his Private Calendar for the period: 1795-1802 Stephen records that Daniel wrote to the Revd John Eyre on the 11th March and the 18th March.1796.

29. It is interesting to note that although Daniel Wilson had the reputation for being outspoken it would appear as reflected both in his letters and his epitaph that he lacked the robust spirituality of Evangelicals such as John Newton or George Whitefield. See however Bateman, J. (1860) Life of Daniel Wilson. London. 2 vols who plays down Wilson's excessive censoriousness and sense of sin. See also: Gibbs, M.E. (1972) The Anglican Church in India. Delhi: SPCK, where she refers to a comment that Bp Wilson made in a letter in which he writes that he never experienced much joy for the first nine years of his episcopacy. This is not borne out by his letters. Whilst he was always conscious of the Holiness of God and his own inward corruptions, there is no evidence to suggest that he experienced no joy in his life. See for example his reaction when he visited Sarawak in 1851 where he was totally lost for words. See: Keppel, H. (1853) A visit to the Indian Archipelago in *HMS Maeander*. London. 2 vols; Letter to the Revd C.D. Brereton from the Bishop of Calcutta, Dr Daniel Wilson. It is probable that what Wilson was opposed to was excessive hilarity of spirits: there was a place for mild gravity with occasional tokens of delight and pleasure not noisy mirth or boisterousness. See: Runciman, S. (1960) The White Rajahs: a History of Sarawak from 1841 to 1946. Cambridge.

30. Stephen Wilson: (1795-1802) Private Calendar: Monday October 23 1797. Bateman is incorrect when he states that Stephen Wilson would not hear any more of the matter as it thwarted all the plans that he had for his son. Likewise, there is no evidence to suggest that Stephen was a cold, distant and austere person indifferent to the needs of his children. Had Bateman consulted Stephen Wilson's Private Calendar for the period 1795-1802 he would not have been inaccurate in his comments.

31. Stephen Wilson. (1795-1802) Private Calendar: Wednesday March 14th 1798. Here it is important to note that it was Stephen who took the initiative in respect of Daniel's decision to enter the Ministry.

32. Stephen Wilson. (1795-1802.) Private Calendar: Sunday March 18th 1798. The Revd Isaac Goode of White Row, Spitalfields is not to be confused with the Revd W. Goode (1762-1816) of St Anne's Blackfriars whom Stephen visited on Tuesday 26th March 1798.

33. John Wilson was Stephen's older brother and on the Selection committee of the

London Missionary Society serving as a Layperson on the examining board. As such, he would have been an ideal person with whom to discuss Daniel's calling. See: Morrison, J. (1839) Fathers and Founders of the London Missionary Society. London. 2 vols. Also: Lovett, R. (1899) The History of the London Missionary Society. London.

34. Clerical Directory. (1829) The Revd George West is cited as being the Rector of Stoke near Guildford (1794) and Perpetual Curate of Seal. (1824)

35. Stephen Wilson: (1795-1802) Private Calendar in which he records that he wrote to Mr Crouch informing him of his proposed visit on Monday the 30th April 1798. Accompanied by his son and eldest daughter Anne, they arrived at Oxford on Tuesday May the 1st. After being examined by Mr Crouch, Daniel was then sworn in by a representative of the Vice Chancellor. Following their return from Oxford he records that Daniel took up residence with the Revd and Mrs J. Pratt at 22 Doughty Street, Holborn, a fashionable area of London.

36. Farewell Sermon to the Clergy in Calcutta: 1845. Josiah Pratt was the Secretary of the CMS and the Eclectic Society that met at St John's Bedford Row where he served as curate to Richard Cecil. His second son, John Henry Pratt was appointed Chaplain to Daniel Wilson, Bishop of Calcutta in 1838 following the resignation of the Revd Josiah Bateman.

37. Daniel Wilson preached Thomas Scott's Funeral Service. (1821)

38. Clerical Guide, (1829) ed., Richard Gilbert. 3rd edition. The living at Chobham was in the hands of the Thornton family. See: Warren, M. (1965) The Missionary Movement from Britain in Modern History. London: SCM who makes the point that Josiah Pratt was by far and away the most important publicist for the missionary cause in the first twenty-five years of the 19th century. See also: DNB, vol. xvi where the contributor notes that Josiah Pratt worked actively to promote an ecclesiastical establishment in India by urging the CMS to give practical aid to Bishop Middleton when he was appointed Bishop of Calcutta.

39. Any knowledge that Daniel Wilson gained about India during his childhood probably came from his maternal grandmother, Mrs Daniel West (née Brooke) his great aunt Mrs Ruth Brooke, her son, cousin Thomas Brooke of Calcutta, father of James Brooke and his three children, Charles, Sophia and Julia by his Bibi who were regular visitors to the home of Stephen and Ann Wilson. Stephen Wilson records that Sophia and Julia Brooke were at the same school as their younger daughters. It seems that Stephen was a merchant dealing with Raw and organzine silk from India. According to his Private Calendar, he made regular visits to the Warehouses of the East India Company, which were in the East India docks at Blackwall. Later, in 1806 new warehouses were built in Fenchurch Street. See: Farrington, A. (2002) Trading Places: The East India Company and Asia: 1600-1834. London: British Library. In addition, we learn that Stephen was auditor to the Fishmongers Company and served on the Livery of the Company.

40. Bishop Wilson's Journal Letters: edited by Daniel Wilson, his son. London: James Nisbet, 1863. Letter dated: Jan 14th 1835. See also: Bateman, J. (1860) Life of Daniel Wilson. London. 2 vols.

41. Richard Cecil (1714-1810) is generally considered one of the most cultivated of all

Evangelical leaders and had a major influence on the next generation of Evangelicals including John Eyre, Josiah Pratt and Daniel Wilson. From 1777 to 1797, he held the living of St Thomas Lewes. In 1797, he held the combined livings of Chobham and Bisley that were in the patronage of the Thornton family. In 1780, he was appointed Rector of St John's Row but resigned on grounds of ill health in 1808 and was succeeded by Daniel Wilson, one time Curate to Cecil in 1803. Wilson preached the Funeral Sermon occasioned by the death of the Revd Richard Cecil, Sunday 26th August and 2nd September 1810.

42. Ann Wilson was the eldest daughter of William and Elizabeth Wilson (née West). The epitaph on her tomb at St Mary Islington reads: *"Sacred to the memory of Ann, the beloved wife of Revd Daniel Wilson, (Vicar of the Parish) who departed this life the 10th day of May, 1827, aged 44 years."* See: Bateman, J. (1860) Life of Daniel Wilson. London. 2 vols.

Of Ann and Daniel Wilson's children, the eldest, Daniel Wilson jnr succeeded his father, now Bishop of Calcutta, to the living and patronage of St Mary, Islington. Whilst Daniel Wilson was in India his son, John died leaving a wife and two young children. Daniel Wilson's only other surviving child Eliza Emma went out with him to India. She married Josiah Bateman her first cousin and her father's Chaplain. Amelia, Ann and William died in childhood.

43. See: Reynolds, J. (1952) The Evangelicals at Oxford: 1735-1871. Oxford.

44. Bateman, J. (1860) Life of Daniel Wilson. London. 2 vols.

45. Bateman, J. (1860) Life of Daniel Wilson. London: 2 vols. William Wilson was a wealthy silk manufacturer who purchased the estates of Over Worton and Nether Worton, Oxfordshire to which he retired in 1810. See: PCC/Prob/11/1649/1821: William Wilson. According to his will, he purchased the livings of Over Worton, Nether Worton, St Mary's Walthamstow, St Mary's Islington and Tooting. In addition, he seems to have obtained the right to presentation at Hampton Gay and Deddington. See also: Victoria County History. (1959) Oxfordshire: vol. iv: Ploughley Hundreds. M. Lobel: also vol. xi. Wooton Hundreds. A. Crossley. (1983).

46. Reynolds, J.S. (1952) The Evangelicals at Oxford: 1735-1871. Oxford. The contrast between Wilson and John Hill could not be greater. Whereas Wilson was formal and distant, John Hill was of a warm nature who made the students feel at ease. Following his appointment as Vice Principal of St Edmund Hall, Hill was presented with the living of Hampton Gay that was in the patronage of William Wilson. See: Stunt, T. (2000) From Awakening to Secession: Radical Evangelicals in Switzerland and Britain: 1815-1835. Edinburgh: T&T Clark., where he describes Hill as being the Calvinist standard bearer of Evangelicals at Oxford.

47. Bateman, J. (1860) The Life of Daniel Wilson. London. 2 vols. See also: Yates, T. (1978) Venn and Victorian Bishops Abroad. London: SPCK. Charles Grant was the father of Charles Grant, later Lord Glenelg who was President of the Board of Control, whilst Zachary Macaulay was the father of Thomas Babington Macaulay who had been appointed Chairman of the Law Commission to the Supreme Council of India. See: Hill, Brian. (1973) Julia Margaret Cameron: a Victorian Family Portrait. London: Peter Owen.

48. See: Stunt, T. (2000) From Awakening to Secession: Radical Evangelicals in

Switzerland and Britain, 1815-1835. Edinburgh: T&T. Clark. where he considers that Wilson's trip to the continent was of the nature of a fact finding tour. This overlooks the fact that he was acting on the advice of his Doctor who probably realized that the skin disorder, Erysipelas from which Wilson suffered would respond to a warmer climate than that found in England. Such a disorder would cause the person to be irritable, and restless. It would also account for the fact that on his return to England he suffered a relapse. See: Beneson, A. S. ed., (1970) Control of Communicable Diseases in Man. 11th edition. New York: The American Public Health Association.

49. Wilson, D. (1823) Letters From an Absent Brother. London: J. Nisbet. Although Wilson makes no mention of the sister it is probable that the letters were addressed to Elizabeth, his youngest sister who was still living with her mother, Mrs Ann Collett Wilson at Daniel's home in Barnsbury, Islington.

50. Lewis, S. (1843) The History and Topography of the Parish of St Mary Islington. London in which Lewis states that the advowson was sold by Benjamin Smith for the sum of £500 to William Wilson of Milk Street, London and Nether Worton, Oxfordshire from whom the property descended to his son-in law, the Rt, Revd Daniel Wilson, Bishop of Calcutta.

51. The three new churches, St John's Holloway, St Paul's, Canonbury and Holy Trinity, Cloudsley Square were designed by Charles Barry. See: Harrison, M.J. Patrons and Church Builders: The Wilsons of Islington: paper given at a study day organized by the Friends of Union chapel and The Victorian Society. September 2005.
See: Woodward, C. (1832) Reminiscences of an Interesting Event Presented to his Friends by the Church Warden of St Mary's Islington. June 1832.

52. Select Committee of the House of Commons. (1832) Sunday Observance, Evidence of John Twells. On the Smithfield market: see: Congregational Magazine. N.S. vol. 4. 1828. On the State of the Cattle Market and Slaughterhouses of London. p.54-55. In 1830 Daniel Wilson founded the Islington Society For the Better Observance of the Lord's Day. See: Wigley, J. (1980) The Rise and Fall of the Victorian Sunday. Manchester: MUP, who incorrectly dates it as being founded in 1827.

53. Blackburn, J. (1829) A Statement on the Awful Profanation of the Lord's Day. London: The Christian Instruction Society. John Blackburn was the secretary of the Christian Instruction Society that was formed in 1825. See also: Congregational Magazine. Vol. 5. 1829. p.684. According to Peel John Blackburn was one of the outstanding men of the Congregational Union. Peel, A. (1931) These Hundred Years. London.

54. That Daniel Wilson declined the invitation of the Deputation led by Revd John Blackburn was due not only to the nature of the constitution of the District Visiting Society but also due to Wilson's sense of Church order: a practice that was set originally by Simeon. On the nature of the constitution of the District Visiting Society see:. See: Blackburn, J. (1829) A Statement on the Awful Profanation of the Lord's Day. in which he refers to the nature of the constitution of the society that probably precluded Anglicans cooperating with Dissenters.

55. Blomfield, C.J. Bishop of London, 1830. A Letter to the Clergy and Laity on the Present Neglect of the Lord's Day. See also: Blomfield, A. (1863) Memoir of Bishop Blomfield. London. There is a reference to the deputation to the Bishop by a group of Dissenters who requested that the Bishop should publish a letter on the subject of the Lord's Day. See: Blackburn, J. (1829) A statement on the awful profanation of the Lord's Day in which he refers to the names of the Deputants who sought the support of the Bishop.

56. See: Wilson, D. (1824) A Sermon Preached at the Parish Church of St Mary, Islington: Sunday July 11, 1824. See also: Wilson, D. (1826) A Sermon Preached at the Parish Church of St Mary, Islington, in aid of the Islington Parochial Schools, in connexion with the National Society to which is prefixed a Pastoral address. December. 11, 1826. also Wilson, D. (1827) The Divine Authority and Perpetual Obligation of the Lord's Day. London: LDOS, 1956. See also: Baylee, J.T. (1852) Statistics and Facts in reference to the Lord's Day. London: LDOS, where he states that the founder of the society was Joseph Wilson.

57. By abolishing pew rent he was establishing a pattern that he would follow in India when he abolished the caste system in the Church. See: Bateman, J. (1860) Life of Daniel Wilson 2 vols. See also: Roberts, J. (1847) Caste: its Religious and Civil Character being a Series of Documents by the Rt Revd Bishops: Heber, Wilson, Corrie and Spencer. London. Also: Hoole, C. (2004) Bishop Wilson and the Origins of Dalit Liberation. Transformation. 21 Jan. 2004. p.42-45.

58. The skin disorder of Erysipelas from which Wilson suffered is common in temperate zones but rare in tropical climates and would explain why his health improved in India. It is not surprising therefore that his doctor gave him a clean bill of health. See: Benenson. A.S. ed., (1970) The Control of Communicable Diseases in Man. 11th edition. New York: The American Public Health Association.

59. On the complex relationship between the Wests, Wilsons, Brookes, Colletts and Pattles see Harrison, M.J. Daniel West: Whitefield's Forgotten Trustee. JURCHS. vol.7. no.8. June. 2006. Also: From Spitalfields to Calcutta: Daniel Wilson's Love of India. M.J. Harrison. Indian Church History Review. June 2006.

60. See: Olsen, V. (2003) From Life: Julia Margaret Cameron & Victorian Photography. London: Aurum Press. By the time that Daniel Wilson arrived in Calcutta in 1832 his cousin, Thomas Brooke had returned to England and settled in Bath. Amongst his mother's cousins still resident in India was James Pattle who had been recalled back to India in 1833 to assist in the transfer of power from the HEIC to the newly formed Supreme Council of India. He was accompanied by his daughter Julia Margaret Pattle: his wife and remaining daughters followed on later. See: Olsen, V. (2003) From Life: Julia Margaret Cameron & Victorian Photography. London: Aurum Press. See also Bateman, J. (1860) Life of Daniel Wilson. London: J. Murray. 2 vols who states that both Thoby and his brother were on the Education Committee.

61. On Dr John Jackson and his wife Maria: See: Boyd, Elizabeth, French. (1976) Bloomsbury Heritage: their Mothers and their Aunts. London: Hamish Hamilton. See also: Olsen, V. (2003) From Life: Julia Margaret Cameron & Victorian Photography. London: Aurum Press. Of James Pattles remaining daughters, they

returned to England where they remained for the rest of their lives. Maria and John Jackson were the grand parents of Vanessa and Virginia Stephen.

62. The apparent speed with which Wilson's appointment was approved was probably due to the fear on the part of Grey that if the Tories were elected they might choose a High Church Bishop or one with High Church leanings to fill the vacant post. On the political situation at the time see: Beales, D.E. (1971) From Castlereagh to Gladstone: 1815-1885. London: Sphere. See also: Bateman, J. (1860) Life of Daniel Wilson. London., who states that Macaulay had written to Grant, jnr urging him to appoint Wilson It is more than likely that they had discussed Wilson's application with Simeon whose real sway was far greater than that of any Primate. See: Hopkins, H.E. (1977) Charles Simeon of Cambridge. London: Hodder & Stoughton.

63. Bateman, J. (1860) Life of Daniel Wilson. London: J. Murray. 2 vols.

64. That Wilson considered he was destined from childhood to go to India is indicated in a letter he wrote to Josiah Pratt quoted by Bateman in his life of Daniel Wilson. On Daniel Wilson junior see: Hincliffe, Tanis, forthcoming: The Building of St Saviour's Aberdeen Park: a paper given at a study day organized by the Friends of Union Chapel in association with the Victorian Society. September 24 2005: also Harrison, M.J. Patrons and Church Builders: The Wilsons of Highbury and Islington. Forthcoming publication. By the terms of his will Daniel Wilson requested to be buried before the High Altar in St Paul's Cathedral, Calcutta. See: Bateman, J. (1860) Life of Daniel Wilson. London: J. Murray, vol.2.

# Index of Tables

Genealogical Tables:

A. The Wilsons of Stenson, Derbyshire.

1. John Wilson [I] (1664-1714) of Stenson, Derbyshire.
2. John Wilson [II] (1696-1747) of Stenson, Derbyshire.
3. John Wilson [III] (1720-1789) of Stenson, Derbyshire.
4. Stephen Wilson [I] (1723-1755) of Coventry.
5. Thomas Wilson [I] (1731-1794) of Highbury, Islington.
6. John Wilson (1751-1826) of Upper Street, Islington.
7. Stephen Wilson [II] (1753-1813) of Church Street, Spitalfields.
8. William Wilson [I] (1756-1821) of Milk Street & TheWortons, Oxfordshire.
9. Thomas Wilson [II] (1764-1843) of Highbury, Islington.
10. Joseph Wilson (1766-1851) of Highbury Place, Islington & Stowlangtoft.
11. Ann Wilson (1776-1821) of Church Street, Spitalfields & Bunhill Fields.
12. Stephen Wilson (1777-1860) of Old Jewry & Bexhill.
13. Daniel Wilson (1778-1858) of Church Street, Spitalfields & Calcutta.
14. William Wilson [II] (1791-1867) of Walthamstow & Oxfordshire.
15. Samuel Wilson (1792-1881) of Aldermanbury & Beckenham.
16. Frances Brereton (1796-1890) of Highbury Place, Islington & Little Massingham.
17. Daniel Wilson (1805-1886) of Barnsbury, Islington.
18. Eliza Emma Wilson (b. 1814) of Islington.
19. Fuller Maitland Wilson (1825-1875) of Stowlangtoft, Suffolk.
20. Joseph William Wilson (1829-1898).

B. Elizabeth Collett and her descendants.

1. Thomas Collett (1676-1743).
2. Elizabeth Collett (c.1700-c.1751).
3. Elizabeth Brooke (1725).
4. Ruth Casson Pattle (1741-1829).
5. Thomas Pattle (1748-1818).
6. Ann Collett West (1754-1829).
7. Elizabeth West (1760-1795).
8. James Pattle (1775-1845).
9. Emma Frances Brooke (1802-1870).
10. Charles Anthoni Brooke (1829-1917).
11. Charles Vyner De Vindt (1874-1963).

# Appendix

## A. THE WILSONS OF STENSON COUNTY DERBYSHIRE 1664-1880

### Table 1: JOHN WILSON (1664-1714)

John Wilson of Stenson the natural and lawful son of Mariae Wilson late of Barrow who succeeded to the farm at Stenson near Barrow upon Trent in 1686. Married Mariae Holden of Barrow upon Trent 1688 at St Peter's Derby.

*issue:*

1. Mariae (Baptized Oct 3rd 1689) Barrow with Twyford
2. Thomas (Baptized May 26th 1693) Barrow with Twyford

*issue:*

    (a) Thomas
    (b) Joseph
    (LJRO/Prob/John Wilson/1714 & Mary Wilson/1718)

3. Joseph (b. 1694) Baptized Feb 12th 1694 Buried Feb 20th 1694
4. John (1696-1747) Baptized Nov 23rd 1696 Barrow with Twyford
   m Aug 16th 1717 Ann Henshaw (Mar 23 1698-Jul 8th 1755) dau of John & Lucy Henshaw (née Couper) of Barrow upon Trent
   had *issue* See: Table 2 John Wilson [II] of Stenson (LJRO/Prob/John Wilson/1714 & Mary Wilson/1718)
5. Sarah (1697-*c.*1712/1713) m Joseph Rolston (Roulson)

*issue:*

    (a) Joseph (n.d.)
    (b) Mary (n.d.) (LJRO/Prob/John Wilson/1714 & Mary Wilson/1718)

6. Rebecca (Baptized Twyford Oct 29th 1699 Buried Nov 1st 1699)

Derbyshire Record Office Matlock Parish Records: Barrow and Twyford 1657-1812.
Litchfield Joint Record Office. Inventory of Mariae Wilson Feb 8th 1686.
Litchfield Joint Record Office. Will John Wilson April 2nd 1714
Litchfield Joint Record Office. Will Mary Wilson Mar 28th 1718.

### Table 2: JOHN WILSON [II] (1696-1747)

John Wilson (II) of Stenson second son of John and Mariae Wilson (née Holden) who succeeded to the farm at Stenson near Barrow cum Twyford Derbyshire.

Married Aug 16th 1717 Ann Henshaw (23rd Mar 1698 d. 8th July 1755) daughter of John and Lucy Henshaw of Barrow upon Trent.

*issue:*

1.  Mary 1718 m Samuel Wilson (not related)
*issue:*
    (a)  Samuel
    (b)  Susanna
    (c)  John
    (d)  Thomas
    (e)  Elizabeth m Thomas Edwards
2.  John (Baptized 7th Sept 1720 d 8th Aug 1789) m Ann Cock (1736-1764)
*issue:* (See: Table 3)
3.  Thomas (1722)
4.  Stephen (Baptized 27 Dec 1723) (1723-1755) m Mary Fullalove
    (See: Table 4) *issue*
    (a)  Ann (d. 1829) m Thomas Oldham (d. 1793) Coventry Master
        Weaver 1774 (See: will Thomas Oldham LJRO Probated 11th
        October 1793) had *issue*
        (i)   Thomas [will of John Wilson 1825]
        (ii)  Stephen
    (b)  John (1751-1826) (See: Table 6)
    (c)  Elizabeth m William Freeman of Coventry had *issue*
        (i)   William
        (ii)  Stephen
        (iii) Edward. (See: will John Wilson 1825)
    (d)  Stephen (1753-1813) (See: Table 7)

5    Ann (1726 Baptized 30th Aug, 1726) m 3rd Sept 1750 Thomas Barton
    of Duffield
*issue:*
    (a)  Stephen
    (b)  Thomas
    (c)  Ann
6    Thomas (1731-1794) m Mary Remington (See: Table 5)
7    William (1733-1793) (Baptized 15 Feb 1733) m Miss Underwood.
8    Joseph (1736) m Ellen Cock St Michael's Coventry June 9th 1763
    (Sister of Ann Cock)
9    Sarah (1739-*c.*1743) (Buried 1st Jan 1743) See: Par.Rec. Barrow and
    Twyford
10   Lucy (1742) (Baptized Barrow and Twyford 11th July 1742 d. 26th Aug
    1742)
11   Sarah (1746 Buried April 8th 1746)

Bateman, J. (1860) Life of Daniel Wilson. London: John Murray. 2 vols.
Derby Record Office, Matlock, Barrow and Twyford: 1657-1812.

Litchfield Joint Record Office. Will: John Wilson: 1747.
Mason, F.B. Family Pedigree of the Wilsons. (n.d.)
PCC/PRO/11/1245. Thomas Wilson. 1793.
Wilson, Harriet, A. (1901) A Family Sketch touching the Wilsons, Moore,
Douglas & Fox Families. (Privately owned)
Wilson, Joshua. (1846) Memoir of Thomas Wilson. London.

Table 3: JOHN WILSON [III] (1720-1789.)

John Wilson (III) of Stenson eldest son of John and Ann Wilson (née
Henshaw) succeeded to the farm at Stenson near Barrow cum Twyford
Derbyshire m Oct 30th 1754 Ann Cock (1736-1764) second dau of Widow
Cock of Champion Derby.

*issue:*

1    John Wilson (1755-1835) d unmarried [Prob/11/396/1836]
2    William [I] (1756-1821) m Elizabeth West (1760-1795) (See: Table 8)
3    Ann (1758-1803) April 30th 1779 by licence at Twyford Ambrose
      Moore (1757-*c*.1798)
*issue:*
   (a)   Ann died young
   (b)   John died young
   (c)   James died young
   (d)   Eleanor (1787-1814 Buried Twyford)
   (e)   Ambrose (1788-1873) m Harriet Ann Fox (1806-1887) had *issue*
         (i)    Harriet Ann (1830-1913) m Joseph W. Wilson (See: Table 20)
         (ii)   Eleanor (1833-1923)
         (iii)  John Wilson Moore (1836-1873) m Nina Gunn Cunningham
         (iv)   Emily (n.d.) m S.H.F.Cox
         (v)    Ambrose Trench (1840-1841)
         (vi)   Edith (1842-1862)
         (vii)  Adeline (1848) m Arthur Marks
   (f)   Sarah (n.d.)
   (g)   Mary Ann (n.d.) m 1st John Hickson had *issue* Elizabeth (n.d.)
         m 2nd George Wayte of Milton nr Repton May
         27th 1824 at Barrow upon Trent
   (h)   Henry Wilson (n.d.)

4    Thomas (1760-1829) m 1st Elizabeth M Edwards (1780-1862 buried
Twyford) marriage dissolved 1803 had *issue*
   (a)   Stenson
   (b)   Rosa

    (c)   Trevor
m 2nd Miss Henfast had *issue*
    (a)   Tudor (n.d.)
    (b)   Melville (n.d.) m Louisa Stephenson (died *c.*1840) had *issue*
        (i)   Henry
        (ii)  Eleanora
        (iii) Charles Rivers Wilson (1831-1916) m 1st Caroline dau of
            R. Cook 2nd Hon Beatrice Violet Mary Mostyn
        (iv) Florence
        (v)  Fanny (Frances)
        (vi) Alice
        (vii) Kathryn (n.d.) m Capt De Moiden had *issue*
            *(i)*     Etienne
            *(ii)*    Joseph
            *(iii)*   Francois.
    (c)   Forrester (n.d.) m Betsy M. Keily had *issue*
        (i)   Thomas
        (ii)  Alexandria

5    Stephen (1761-1814) m Jane Mason (1765-1825) had *issue*
    (a)   Fletcher (1788-1860) m Ann Morley (1795-1847)
    had *issue*
        (i)   Arthur (1823-1847) d unm.
    (b)   Jane (n.d.) m 1st Mr Owen 2nd Mr Stephenson had *issue*
        (i)   Eliza
        (ii)  Mary Jane
    (c)   George
    (d)   Ann (n.d.)
    (e)   Mary (1793-1818) Buried Twyford Derbyshire July 2nd 1818.
    (f)   Susanna (n.d.) still alive after 1847 (See: H.A. Wilson.
        A Family Sketch. 1901 (privately owned)
6    Mary (1763-1796 dsp buried Twyford 14 Feb 1796) m Willam Green

Bateman, J. (1860) Life of Daniel Wilson. London: J. Murray. 2 vols.
Derby Record Office, Matlock, Parish Records: Barrow and Twyford:
    1655-1812.
Foster, J, ed. Alumni Oxonienses. 1715-1886. Oxford.
JWW. (n.d.) The Legend of the Wolfsons.
LJRO: John Wilson: 13 Oct 1789; Twyford
PRO/11/396/1836: John Wilson.

Venn, J.A, (1953) Alumni Cantabrigienses. Part II. Vol. VI. Cambridge.
Vestry House Museum. Walthamstow: Parish Records. (Fletcher Wilson and Jane Mason)
Wilson, Harriet Ann. (1901) A Family Sketch touching the Wilsons, Moore, Douglas & Fox Families. (Privately owned)

Table 4: STEPHEN WILSON [I] (1723-1755) of Coventry.

Stephen Wilson 2nd son of John and Ann Wilson (née Henshaw) of Stenson near Barrow cum Twyford m Mary Fullalove (d. 1786) had *issue*

1    John (1751-1826) m Elizabeth Wight (d. 14 Jan 1830) m Feb 1774 St Matthew Friday Street (See: Table 6)
2    Elizabeth (n.d.) m William Freeman (n.d.) June 26th 1769 St Michael's Coventry had *issue*
     (a)   William
     (b)   Stephen
     (c)   Edward
3    Stephen Wilson (1753-1813) m Ann Collett West (1756-1829) eldest daughter of Daniel and Ann West (née Brooke) of Church Street Spitalfields 20th June 1774 (See: Table 7)
4    Ann (d. 1829) m Thomas Oldham (d. 1793) of Coventry St Michael Coventry April 19th 1774 had *issue*
     (a)   Thomas (See: will of John Wilson [IV] 1835)
     (b)   Stephen

Bateman, J. (1860) Life of Daniel Wilson. London: John Murray, 2. vols.
Hinman, M.J. (1988) Men who ruled Coventry: 1725-1780. Coventry & Warwickshire Historical Association.
LJRO. Prob: 11. Oct 1793: Thomas Oldham.
PCC/Prob/11/878/1762. Robert Brooke of Goodmanfields, Whitechapel.
PCC/Prob/1148/1786 Mary Wilson (née Fullalove) of Stenson.
PCC/Prob/11/819/Stephen Wilson
Wilson, Joshua. (1846) Memoir of Thomas Wilson. London.
Wilson, Stephen. Private Calendar. 1795-1802. (Privately Owned)

Table 5: THOMAS WILSON [I] (1731-1794) of Highbury, Islington.

Thomas Wilson, 3rd son of John and Ann Wilson (née Henshaw) of Stenson Derbyshire, m Mary Remington (1726-1816), only daughter of John Remington. Merchant of Coventry had *issue*
1-6 died in infancy

7    Thomas Wilson (1764-1843) m Elizabeth Clegg younger daughter of
     Arthur and Mary Clegg of Manchester (See: Table 9 Thomas Wilson [II]
     of Highbury Islington) had *issue*
     (a)  Joshua (1795-1874) m Mary Bulley had *issue*
          (i)   Thomas (1841-1915) m Jessica Taylor had *issue* See: Table 9
          (ii)  Mary (d. 1906)
          (iii) John Remington (1847-1904)

     (b)  Elizabeth (b. 1793) Revd J Coombes (1784-1872) had *issue*
          (i)   Thomas Addison (1824)
          (ii)  Eliza Wilson
          (iii) Joshua Wilson (1829-1911) m Charlotte Clapperton
                (1830-1897) had *issue*
          (iv)  Mary Ann Coombes (b. 1834) m James French
          (v)   Jane Coombes (b. 1836)
          (vi)  John Howard (d. 1829)

     (c)  Rebecca (b. 1796) m Revd James Stratten had *issue*
          (i)   Thomas Wilson
          (ii)  Arthur m Gertrude Frances Dew (1863-1960)
          (iii) John m Augusta Hope
          (iv)  Frances
          (v)   Charlotte (d. 1841)

8    Joseph Wilson (1766-1851) m.1st Mary Ann Maitland (1771-1798)
     had *issue*
     m 2nd Emma Welford (d. 1851 dsp)
     (See: Table 10 Joseph Wilson of Highbury Hill)

9    Mary m Samuel Mills (1769-1847) had *issue*
     (a)  Thomas (d. 1862 dsp) m 1st Eliza King 2nd Laura Wiltshire
     (b)  John Remington Mills (1797-1879) m Louisa M. Trueman had *issue*

Burkes Landed Gentry: Remington Mills of Tolmers Herts.
Creasey, J. The Congregational Library: The Congregational Lecture, 1992.
Harrison, M. J. Patrons and Church Builders: The Wilsons of Highbury and
     Islington: Paper given at a Study Day, Sept 2006: Friends of Union Chapel
     and the Victorian Society.
Larsen, T, ed. (20003) Biographical Dictionary of Evangelicals. Leicester: IVP.
Morison, J (1884) The Fathers and Founders of the London Missionary
     Society. London.

Oxford Dictionary of National Biography. Oxford: OUP. 2004. ed. Matthew, C & B. Harrison.
PRO/11/1543/1813/John Remington of Clapton
PRO/11/1245/1793/Thomas Wilson of Highbury Place.
Wilson, J. (1846) Memoir of Thomas Wilson. London.
Wilson, Thomas: Autobiographical Notes: Dr Williams's Library. DWL. CL. II. D.3.

Table 6: JOHN WILSON (1751-1826) of Upper Street Islington

1st son of Stephen and Mary Wilson (née Fullalove) of Coventry m Elizabeth Wight (d January 14th 1830) had *issue*

1　John (1775) m Ann Allnutt had *issue*
2　Stephen (1777-1860) m Sarah Lea. had *issue* (See: Table 12 Stephen Wilson of Old Jewry)
3　Jemima (1779) m Thomas Osborne Stock
4　Maria (1781) m Joseph Oldham (1780-c.1849) eldest son of James Oldham of Holborn had *issue*

(a)　Eliza (1803) m Alfred Wilson
(b)　Maria (1810)
(c)　Joseph (1812.) m Ellen Haslobe
(d)　Benjamin (1814) m Mary Baker
(e)　William (b. Jul. 4th 1816 d Sept 5th 1816)
(f)　Joshua (1819) m Agnes Bailey
(g)　Ellen (1822) m W. Hughes.

5　Abraham (1782- 1824) m Eliza Jane Kemp had *issue*
(a)　Clement Abraham (1813)
(b)　Abraham (1817)
6　Eliza (Sept 1st 1784-Aug 14th 1787)
7　Hannah (April 5th 1786-Sept 6th 1787)
8　Susanna (April 5th 1786-April 7th 1786)
9　Lydia (April 3rd 1787-Aug 1st 1787)
10　Julia (July 11th 1788) m George Wilkins
11　Sophia (July 13th 1790-Jan 30th 1814) m J. Blackett had *issue*
12　Samuel (Dec 18th 1791-1881) m Jemima Lea (See: Table 15)
13　Josiah (May 15th 1793) m Amelia Collins (m Sept 28th 1828 Tottenham) had *issue*
14　Benjamin (Aug 16th 1794-Aug 23rd 1794)
15　Ford (July 3rd 1796) m Eliza J Collins. (m July 31st 1834 Tottenham) had *issue*

16    Ruhamah (Nov 29th 1797)
17    Laetitia (May 13th 1799)
18    David (Sept 21st 1803)

Arnold M. (1978) Culture and Anarchy. Ed. J Dover Wilson. Cambridge: CUP.
Morrison, J. (1844) The Fathers and Founders of the London Missionary
    Society. London. 2 vols
Plummer, A. (1972) The London Weavers Company: 1600-1970. London:
    Routledge & Kegan Paul
Wilson, Harriet, Ann. (1901) A Family Sketch touching the Wilsons, Moore,
    Douglas & Fox Families. (Privately owned).
Wilson, John. Family Bible: (Privately owned).
Wilson, Joshua. (1846) Memoirs of Thomas Wilson. London.
Wilson, Stephen Private Calendar: 1795-1802. (Privately Owned).

Table 7: STEPHEN WILSON [II] (1753-1813) of Church Street Spitalfields

2nd son of Stephen and Mary Wilson (née Fullalove) of Coventry m Ann
Collett West (1754-1829) eldest daughter of Daniel and Ann West (née
Brooke) of Church Street Spitalfields and great grand-daughter of Thomas
Collett of Barking Essex.
*issue:*

1    Mary (May 23rd 1775 Baptized June 12 1775 Christ Church Spitalfields
     d. July 2nd 1790)
2    Ann (Oct 5th 1776-Aug 21st 1842) Baptized Bull Lane Independent
     Chapel 10th Oct 1776 m Feb 21st 1800 William Bateman (1774-1850)
     St Matthew's Friday Street had *issue* (See: Table 11)
3    Daniel (Thurs 2nd July 1778: Baptized Bull Lane Independent Chapel
     Stepney Green July 23rd 1778 d. 1858 India) m Ann Wilson
     (1785-1827) eldest daughter of William and Elizabeth Wilson
     (née West) (See: Table 13)
4    Robert Brooke (24th Dec 1779 Baptized Bull Lane Chapel 20 Jan 1780
     d. 21 Nov 21st 1829)
5    Ruth (Feb 6th 1782 Baptized Bull Lane Chapel Mar 4th 1782 d Sept 6th
     1844) m Major Blundell had *issue* (See: A Family Sketch by Harriet
     A. Wilson, 1901 Privately owned)
6    Elizabeth (Eliza) (Sat Mar 14th 1784 Baptized Bull Lane Chapel)
     m Percival White (d. 1851)
7    Stephen (Aug 24th 1787 Baptized Bull Lane Chapel Sept 7th 1787
     d. 1826) m Mary Wigg had *issue*

8    Thomas (July 19th 1790-Oct 29th 1826) [Baptized Bull Lane Chapel
     Aug 16th 1790] m Sarah Hayter she married 2nd Mr Sutton (See: Table
     12 Stephen Wilson of Old Jewry)
9    George (April 17th 1793-June 8th 1846) (Baptized Bull Lane Chapel
     May 13th 1793) m Harriet Wilson had *issue*
     (a)  Christopher
     (b)  Eleanor m Revd Professor H.M. Hart
     (c)  Margaret m Revd Prof H. Drew

Bateman, J. (1860) Life of Daniel Wilson. London: John Murray.
Foster, J. ed. Alumni Oxonienses, 1715-1886. Oxford.
Oxford Dictionary of National Biography. Oxford: OUP. 2004. ed. Matthew,
     C & B. Harrison.
PCC/Prob/1148/1786/Mary Wilson (née Fullalove)
PCC/Prob/152/1814/Stephen Wilson.
Venn, J.A, ed. Alumni Cantabrigiensis. 2 vols. Cambridge, 1953
Wilson, Harriet Ann. (1901) A Family Sketch touching the Wilsons, Moore,
     Douglas & Fox Families. (Privately owned).
Wilson, S. 1795-1802: Private Calendar (Privately Owned)

Table 8: WILLIAM WILSON [I] (1756-1821) of Milk Street &
The Wortons Oxfordshire

William Wilson [I] 2nd son of John and Ann Wilson (née Cocks) of
Stenson m Elizabeth West (1760-1795) 2nd daughter of Daniel and Ann West
(née Brooke).
*issue:*
1    Ann (1785-1827) m Daniel Wilson (1778-1858) had *issue* (See: Table 13)
2    Joseph (1786-1855) m Emma Aplin (1784-1870) had *issue*
     (a)  Edward (1810)
     (b)  Nathaniel (1812) m Agnes Wilson (1827) had *issue*
     (c)  Cornelius William. m Eliza Prinsep
     (d)  Frederick William (Nov 24th 1818-Apr 14th 1827)
     (e)  Joseph Henry (1821-1896) m Henricia Haigh had *issue*
          Frances Henricia
     (f)  Louisa Emma (Jan 22 1826-Aug 8 1827)
3    Selina (1788-1863) m Revd J. Davies (1789-1858) had *issue*
     (a)  Jane
     (b)  Charlotte
     (c)  Clementina (1823-1904) m Dr Robert Martin (1815-1896)
          had *issue* Charlotte (1854-1944) m Arthur Wilson (1846-1932)

4  Charlotte (n.d.) m Revd Charles Wetherall had *issue* Mary (married)
5  William [II] (1791-1867) m Mary Garratt had *issue* (See: Table 14)
6  Sophia (1792-1852) m Revd R. Greaves (1793-1870) had *issue*
  (a) Evelyn (Aug 6 1818 Baptized Aug 30 1818)
  (b) Richard Wilson (1819-1891) m 1st Sophia Corbett (d. 1822)
  m 2nd Charlotte White
  (c) Joshua (1820-1885) m Frances Sara Dent
  (d) Francis William (April 4 1822 Baptized May 11 1822)
  (e) Sophia (1824-1903) m Dr Hoadley Gabb
7  Eliza (1793-1817)

Bateman, J. (1860) Life of Daniel Wilson. London: J. Murray. 2 vols.
Hill, Revd John. Diary of Revd John Hill MSS67/9. Bodleian Library, Oxford.
Hole, C. (1896) The Early History of the Church Missionary society for Africa and the East to the end of Anno Domini, 1814. London.
Latham, J.E.M (1999) Search for a New Eden. London: Associated University Press.
Owen. J. (1816) History of the British and Foreign Bible Society. London. 2 vols.
Oxford Dictionary of National Biography: Charlotte Wilson (née Martin)
Oxford Dictionary of National Biography: John Dover Wilson.
PRO/Prob/11/1645/William Wilson/1821
Reynolds, J. S. (1953) The Evangelicals at Oxford: 1735-1871. Oxford.
Victoria History of the Counties of England, a History of the County of Oxford. vol. 11. ed. A. Crossley. London: Oxford University Wilson,
Wilson, Harriet Ann. (1901) A Family Sketch touching the Wilsons, Moore, Douglas & Fox Families. (Privately owned).
Wilson, John Dover. (1969) Milestones on the Dover Road. London: Faber.
JWW (n.d.) The Legend of the Wolfsons
Wilson, Stephen: 1795-1802. Private Calendar. (Privately owned.)
Wilson, William (senior) Letter to the Revd T. Lancaster. January 3rd 1818.
Wintringham, Elizabeth. (n.d.) Brief notes on the Wilsons of Over Worton.)

Table 9: THOMAS WILSON [II] (1764-1843) of Highbury Islington

Eldest son of Thomas and Mary Wilson (née Remington) of Highbury Islington. (Born 11 Nov 1764. Died 17th June 1843 and buried at Abney Park Cemetery).
  m Elizabeth Clegg youngest daughter of Arthur and Elizabeth Clegg of Manchester Mar 31st 1791 had *issue*

1    Joshua (11 Nov 1795-14 Aug 1874) m Mary Bulley Wood had *issue*
     (a)  Thomas (Feb 10th 1841-1915) m Jessie Taylor of Ongar had *issue*
          (i)   Geoffrey Remington (Aug 21 1874-Oct 7 1943) m Eileen
                Margaret Georgina Gratton, youngest daughter of Dr Matthew
                Henry Gratton
     (b)  Harold Remington
          (ii)  John Remington (Oct 15 1847-May 28 1904)
     (c)  Mary Elizabeth (d. 1906)


2    Elizabeth (1793) m Revd John Addison Coombes had *issue*
     (a)  Thomas (1824)
     (b)  Eliza (1828) m Edward Burkitt
     (c)  Joshua (1829-1911) Charlotte Mapperton (1830-1897) had *issue*
          Howard Addison Coombs (1872-1934) m Elizabeth Gardner
          (1878-1934) had *issue*
          Elizabeth Ann (1903-1984) m Hubert King (1901-1959) had *issue*
          Elizabeth Ann King. (1928) m William Waller (1935-1990)
     (d)  Mary Ann (1834) m James French
     (e)  Jessie (1832)
     (f)  Jane (1836)
     (g)  John Howard (d. 1829)


3    Rebecca (1796-) m Revd John Stratten had *issue*
     (a)  Thomas Wilson
     (b)  Arthur m Gertrude Frances Dew (1863-1960) She married as her
          second husband Revd Thomas Williams.
     (c)  John m Augusta Hope
     (d)  Frances
     (e)  Charlotte (d. 1841)


Burkes Landed Gentry. Maitland Wilson of Highbury and Stowlangtoft. Also
     Burkes Peerage and Baronetage.
Burkes Landed Gentry. Remington Mills of Tolmers, Herts.
Creasey, J. The Congregational Library. The Congregational Lecture. 1992.
Harrison, M. J. Patrons and Church Builders: The Wilsons of Highbury and
     Islington.
Larsen, T. (2003) Biographical Dictionary of Evangelicals. Leicester: IVP.
Morison, J. (1844)The Fathers and Founders of the London Missionary
     Society. London.
Oxford Dictionary of National Biography. Revised Edition. Vol. 59. Oxford:

OUP, 2004. ed., Matthew, C & B Harrison.
PCC/Prob/11/1245/1793. Thomas Wilson (I)
Venn, J.A, ed. Alumni Cantabrigienses. 2 vols. Cambridge, 1953.
Wilson, J. (1846) Memoir of Thomas Wilson. London.
Wilson, Thomas Autobiographical Notes: Dr Williams's Library. DWL CL II. D. 3.

Table10: JOSEPH WILSON (1766-1851) of Highbury Place & Stowlangtoft

2nd son of Thomas and Mary Wilson (née Remington) m 1st Mary Maitland eldest daughter of Robert and Elizabeth Maitland of Blue Ridge, Greenwich had *issue*

1   Mary (1794-1865) m Henry Grace Sperling (1792-1821) had *issue*
    Henry Grace Wilson Sperling (1820-1879) m 1st Anna Marguaretta Brereton (1823-1847) dsp
    m 2nd Mary Maitland Wilson (1824-1875) had *issue* (See: Burkes Landed Gentry)

2   Frances (1796-1890) m Revd Charles David Brereton (1790-1863) of Little Massingham Norfolk had *issue* (See: Table 16)

3   Henry Wilson (1797-1866) m 1st Mary Fuller Maitland (1802-1834) eldest daughter of Ebenezer and Bethia Fuller Maitland of Stansted Hall Stansted Mountfitchet Essex (See: Burkes Landed Gentry also Burkes Peerage 1963) had *issue*

    (a)   Mary Maitland Wilson (1824-1875) m Henry Grace Wilson Sperling only son of Revd Henry Grace Sperling and Mary dau of Joseph Wilson. She was the second wife of Henry Grace Wilson Sperling. (See: Burkes Landed Gentry)
    (b)   Fuller Maitland Wilson heir (1825-1875) m Caroline Agnes Kindersley (1829-1913) 2nd dau of Sir R. T. Kindersley (See: Burkes Landed Gentry)
    (c)   Henry (1827-1888) m Mary Digby (1833-1857) Mary (1856)
    (d)   Adela Maitland. (1830-1910) unm
    (e)   Ellen (1832-1919) m W.A. Smith had *issue*
    (f)   Frances (1832-1913) m Edward Leigh Kindersley only son and heir of Rt Hon Sir R. T. Kindersley. (See: Burkes Landed Gentry)
    (g)   Joseph Edward R.N. (1833-1920) m Mary Kelly dau of Arthur and Sophia Kelly (née Maitland) of Devon had *issue* (See: Burkes Landed Gentry 1863)
    (h)   Janet (1834-1911) m Reginald Kelly of Kelly son of Arthur & Sophia Kelly (née Maitland) of Devon dsp (See: Burkes Landed Gentry 1863)

Married 2nd Caroline Fitzroy (1809-1891) only daughter of Revd
Lord Henry Fitzroy Prebendary of Westminster and Rector of
Euston Hall Suffolk and Caroline Fitzroy (née Pigot) Date of
marriage 18th May 1839.

*issue:*
(a) Fitzroy (1840-1887) m Annie Laughton daughter of Col. Laughton
    had *issue*
(b) Cyril Fitzroy (1841-1898) [Rector Stowlangtoft] m Frances Smith
    (1844-1887) had *issue*
(c) Caroline Fitzroy (1844-1888) unm
(d) Amy Fitzroy (n.d.)

NOTE:
Caroline Fitzroy's brother, Revd Augustus Fitzroy married as his second
wife: Emma Joanna the 6th daughter of Ebenezer Fuller Maitland. See: The
Genealogical and Historical Account of the Maitland Family: compiled by
George Harrison Rogers-Harrison. (1869) See also: Burkes Peerage & Co.
Grafton.

ARMS: Sa: a Wolf salient, or on a chief of the last pale of the first charged
with a fleur-de-lis arg. between two pellets.

Crest – a demi wolf or, the sinister paw resting on a pellet charge with a
fleur-de-lis gold. Motto:– Wil sone Wil.

Burkes Landed Gentry & Burkes Peerage and Baronetage.
Barker, H.R. West Suffolk Illustrated.
Copinger, W.A. (1905) The Manors of Suffolk: notes on their history and
    devolution: The Hundreds of Babeigh & Blackburn.
DNB. art. Field Marshall Maitland Wilson.
PRO/Prob/11/2131/Joseph Wilson of Highbury Hill/1851


Table 11: ANN WILSON (1776-1842) of Church Street Spitalfields
and Bunhill Fields.

2nd daughter of Stephen and Ann Collett Wilson (née West) of Church Street
Spitalfields m William Bateman 2nd son of Jonathan and Ann Bateman (née
Dowling) of Bunhill Row had *issue*
1   William (b. 1801) m Elizabeth Parrat
2   Henry (b. 1802) m Mary Piper had *issue*
3   Josiah (1803-1893) m Eliza Emma Wilson (b. 1814) had *issue*
4   Louisa
5   Mary

6    Eliza m Thomas Piper had *issue* (It is from the Pipers that the
     Rushbrook-Williams are descended.)
7    Emma
8    Augusta Emily

Lever, Christopher. (1975) Goldsmiths and Silversmiths: Hester Bateman and
    her Family. London: Hutchinson.
Shure, David. S. (1959) Hester Bateman: Queen of English Silversmiths.
    London: W. H. Allen.
Wilson, S. Private Calendar: 1795-1802. (Privately owned)

Table 12: STEPHEN WILSON (1777-1860) of Old Jewry and Bexhill

2nd son of John and Elizabeth Wilson (née Wight) of Upper Street
Islington m Sarah Lea eldest daughter of Richard and Mary Lea of Old
Jewry and Beckenham.
*issue:*
1    Sarah (b. Sept 18th 1799)
2    Lea (b. March 5th 1801) m Mary Bacchus had *issue*
3    Edward (b. Dec 2nd 1801) m Mary Hayter
4    Richard Lea (b. Jan 21st 1808)
5    Elizabeth (b. Jan 6th 1810) m Mr Jennings had *issue*
6    Julia (b. Sept 11th 1812)
7    Mary Lea (b. Sept 4th 1814)
8    Maria (b. June 30th 1816)
9    Stephen Lea (b. Oct 17th 1818) m Caroline Kelk had *issue*

Rothstein, N.K.A. (1990) Silk Designs of the 18th century in the Collection
    of the Victoria and Albert Museum. London: Thames and Hudson.
Wilson, Harriet Ann. (1901) A Family Sketch touching the Wilsons, Moore,
    Douglas & Fox Families. (Privately owned).
Wilson, John. Family Bible: (Privately owned).

Table 13: DANIEL WILSON (1778-1858) of Spitalfields and Calcutta

1st son of Stephen and Ann Collett Wilson (née West) of Church Street
Spitalfields m Ann Wilson (1785-1827) eldest daughter of William and
Elizabeth Wilson (née West).
*issue:*
1    Daniel (1805-1886) m Lucy Sarah Atkins had *issue* (See: Table 16)
2    John (1807-1833) m Jane Roats
3    Amelia (Sept 1809) died young.

4    Ann Margaret (1811-1818)
5    Eliza Emma (1814) m Josiah Bateman had *issue* (See: Table 18)
6    William (1816-1821)

Bateman, J. (1860) Life of Daniel Wilson. London: John Murray. 2 vols.
Harrison, M. J. From Spitalfields to Calcutta: Daniel Wilson's Love of India.
    Indian Church History Review. June 2006.
Harrison, M. J. Patrons and Church Builders: the Wilsons of Islington. Paper
    given at a seminar, September 2005 organized by the Friends of Union
    Chapel and the Victorian Society. (to be published 2008)
Oxford Dictionary of National Biography. (2005) entry by Andrew Porter.
Reynolds. J.S. (1952) The Evangelicals at Oxford: 1735-1871. Oxford:
    Clarendon Press.
Wilson, Harriet Ann. (1901)A Family Sketch touching the Wilsons, Moore,
    Douglas & Fox Families. (Privately owned).

Table 14: WILLIAM WILSON [II] (1791-1867) of Walthamstow
and Oxfordshire

William Wilson (1791-1867) 2nd son of William and Elizabeth Wilson
(née West) m Mary Garratt (1794-1878)
*issue:*
1    Lydia Mary (1816-1890) m Charles Giberne had *issue*
2    Emily Mary (1817-1900) m Revd Richard Harris had *issue*
3    Eliza Mary (1818-1865) m Francis Bedwell (1804-1855) had *issue*
4    Harriet Mary (1819-1820)
5    William (1821-1860) m Anne Corbett had *issue*
6    Alfred William (1822-1894) m E.M. Cox had *issue*
7    Mary Frances (1824-1864) m 1st Wm Davis Wilson 2nd Charles
     Saunders
8    Francis Garratt (1825-1885) m Susannah Dover Davies (1824-1885)
     had *issue*
9    Agnes Mary (1827-1899) m Nathaniel Wilson had *issue*
10   Joseph William (1829-1898) m Harriet Ann Moore (1830-1913)
     had *issue* (See: Table 20)
11   Frances Mary (1831-1852) m S.M.F Cox
12   Ernest William (1833-1886) m Eliza Preston

Bateman, J. (1860) Life of Daniel Wilson. London. 2 vols.
McCann, P. & F.A. Young. (1982) Samuel Wilderspin and the Infant
    Education system. London: Croom Helm.

JWW. (n.d.) The Legend of the Wolfsons.
PRO/Prob/William Wilson/1868
Wilson, Harriet Ann (1901) A Family Sketch touching the Wilsons, Moore, Douglas & Fox Families. (Privately owned).
Wilson, John Dover. (1969) Along the Dover Road. London: Faber.

### Table 15: SAMUEL WILSON (1792-1881) of Aldermanbury and Beckenham

Youngest son of John and Elizabeth Wilson (née Wight) of Upper Street Islington m Jemima Lea (1793-1864) 9th child of Richard and Mary Lea of Old Jewry had *issue*

1    Cornelius Lea Wilson (1815-1911) m Mary Ann Wilcox had *issue*
   (a)    Cornelius (1844-1932) m Julia Adel Mais had *issue*
   (b)    Mary Ann (1846-1897)
   (c)    Maria (1848-1935)
   (d)    Charles Lea (1851-1936) m Neville Juliana Barclay had *issue*
   (e)    Samuel Henry (1853-1894) m Honor Victoria Doll
       had *issue*
   (f)    Arthur Lea (1858-1943) m Ethel Mary Higgen had *issue*

2    Arthur Lea Wilson (1818-1821)
3    Ernest Francis Wight (1828-1828)

Other children born to them included a daughter, who was born on July 17th 1814 but died at birth. Jemima also gave birth to a son, *c*.1827 who died aged 5 months 5 days.

Arnold, Matthew. (1979) Culture and Anarchy. Ed. John Dover Wilson. Cambridge: CUP.
Plummer, A. (1972) The History of the London Weavers Company: 1600-1970. London: Routledge, Kegan and Paul.
Rothstein, N.K.A. (1990) Silk Designs of the 18th century in the Collection of the Victoria and Albert Museum. London: Thames and Hudson.
Wilson, Harriet Ann. (1901) A Family Sketch touching the Wilsons, Moore, Douglas & Fox Families. (Privately owned).
Wilson, J. (1846) Memoirs of Thomas Wilson. London.

### Table 16: FRANCES WILSON (1796-1890) of Highbury Islington

Frances Wilson was the second daughter of Joseph and Mary Wilson, (née Maitland) of Highbury Hill Middlesex. She married the Revd Charles David

Brereton (1790-1868) second son of John and Ann Margaretta Brereton (née Lloyd) of Brinton Norfolk had *issue*

1   Charles David (1820 1870) m Eliza Kent (n.d.) had *issue*
    (a)   Alice (1844) m William E Langhorne
    (b)   Mary (1846)
    (c)   Clement 1848)
    (d)   Alfred (1849) Maud Shaw had *issue*
    (e)   Charles Harold (1852)
    (f)   Cecil (Revd) (1856-1939) m Rose Temple had *issue*

2   Henry (1821-1852) m Emily Jane Boulderson had *issue*
3   Joseph Lloyd (1822-1901) m Frances Martin (1834-1891) had *issue*
4   Anna Margaretta (1823-1847) m Henry Grace Sperling (see Table 10)
5   Frances Mary (1826-1845)
6   John Alfred (Major General) (1827-1913) m Marion Gillespie had *issue*
7   Mary Anne Louise (1828-1855) unm
8   William Wilson (1830-1854) died Sarawak whilst serving for James Brooke 1st White Rajah of Sarawak.
9   Emma Matilda (1832-1887)
10  Robert Lloyd Maitland (1834-1911)
11  Henrietta Lucy (1835-1898) m Frederick Dew (See: Table 9) had *issue* (They were cousins)

Brereton, Robert Lloyd Maitland. (1834-1911) The Brereton Family of Cheshire.
McLeod. Revd Ronald F. Massingham Parva: Past and Present. London. 1882.
Norfolk Record Office: Brereton Papers.
Runciman, S. (1960) The White Rajah. Cambridge: CUP.

Table 17: DANIEL WILSON (1805-1886) of Barnsbury Islington

Eldest son of Daniel and Ann Wilson of Islington m Lucy Sarah Atkins (1821-1863) had *issue*
1   Daniel Frederick (1830-1918) m 1st Katherine Leathes had *issue*
    m 2nd Sarah Maria Johnstone (1841-1935) daughter of Andrew & Priscilla Johnston (née Buxton) had *issue*
2   Lucy Ann (1832-1835)
3   Wilberforce (1836-) m Jessie Ransome (d.1894) had *issue*
4   Emily (n.d.) m Revd D.C. Hankin had *issue*

5    Fanny (Frances) died young
6    Mary Louisa m Revd W. Martin had *issue*
7    Ellen Richenda m Revd Robert Browne had *issue*
8    Edward Francis (1845-1915) Missionary to Indians at Algoma Canada
     m Frances Spooner (b. 1841) had *issue*
9    Arthur (1846-1932) m Charlotte Martin (cousin) (1854-1955 dsp)
Boase. F. Modern English Biography. Truro, 1892-1921. 2. vols.
Buxton, Ellen. Ellen Buxton's Journal, 1860-1864.
Harrison, M. J. Patrons and Church Builders: The Wilsons of Highbury and
     Islington. Paper given at a seminar: Union Chapel, Islington. Sept 26th
     2005; to be published 2008.
Hinchcliffe, Tanis St Saviour's Highbury: Paper given at a seminar: Union
     chapel Islington, 2005: to be published: 2008.
Nock, D. E.F. Wilson: Early years as a Missionary in Huron and Algoma.
     Journal of the Canadian Church Historical Society. vol. xv no.4
     Dec. 1973.
Stock, E. The Islington Centenary. The Record: Thursday June 26th 1924.

Table 18: ELIZA EMMA WILSON (b. 1814) of Islington

Youngest surviving daughter of Daniel and Ann Wilson (née Wilson)
m Josiah Bateman 3rd son of William and Ann Bateman (née Wilson)
See: Table 12.
*issue:*
1    Alice (Alison) Wilson (1840-1903) m Revd James Henry Morley (b. 1835)
     had *issue*
2    Hugh (1842) m Georgina Wrench
3    Gertrude Anne m Revd William Francis Shaw
4    Marion Amy (1848-1900) unm

Bateman, J. (1860) Life of Daniel Wilson. London: 2 vols.
Blackwell Dictionary of Evangelical Biography 1730-1860, ed. D.M. Lewis.
     2 vols Oxford. entry Ian Rennie.
Boase, F. ed. Modern English Biography. Truro, 1892-1921. 2.vols.
McNally, S.J. (1976) Biographical Notes of East India Chaplains: 1600-1858.
     London: British Library.

Table 19: FULLER MAITLAND WILSON (1825-1875)
of Stowlangtoft Suffolk

The eldest son of Henry and Mary Wilson (née Fuller Maitland) On the
24th April 1852 Fuller Maitland Wilson married Caroline Agnes Kindersley

the second daughter of Sir Richard and Lady Mary Ann Kindersley (née Leigh) of Clyffe Dorset had *issue*

1   Mary (1854-1860)
2   Kindersley (1856-1859)
3   Arthur Maitland Wilson (1857-1934) married Harriet Maude Isabella Kingscote (d.1906) and had *issue*
   (a)   Henry Maitland Wilson (1881-1964) Field Marshall 1st Baron Wilson m Hester Mary Digby (see: Burkes Landed Gentry Digby Wykham of Tythrop House Oxon) had *issue*
      (i)   Patrick 2nd Baron (b. 1915) m Storeen Violet Douglas Campbell *issue* Gordon (1945-2000) (See Burkes Peerage)
      (ii)   Maude (1917-2001)
   (b)   Nigel (1884-1950) m Lady Violet Freddy (1888-1960) daughter of Revd Lord Charles Edward Fitzroy and sister of the 10th Duke of Grafton had *issue*
   (c)   Reginald Maitland (1889-1945) m Monica only daughter of William Towers Mynors dsp.
4   Henry Fuller Maitland (1859-1941) [Sir] KCMG: Lt General m Charlotte Elise Gough had *issue* (a) Arthur Henry (1885-1918) (b) Hugh, (Major) (1886-1955) (c) Muriel (d. 1950)
5   Ethel Maitland (1860-1950) died unm
6   Ellen (1861-1955)
7   Constance (1862-1939) m H.W. Smith (1862-1925)
8   Ida (1864-1943) m Major John Daniell (See Burkes L.G. Daniell formerly of Daresbury and then of Eyston Hall Sudbury Suffolk)
9   Amy (1866-1959) unm
10   Joseph Maitland (1868-1940) m Constance Eagle dsp
11   Agnes Katherine (1870-1954) m Revd Canon J.W.D. Brown (d. 1922) Rector of Stowlangtoft (1893-1919)
12   Alice (1876-1954)

Crest – a demi wolf or, the sinister paw resting on a pellet charge with a fleur-de-lis gold. Motto:- Wil sone Wil.

Burkes Landed Gentry
Burkes Peerage and Baronetage.
Barker, H.R. West Suffolk illustrated.
Copinger, W.A. (1905) The Manors of Suffolk: notes on their history and devolution: The Hundreds of Babeigh & Blackburn.
DNB. art. Field Marshall Maitland Wilson.

Table 20: JOSEPH WILLIAM WILSON (1829-1898)

Fourth son of Revd William and Mary Wilson (née Garratt) of Walthamstow and the Over Worton Oxfordshire m Harriet Ann Moore daughter of Ambrose and Harriet Ann Moore (née Fox)
*issue:*

1   Joseph William (b. Oct 22nd 1851-1930) m Mabel Isabel Hanson had *issue*

2   Ambrose John (Jan 13th 18531929) m 1st Julia Lawrence had issue m 2nd Irma Rowntree had *issue*

3   Edwin Wilson (1855-1915) m Elizabeth Dover had *issue*

4   Harriet Mary (1857 1937) unm

5   Walter Noel (1858-1924) m Edith Eames had *issue*

6   Ruth (1860-1950) m Joseph Arthur Arkwright (later Sir) had *issue*
    (a)   Elizabeth Emma Arkwright (1894-1972)
          m 1st Thomas Wintringham had *issue*
          m 2nd John Dover Wilson (cousin)
    (b)   Ruth Mildred (1896) m Cuthwin Donaldson
          had *issue*
    (c)   Eleanor Mary (1902) m Leslie Haworth
          had *issue*

7   Maurice (1862-1936) m Maria Brena Bloyd had *issue*

8   Basil (1864-1936) m Katharine Marian Maynard

9   Ernest Moore (1865-1951) m Kate Adelina Lawrence had *issue*

10  Edith Amy (1868-1951) unm

11  Norman Octavius (1870-1940) m Margaret Louise White had *issue*


Barlow Gardiner, Robert, Revd ed. The Registers of Wadham College, Oxford. London: 1895.
Boase. F. ed. Modern English Biography.
Foster, J, ed. Alumni Oxonienses: 1715-1886.
ILN. 19 Nov. 1898. p 737 including portrait.
Proceedings of the Institute of Civil Engineers. Vol. 135. p. 359-80. 1898.
Wilson, Harriet Ann. (1901) A Family Sketch touching the Wilsons, Moore, Douglas & Fox Families. (Privately owned).

B. Family tree of the Colletts, Wests, Brookes, Wilsons and Pattles.

Elizabeth Collett and her descendents.

Elizabeth Collett was the second daughter of Captain Thomas Collett of the EIC maritime services. Married to Robert Brooke (*c.*1700-1762) it was from them that Daniel Wilson (1778-1858), James Brooke (1803-1868), Emma Johnson (née Brooke) including succeeding generations of Rajahs and the 7 daughters of James Pattle were descended.

(1)  Thomas Collett (1676-1743) m Isabella Castle of Goodmanfields & Barking had *issue*

1  Grisella (1699-1759) m as second wife Captain Jonathan Pelly (1683-1762)
2  Elizabeth (*c*.1700-1751) m Robert Brooke (*c*.1700-1762) had *issue* (See: Table 1)
3  Thomas (1704-1718) Buried: Fort William Calcutta 2nd Nov 1718
4  Susanna (1707-1757) m Mr Court

(2)  Elizabeth Collett (*c*.1700-1751) m Robert Brooke (*c*.1700-1762) of Goodmanfields Whitechapel

1  Ann (1722) m Daniel West (1726-1796) had *issue*
   (a)  Elizabeth Brooke (1752-*c*.1765)
   (b)  Ann Collett (1754-1829) m Stephen Wilson (See: Table 6)
   (c)  Daniel (1755 *c*.1765)
   (d)  Catherine (n.d. died *c*.1765)
   (e)  Elizabeth (1760-1795) m William Wilson had *issue* (See Table 7)
   (f)  Charlotte (1762) unm still alive *c*.1803.
   (g)  Catherine (1764) m William Whitewell had *issue*
2  Elizabeth (1725) m Thomas Pattle (1710-1770) had *issue* (See: Table 3)
3  Robert (1727) m Ruth Casson Pattle (1741-1829) had *issue* (See: Table 4)
4  Thomas (1731) died young
5  Jonathan (1733) died young

(3)  Elizabeth Brooke second daughter of Elizabeth and Robert Brooke m Thomas Pattle had *issue*

1  Mary Ann (1740) died young
2  Ruth Casson (1741-1829) m Robert Brooke (1727) (See: Table 4)
3  Thomas (1748-1818) m 1st Sarah Hasleby (1755-1813) (See: Table 5)
4  Elizabeth (1752) died young

(4)  Ruth Casson Pattle (1741-1829) eldest surviving daughter of Elizabeth and Thomas Pattle m Robert Brooke (1727) only surviving son of Elizabeth Collett and Robert Brooke of Goodmanfields Whitechapel had *issue*

1   Thomas (1760-1835) He had *issue* by the Moher Bibi of Arah in Bihar
    (a)   Charles William (1784-1836) m Charlotte Dyson had *issue*
    (b)   Sophia (*c*.1785) m David Morrieson (1783-1821) had *issue*
    (c)   Julia (*c*.1786-*c*.1829)
    Married February 1st 1793 Anna Maria Stuart (1773-1843)
    (a)   Harriet Grace (1794-*c*.1836) unm
    (b)   Anna Matilda (1795-1816)
    (c)   Eliza (1797)
    (d)   Henry Stuart (1798-1820) unm
    (f)   Emma (1802-1870) m Revd F.C. Johnson had *issue* (See: Table 9)
    (g)   James (1803-1868) unm 1st White Rajah
    (f)   Margaret (1805-*c*.1864) m Revd Anthony Savage had *issue*
    (g)   Henrietta (1818-1816)

    (5)   Thomas Pattle (1748-1818) only son of Thomas and Elizabeth
          Pattle (née Brooke) m 1st Sarah Hasleby (1755-1812) had *issue*

1   Thomas Charles (1773-1815) m Elizabeth Middleton (d. 1820) had *issue*
    Eliza Ann Middleton.
2   James (1775-1845) m Adeline Maria De L'Etang (1793-1845)
    (See: Table 6)
3   Sophie (n.d.) m Mr Day
4   Sarah (n.d.) m Mr Roche
5   Louisa Ann (Baptized Feb 12 1781)
6   Richard William (died young)
7   Henry John (died *c*.1813)
8   William (1783-1865)
9   Eliza Ann (Elizabeth n.d.)

    (6)   Ann Collett West eldest daughter of Ann West (née Brooke) and
          Daniel West married Stephen Wilson second son of Stephen and
          Mary Wilson (née Fullalove) of Coventry had *issue*

1   Mary (1775-1790)
2   Ann (1776-1842) m William Bateman (1774-1850) had *issue*
3   Daniel (1778-1858) 5th Bishop of Calcutta m Ann Wilson (1785-1827)
    had *issue*
4   Robert Brooke (1779-1829) unm
5   Ruth (1782-1824) m Major Blundell had *issue*
6   Elizabeth (b.1784-*c*.1860) m Percival White (d. 1851)
7.  Stephen (1787-1826) m Mary Wigg had *issue*
8   Thomas (1790-1826) unm

9   George (1793-1846) m Harriet Wilson had *issue*

(7)   Elizabeth West 2nd daughter of Ann West (née Brooke) and Daniel West married William Wilson: had *issue*

1   Ann (1785–1827) m Daniel Wilson (1778-1858) eldest son of Ann Collett and Stephen Wilson had *issue*
2   Joseph (1786-1855) m Emma Aplin (1784-1870) had *issue*
   (a)   Edward (1810)
   (b)   Nathaniel (1812) m Agnes Wilson (1827) had *issue*
   (c)   Cornelius William m Eliza Prinsep
   (d)   Frederick William (Nov 24th 1818-Apr 14th 1827)
   (e)   Joseph Henry (1821-1896) m Henricia Haigh had *issue*
      Frances Henricia
   (f)   Louisa Emma (Jan 22 1826-Aug 8 1827)
3   Selina (1788-1863) m Revd J. Davies (1789-1858) had *issue*
   (a)   Jane
   (b)   Charlotte
   (c)   Clementina (1823-1904) m Dr Robert Martin (1815-1896) had *issue*
   Charlotte (1854-1944) m Arthur Wilson (1846-1932)
4   William (1791-1867) m Mary Garratt had *issue*
5   Sophia (1792-1852) m Revd R. Greaves (1793-1870) had *issue*
   (a)   Evelyn (Aug 6 1818 Baptized Aug 30 1818)
   (b)   Richard Wilson (1819-1891) m 1st Sophia Corbett (d. 1822) m 2nd Charlotte White
   (c)   Joshua (1820-1885) m Frances Sara Dent
   (d)   Francis William (April 4 1822 Baptized May 11 1822)
   (e)   Sophia (1824-1903) m Dr Hoadley Gabb
6   Eliza (1793-1817)
7   Charlotte (n.d.) m Revd Charles Wetherall had *issue* Mary

(8)   James Pattle second son of Thomas and Sarah Pattle (née Hasleby) m Adeline Maria De L'Etang

1   Adeline (1812-1836) m Colin Mackenzie had *issue*
2   James (b. 1813 died young)
3   Eliza (1814-1818)
4   Julia Margaret (1815-1879) m Charles Hay Cameron had *issue*
5   Sara (1816-1887) m Thoby Prinsep had *issue*
6   Maria (1818-1892) m Dr Jackson had *issue*

7   Louisa (1821-1873) m H.V. Bayley had *issue*
8   Virginia (1827-1910) m Viscount Eastnor 3rd Earl Somers had *issue*
9   Harriet Trevor (1828)
10  Sophia (1829-1911) m Sir John Dalrymple Bt had *issue*

(9)  Emma Frances Brooke 5th daughter of Thomas and Anna Maria Brooke (née Stuart) married the Revd Francis Charles Johnson Vicar of White Lackington Somerset.

1   John Brooke (1823-1868) [Later: Brooke=Rajah Muda] m 1st Annie Grant (1834-1858) of Kilgraston
    (a)  Basil (1857-1860)
    (b)  John Evelyn Hope (1858-1935) m Hon Violet Barrington had *issue*
    m 2nd Julia Welstead (d. 1862) had *issue*

2   Mary Anna (1825-1901) m Gilbert Nicholetts (Colonel) dsp
3   Harriett Helena (1826-1906)
4   Charles Anthoni (1829-1917) [Later Brooke 2nd Rajah of Sarawak] m Margaret De Windt See: Table. 10
5   William Frederick (1830-1916) Captain RN m Caroline Hope Toller (1865) had *issue*
6   Emma Lucy (n.d.) m Revd Edmund Eveleyn dsp
7   Henry Stuart (n.d.) m Mary Barnard had *issue*

(10) Charles Anthoni later Brooke, 4th son of Emma and Francis Johnson [2nd Rajah of Sarawak] m Margaret De Windt

1   Ghita (1870-1873)
2   Charles (Harry) & James (Clayton) twins (1872-1873)
3   Charles Vyner De Windt (1874-1963) 3rd Rajah m Hon Sylvia Brett had *issue*
4   Bertram Willes Dayrell (1876-1965) Tuan Muda m Gladys Palmer had *issue*

(11) Charles Vyner De Vindt 3rd son of Charles Anthoni and Margaret Brooke (née De Vindt) 3rd Rajah of Sarawak m Hon Sylvia Brett 2nd Daughter of Viscount Esher

1   Leonora (1911) m as his 2nd wife, Kenneth William Lyle 2nd Earl of Inchcape (1887-1939) had *issue*

(a) Simon Brooke Mackay (1934) Lord Tanlaw m 1st Joanna Susan Hirsch had *issue*
    (i)   Iona Heloise (1960)
    (ii)  James Brooke (1961)
    (iii) Joshua Alex Brooke (1964-7)
    (iv) Rebecca Alexandra (1967)
    m 2nd Rine Siew Yang Tew had *issue*
    (i)   Asia Mackay (1960)
    (ii)  Brooke Mackay (1962)
(b) Rosemary (1936) m Francis Martin French had *issue*
    (i)   Ewan Alex Francis (1959)
    (ii)  Anna Louise Rosemary (1961)
    (iii) Nicola Catherine (1967)
    (iv) Kirsty Elizabeth (1970)
2    Elizabeth (n.d.) m Harry Roy
3    Valerie (n.d.) m Rob Gregory

Boyd, Elizabeth French. (1976) Bloomsbury Heritage: Their Mothers & Their Aunts. London: Hamish Hamilton.

Harrison, M. J. Daniel West: Whitefield's Forgotten Trustee. Journal of the United Reformed Church History Society. vol. 7. no. 8. June 2006.

Harrison, M.J. From Spitalfields to Calcutta: Daniel Wilson's Love of India. Indian Church History Review. June 2006.

Olsen, Victoria. (2003) From Life: Julia Margaret Cameron and Victorian Photography. London: Aurum Press.

Runciman, S. (1960) The White Rajahs A History of Sarawak from 1841 to 1946. Cambridge: Cambridge University Press.

# Select Bibliography

Arnold, M. (1978) Culture and Anarchy: edited with an introduction by John Dover Wilson. Cambridge: Cambridge University Press.

Bateman, J. (1860) The Life of the Right Revd Daniel Wilson, D.D. London: John Murray. 2 vols.

Barley, N. (2003) White Rajah: a Biography of Sir James Brooke. London: Abacus.

Beales, D. (1971) From Castlereagh to Gladstone: 1815-1855. London: Sphere.

Bebbington, D. (1989) Evangelicals in Modern Britain: a History from 1730s to the 1980s. London: Unwin Hyman.

Beneson, A.S. ed., (1970) Control of Communicable Diseases in Man. 11th ed. New York: The American Public Health Association.

Boyd, Elizabeth French. (1976) Bloomsbury Heritage: their Mothers and their Aunts. London: Hamish Hamilton.

Brooke, G.E. (1918) The Brookes of Horton in the Cotswolds. Singapore: Methodist Publishing House.

Brown, F.K. (1960) Fathers of the Victorians: the Age of Wilberforce. Cambridge: Cambridge University Press.

Coleman, D.C. (1969) Courtaulds: an Economic and Social History. Oxford: Clarendon Press.

Dallimore, A. (1970) George Whitefield: the Life and Times of the Great Evangelists of the 18th century revival. London: Banner of Truth Trust.

Dalrymple, William. (2003) White Mughuls: London: Harper Collins.

Davidoff, L & C. Hall. (1987) Family Fortunes: Men and Women of the English Middle Class: 1780-1850. London: Hutchinson.

Eden, Emily, Hon. (1872) Letters from India: edited by Eleanor Eden. London: 2 vols.

Farrington, A. (1999) Biographical Index of EIC Ships 1600-1834. London: British Library.

Farrington, A. (1999) Biographical Index of EIC Maritime Service Officers: 1600-1834. London: British Library.

Farrington, A. (2002) Trading Places: the East India Company and Asia: 1600-1834. London: British Library.

Forster, E.M. (1974) Two Cheers for Democracy. Harmondsworth: Penguin.

Galinou, M. ed., (2004) City Merchants and the Arts: 1670-1720. Wetherby: Oblong Creative Ltd in conjunction with the Corporation of London.

George, Dorothy, M. (1965) London Life in the 18th century. Harmondsworth: Penguin.

Gordon, Caroline. & W. Dewhirst. (1985) The Ward of Cripplegate in the City of London. with a foreword by Lord Briggs. London: Cripplegate Ward Club.

Green, H and Wigram, R. (1881) The Chronicles of the Blackwall Yard. London.

Harrison, M.J. Patrons and Church Builders: The Wilsons of Highbury and Islington: a paper given at a seminar organised by the Friends of Union Chapel and the Victorian Society. London. September 24th 2005. Forthcoming publication 2008.

Harrison, M.J. Daniel West: Whitefield's Forgotten Trustee. Journal of the United Reformed Church History Society. Vol 7 No. 8 June 2006.

Harrison, M.J. Daniel Wilson and his Love of India. Indian Church History Review. June 2006.

Harrison, M.J. The Wilsons of Derbyshire: a note. Journal of the United Reformed Church History Society. January 2008

Hill, Brian. (1973) Julia Margaret Cameron: a Victorian Family Portrait. London: Peter Owen.

Hodder, E. (1887) The Life of Samuel Morley. London.

Jacob, G. L. (1876) The Raja of Sarawak: an Account of Sir James Brooke, KCB, LL D. London: Macmillan.

James, Lawrence. (1998) Raj: the Making and Unmaking of British India. London: Abacus.

Keppel, H. (1846) The Expedition to Borneo of *HMS Dido* for the Suppression of Pirates. London: Chapman and Hall. 2 vols.

Keppel, H. (1853) A Visit to the Indian Archipelago in *HMS Meander.* London: Bentley. 2 vols.

Latham, J.E.M. (1999) Search For a New Eden: James Pierepoint Greaves 1777-1842: the Sacred Socialist and his Followers. London: Associated University Press.

Loane, Marcus. (1951) Oxford and the Evangelical Succession. London: Lutterworth Press.

Lovett, R. (1899) The History of the London Missionary Society. London.

McCann P & F.A. Young. (1982) Samuel Wilderspin and the Infant School Movement. London & Canberra: Croom Helm.

McClatchy, D. (1960) Oxfordshire Clergy. Oxford: Oxford University Press.

McNally, S.J. (1976) Biographical Notes of East India Company Chaplains: 1600-1858. London: British Library.

Mathias, P. (1989) The First Industrial Nation: the Economic History of Britain: 1700-1914. 2nd edition. London: Routledge.

Morrison, J. (1839) The Fathers and Founders of the London Missionary Society. London: Fisher and Son. 2 vols.

Noll, M. (2004) The Rise of Evangelicalism: the Age of Edwards, Whitefield and the Wesleys. Leicester: Inter Varsity Press.

Olsen, Victoria. (2003) From Life: Julia Margaret Cameron and Victorian Photography. London: Aurum Press.

Overton, M. (1996) Agricultural Revolution in England: The Transformation of the Agrarian Economy 1500-1850. Cambridge: Cambridge University Press.

Owen, J. (1816) History and Origin of the First Ten years of the British and Foreign Bible Society. London. 2 vols

Plummer, A. (1972) The London Weavers Company: 1600-1760. London: Routledge, Kegan and Paul.

Reynolds, J.S. (1953) The Evangelicals at Oxford 1735-1871. Oxford: Clarendon Press.

Rothstein, N.K.A. (1985 The Quiet Conquest: The Hugenots 1685-1985. London: Museum of London.

Rothstein, N.K.A. (1990) Silk Designs of the 18th century in the Collection of the Victoria and Albert Museum. London: Thames and Hudson.

Rothstein, N.K.A. ed. (1992) Four Hundred Years of Fashion. London: Victoria and Albert Museum.

Runciman, S. (1960) The White Rajah: a History of Sarawak from 1841-1946. Cambridge: Cambridge University Press.

Saunders, G. (1992) Bishops and Brookes: the Anglican Mission and the Brooke Raj in Sarawak: 1848-1941. London: Oxford University Press.

Skevington Wood, A. (1969) The Inextinguishable Blaze: Spiritual Renewal and Advance in the 18th century. Exeter: Paternoster Press. Paternoster Church History. vol. viii.

Stunt, T. (2000) From Awakening to Secession: Radical Evangelicals in Switzerland and Britain, 1815-1835. Edinburgh: T&T Clark.

Tyerman, L. (1890) The Life of George Whitefield. 2nd edition. London: Hodder and Stoughton.

Vyner, C. (1887) The Vyners: a Family History. Leamington

Welch, E. 91975) Two Calvinistic Methodist Chapels 1743-1811: The London Tabernacle and Spa Fields. London: London Record Society.

Wilson, John Dover. (1969) Along the Dover Road. London: Faber.

Wilson, J. (1846). Memoir of the Life and Character of Thomas Wilson. Esq., by his son. London.

Yates, T. (1978) Venn and Victorian Bishops Abroad. London: SPCK.